Defining Physical Education

Studies in Curriculum History Series

General Editor: **Professor Ivor Goodson**, Faculty of Education, University of Western Ontario, London, Canada N6G 1G7

Studies in Curriculum History Series: 18

Defining Physical Education:
The Social Construction of a School Subject in Postwar Britain

David Kirk

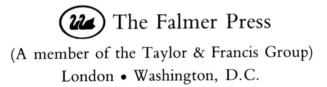 The Falmer Press

(A member of the Taylor & Francis Group)
London • Washington, D.C.

UK   The Falmer Press, 4 John St., London WC1N 2ET
USA The Falmer Press, Taylor & Francis Inc., 1990 Frost Road, Suite 101, Bristol, PA 19007

First published in 1992

A catalogue record of this book is held by the British Library

Library Congress Cataloging-in-Publication Data are available on request

ISBN 0 75070 024 6 Cased

Jacket design by Caroline Archer

Typeset in 9.5/11 pt Bembo
by Graphicraft Typesetters Ltd., Hong Kong
Printed and bound in Great Britain by
Burgess Science Press
Basingstoke

Contents

Contents

Acknowledgements

A large number of people have played a part in the production of this book, and to each of them I am extremely grateful for their assistance. The project on which the book is based began formally in August 1987 during a study leave from the University of Queensland. I wish to thank Ian Jobling and the Department of Human Movement Studies for funding the leave and supplying other financial assistance at various times, and the University of Glasgow for providing me with office space during the leave. Special thanks are due to David Hamilton for very generously allowing me access to his computer, personal library and his time during my stay in Glasgow, and to Christine Midgeley, who was extremely helpful during my visit to the Physical Education Association Library in London. Louise Campbell, Annette Corrigan, John Evans, Lindsay Fitzclarence, Ivor Goodson, Bill Green, Neil Kelly, Jane Kenway, Tony Mangan, Gail Reekie, and Ian Thomson each provided helpful comments and suggestions at various stages of drafting chapters. Bernadette Baker, Jim McKay and Fazal Rizvi read an earlier draft of the complete manuscript and gave me some excellent and detailed advice, most of which I tried to follow. Gordon Tait collected some of the historical material on which the study is based. Susan Kirk is due special thanks for her encouragement, support and lessons in basic grammar. My final thank you is to my colleagues in physical education at Deakin University who made it possible for me to write the bulk of this book during the second half of 1989. Despite all of this assistance, shortcomings invariably remain, and for those I take sole responsibility.

Foreword

This is a book about ideas in British physical education and the processes by which these ideas were created and became established as orthodoxies and conventions over a period spanning the end of the second world war up to the present. It is also about the relationship of these ideas to beliefs in more general circulation in society concerning the value and uses of sport and other forms of organized physical activity in schools, and the part this configuration of notions played in a public debate centred on physical education which preceded the 1987 General Election in Britain. I hasten to add that I don't wish to make too much of this debate in itself, nor to claim for it greater significance than I believe it merits. Rather, the debate is a point of focus for the book and a means of organizing the arguments it presents, chosen as much for its topicality as for its suitability to illustrate a matter of much more general social and professional significance, which is the social construction of school knowledge.

At the same time, I think there is currently a growing public awareness and a multiplicity of interest in the body and physical activity, particularly in terms of health, physical fitness, slenderness and well-being, and school physical education is a part of the constellation of forces which fuel this awareness and interest. The very public airing of this recent debate centred on physical education is evidence of the strong connections between what goes on in educational institutions and the workings of society more broadly. But these connections are often far from obvious or direct; even for those people who are daily involved in teaching physical education, the relationship between what they teach and the outcomes of their work at the level of culture is extremely difficult to discern. This is because the interconnections between physical education and culture are complex and convoluted, and the nature of the evidence of these connections is highly problematic. But, as this study aims to show in a delimited way, these connections do exist, events in school physical education lessons and in society more broadly are interconnected, and the consequences of this interaction are far from trivial, socially, culturally and politically.

The delimitations of this study do require some brief explanation in order to avoid, as far as might be possible, confusion over the status of the arguments presented in this book.

The first delimitation concerns the use of historical material. The book does resemble a history in so far as it utilizes historical material as the basis for analysis. But I don't want to claim any more for it, as a history, than this. It differs most markedly from more conventional histories of physical education by its concern to use this material to interrogate a set of contemporary curriculum problems. This is not meant to be read as a comment on conventional histories, but as a statement of difference of purpose. Moreover, by focusing the analysis on current or recent concerns, I am not presenting a version of presentism (the reading — and distortion — of past events through contemporary lenses). Rather, my concern here is to better understand our current circumstances by understanding how we arrived at the present state of affairs, in the hope that such understanding might inform our judgments about future courses of action.

A second delimitation relates to my choice of material which forms this historical record. The concern for ideas and their expression in the language and actions of physical educators and other (adult) parties should not be interpreted as a neglect of the crucially important role of pupils as the recipients of school physical education, but rather as a necessary methodological strategy. Since the masses of children who experienced physical education programmes in Britain since 1945 have left few if any publically accessible records or accounts of their involvement, the best that can be done is to make inferences from indirect evidence of the effects of programmes where this is available. But this strategy, at best, allows only very tentative and provisional conclusions to be drawn. This study explores the ideas about physical education that became conventional wisdom, but it can say very little about the role physical education programmes played in the formation of individual subjectivities. Moreover, the selection of discourse as a focusing concept for the study is not intended to convey a lack of interest in empirical events. It does suggest a hierarchy of sorts, though, in terms of my interests. Events and actions are certainly not neglected in this study, but I have deliberately chosen to focus on various individuals' and groups' interpretations of these events, and the socio-cultural context in which they occurred, rather than merely documenting the facts themselves.

A third delimitation relates to my rather general definition of 'British' physical education in places and a decision not to delineate too finely the differences between English, Irish, Scottish and Welsh experiences. This is not to diminish the significance of these differences. Being born and brought up a Scot, I am finely tuned to national sensitivities in Britain, and well aware of the political and cultural importance of the equation that English means British. I have, where I considered it relevant, made distinctions. But I do believe that there was much more similarity than difference between the ideas in physical education in general circulation in Britain, especially so since the beginning of the postwar period when mass communications and transport began to take on their more familiar contemporary form. It is here, perhaps, that some historians may feel most aggrieved at what they may consider to be a lack of attention to detail. But, in the face of such a view, I maintain that the very fact an idea originating in one place can become an orthodoxy in another is a matter of central interest to a study of the social construction of school knowledge.

This book appears at a time of considerable social and political turmoil in the world generally and, in the academic world, in social and cultural theory in particular. New notions, loosely grouped under the label postmodernism, have challenged a range of well established ideas about social change, human progress, scientific rationality and environmental stability. Many of these ideas were beginning to enter the communications of educational and other social researchers while I was framing and carrying out the project this book reports, and some have had a quite profound impact on my understanding of why this book should be written and what it is intended to do. As I will go on to discuss in some detail in the second chapter, the theoretical framework and my interpretations of the postwar development of ieas in physical education have shifted somewhat from my initial position. In this respect, the arguments presented here need to be viewed as part of a provisional analysis of an ongoing process, and the theoretical position seen as contingent on my current understanding of the state of play.

At the same time, what has not changed is my conviction that knowledge is a powerful human resource for change and for social good, and that the problematization of orthodoxies and conventions is one necessary means of coming to understand more about the social world and the consequences of our actions within it. One of the purposes of this book is to inform; but far more important to me is its capacity to provoke, trouble, question, agitate, challenge. It is aimed at undermining simplistic and reductionist truths about the world and the role of physical education within it. But all of the work the book is intended to do is not negative, in the sense of providing no answers or resolutions. It also attempts to move beyond critique, to provide a framework of ideas for thinking about the social construction of knowledge in physical education and its selection, organization and evaluation in institutionalized settings. It attempts to promote the optimistic view that knowledge itself has power, and can be a force for good. But it can also be a source of oppression in some circumstances, disproportionately and unjustly advantaging some people over others.

This is the point at which this book and the project it represents reaches its limit. Knowledge and understanding by themselves cannot create a good and just society. This is only possible through the uses to which the knowledge contained in this book are put by its readers. It cannot empower and it cannot bestow wisdom, but can only provide some of the means by which empowerment and wisdom might, under particular circumstances, be possible.

David Kirk
September 1991

For Murray and the future

Unless teachers of physical education can open their minds and hearts to the boundless possibilities involved in this wider contribution they can make to education, they are forever doomed to skulk behind the palisade of their own specialism, fighting amongst themselves about which of them can offer the most powerful form of defence.

J Myrle-James, 1970

It has been said, of the world of fashion, that if one resists change long enough one would eventually come back into vogue. To some extent, this can be said of educational thought, as it would seem to be continually in a state of flux.

James Livingstone, 1970

Chapter 1

Defining Physical Education:
Crisis, Conflict and a Recent Debate

For physical educators used to thinking of themselves as 'survivors in a marginal role',[1] the events of the second half of the 1980s will have come as an unexpected and rather unpleasant surprise. Suddenly, or so it seemed, school physical education had become news-worthy, catapulted on to the front pages of the tabloid press[2] and publicly scrutinized by a prime-time current affairs programme.[3] Sadly for the physical education profession, this media attention was not over-due recognition of teachers' work. Rather than achieving instant stardom as unsung heroes, physical educators suffered instead the ignominy of notoriety. According to some very prominent and powerful critics, they had not been doing their jobs at all well. The reasons for this were not so much incompetence, the critics claimed, but were more to do with misguided idealism, so misguided that it risked undermining the entire structure of British sport and in turn damaging the morale of the British people.

At the height of this public debate about school physical education, which reached a peak leading up to the 1987 General Election, articles were appearing frequently in newspapers and professional journals, defending or attacking one point of view or another, speeches were being made, seminars were being held, commissions of inquiry were being organized, and letters to various editors were flying thick and fast through the postal system. What had happened to generate all of this furore and passion among the normally apathetic and docile British public? What heinous crime had physical educators committed that could raise the hackles of a number of prominent politicians? How could a subject so often ignored by political strategists and civil servants in their official plans for the school curriculum, and generally viewed as a means of light and harmless relief by many members of the (non-physical education) teaching profession and general public, so offend the sensibilities of newspaper editors and television journalists?

The answers to these questions occupy this first chapter, since they expose a range of broader issues that are the subject of investigation in this book. Indeed, the recent public debate over physical education in Britain has provided a useful context in which to locate this investigation because, although the debate is not the subject of the study in itself, it provides a dramatic demonstration of con-testation and struggle to control the ideological terrain that school subjects occupy. The issues the debate has exposed relate most broadly to the social construction of school knowledge, and specifically to the definition of physical education, what the subject *is*, and how its aims, subject matter and pedagogy have been defined by competing interest groups. Recent developments in the sociology of school knowledge[4] and particularly the history of school subjects[5] have shown that school knowledge is not fixed and unchanging, but is instead constantly in process, shaped by social, political and cultural, as well as educational, forces. School knowledge is not politically and culturally neutral, but on the contrary embodies and communicates the interests and values of those parties who have a major hand in constructing the school curriculum, a process which unjustly disadvantages some categories of pupils in relation to others. A number of historical studies have appeared within this literature on most of the subjects and topics that comprise the school curriculum, but none as yet have focused on physical education. Part of this neglect is due to the traditional style of historical work in school physical education,[6] and part of it to the marginalization of practical activities in a curriculum dominated by 'academic' subjects.[7] This public debate reveals, however, that the lowly educational status often imputed to physical education significantly underestimates the political and cultural significance of this field of knowledge.

This chapter outlines the purpose and the scope of this book within the context of the public debate over physical education in Britain from the mid to late 1980s, and argues the case for a study of the social construction of physical education during the immediate post-second world war period, in which the underpinning or 'structuring' discourses of contemporary physical education programmes were contested and put in place. I want to argue in this and subsequent chapters that this period represents a watershed in British physical education discourse, a new moment in the production of definitions of physical education. As I will go on to argue later in this chapter and in Chapter 7, the 1970s and early 1980s witnessed the application, consolidation and further development of these discourses, a process which has only recently been disturbed in any radical way by a new crisis which first manifested itself in the public domain in the mid 1980s. The first section of this chapter considers some of the key issues exposed by this recent public debate which, as I will suggest later in this book, represents only the beginning in a new period of conflict and contestation among physical educators and other interested parties that heralds the construction of new definitions of physical education.

A Recent Public Debate

There had been some sporadic criticisms through the 1960s and 1970s of the extent to which competitive sports and games dominated physical education programmes, but this had made little impression on practice in schools. There had also been a degree of tension, which had been growing steadily since the 1950s, between some physical education teachers and youth sports bodies over who should take responsibility for elite sport. In the early 1980s, though, the dissatisfaction with team games as the main form of activity in physical education began to grow, finding expression in journals like the *Bulletin of Physical Education*.[8] Most of this criticism continued to be contained within professional discourse in physical education and aimed primarily at physical education teachers and teacher educators, while the antagonism between teachers and sports coaches and administrators often amounted to little more than a stand-off, and their problems rarely, if ever, aired in public. The events between 1985 and 1988 marked a new phase in this process, when the debate over the relationship between school physical education and elite sport entered a much more public arena.

One of the first indications of the shift in scale of the debate appeared late in 1985 when *The Times Educational Supplement* reported on an attempt by representatives of the Football Association, the Rugby Union and the Cricket Board in collaboration with the Central Council for Physical Recreation's (CCPR) Peter Lawson to lobby the Minister for Sport Dick Tracey for government co-ordination of physical education and sport in and out of schools. Their request was based on the claim that the expansion of activities on offer in school programmes had led to neglect of their respective sports.[9] Very quickly, this alleged decline in team games was being touted as a symptom of ambivalence, even open hostility, among physical educators towards school sport in general and competition more specifically, and an outcome of dangerously misguided ideas about promoting co-operative and individualistic activities among pupils.[10] By July 1986, the Editor of *The Times Educational Supplement* had joined the fray, claiming that 'traditional competitive sports in schools are under a cloud'. Sport was a popular and widespread cultural activity, the Editor argued, and yet schools were turning their backs on this fact and 'moving in the opposite direction'.

> What is to be made of the 1960-ish ideology which prompts ageing PE organizers to decry traditional forms of sporting competition on the basis of value-judgments that are wildly at odds with those of the society the schools exist to serve? Last weekend, London TV viewers were treated to a comprehensive school where pupils engaged in stool-ball, a primitive forerunner to cricket played with a soft ball which, *The Times* man said, 'allows both sexes to play and is not competitive'. Viewers must have reflected that one thing is fairly certain; the West Indian pace attack was not reared on stool-ball and stool-ball is not going to help England find a quick bowler.[11]

Physical educators had been neglecting their traditional responsibilities, which the Editor implied were primarily to service the needs of elite sport in England, by their adoption of some very doubtful ideas about participation and 'sport for all'. The Editor suggested that physical education teachers were letting down 'the exasperated public', and went on to argue that if 'schools are not going to serve as the nurseries of sporting talent', then this must be fostered in the youth clubs and youth sections of adult sports clubs. Similar themes were picked up elsewhere, most notably the following month by Denis Howell, a former Labour Minister for Sport, in an address at Loughborough's golden jubilee. Howell stated bluntly that 'school sport is the foundation of British sport'. In response to the idea that school sport ought to be less competitive, Howell was quoted as saying 'I have never heard such nonsense. It is impossible to play games unless someone is seeking to win — which inevitably means that someone should lose. This is a fact of life...I suppose people opposed to team games will try to ban ring-a-ring o' roses next on the extraordinary grounds that the last one to fall down is a failure'.[12]

During 1986, the popular press, from the 'respectable' dailies down to the tabloids, had begun to enter the debate, fuelling what Andrew Pollard has referred to as 'the moral panic of 1986' in which the press conveyed the impression that the decline of games playing in schools was now a matter of grave public concern.[13] This conclusion seemed to be confirmed when the BBC's *Panorama* went to air in March 1987 with an investigative documentary which posed the question 'Is Your Child Fit for Life?'. Richard Lindley, the writer and presenter asserted, in an article in *The Listener* which accompanied the programme, that:

> There has been a drastic decline in team-game fixtures between state secondary schools, a decline that, in many schools, has not been arrested by the end of the teachers' strike. And a significant reason for that seems to be a change in the attitude of physical education teachers. 'Team spirit?' snorted Richard Swinnerton, a young PE teacher at Bill Colely's school. 'You mean the team spirit that managed to get so many thousands and millions of people killed in World War 1? I hope we've replaced it with something a little better'.[14]

In the programme, Lindley skilfully counter-posed images of expansive, cold, bleak and empty playing fields, and boys and girls of a variety of races from a London comprehensive school dressed in a mixture of sports clothing playing small-side games, with the purposeful activity of uniformly and immaculately kitted white, Anglo-Saxon private school boys playing rugby union, and enthusiastic primary school children exercising under the scrutinizing gaze of a sports scientist surrounded by expensive-looking technical equipment. The message he wanted to convey through this imagery was that traditional values and standards of excellence in games playing, presumably represented by the grammar school pupils, were being undermined by 'ideologically motivated' teachers who wished to promote equality by dispensing with failure. In the 'new PE' as he named it, there seemed to be 'a variety of experience, but not always much achievement'. Later in the programme, he turned his attention to the recent concern for health-related activity in physical education, which some critics[15] had claimed was in part responsible for distracting physical education teachers from their responsibilities towards team games, and marshalled evidence which suggested children were less fit than they had been at some unspecified point in the past.

At this point in the programme, Lindley's messages did seem to become a little tangled and confusing. It was not clear, for example, whether the new health orientation was meant to be viewed as a 'good thing', and the extent to which its arrival might be significant for team games. This confusion was also clear from his comments in the *Listener* article, where he suggested that:

> at their best, traditional team games stretch and exercise only a minority of children, even if the teachers are prepared to make the effort of organizing them. "Sport for all" offers a theoretical opportunity to involve more children, but in practice may be too thinly spread to offer any really good physical education. So how can we help children acquire

the habit of exercise that could offer them both pleasure and health throughout life?'[16]

Despite this confusion, which perhaps was a result of his attempt to impose his own 'ideologically motivated' view on a far from simple set of issues,[17] Lindley's use of imagery and language successfully conveyed the impression that something was badly amiss with school physical education, providing confirmation of the barrage of criticisms during 1986 that had preceded the *Panorama* presentation.

John Evans has argued that following the *Panorama* programme, 'the public at large could be forgiven for thinking that something both radical and widespread was happening, as damaging to the country's economic well-being as it was to its performance on various national and international sporting scenes'. The sheer weight of criticism, its often high-ranking sources and wide public exposure these criticisms were given through the popular press all contributed to lend credence and legitimacy to the debate over physical education. But just as the noise and acrimony of the conflict seemed to be reaching a crescendo, the 'problem' appears to have been solved. As Evans went on to remark:

> Less than twelve months after the BBC *Panorama* programme was shown, many of the national newspapers could carry the story...rarely given front page position, that the place and position of competitive team games in schools was not only alive and secure but also strongly endorsed by no less than the Inner London Education Authority, which most of the press had previously taken great delight in characterizing as amongst the most politically radical and dangerously extreme in Britain. The crisis, it seemed, was over. The profession had come to its senses, even that lion of radicalism (the) ILEA had been tamed.[18]

According to Evans, the critics seemed to have achieved victory, or at the very least, a number of potentially 'radical' forces had been neutralized. However, the suddenness with which the problems in school physical education appeared to be 'resolved' should not be permitted to disguise the fact that something quite dramatic and significant had happened to physical education and the way in which it had been viewed both inside the profession and out. In the first place, and while there should be no suggestion that physical education's critics collaborated in this exercise, nor that there was any conscious attempt to form a coalition to defend the status of team games in schools beyond the loose affiliations represented by bodies like the CCPR, there were nevertheless a number of common themes articulated by the critics. The demise of school sport was equated with Britain's poor showing in international sport. The assumption was clearly made by many of the contributors to the debate that sport is part of Britain's cultural heritage and an emblem of national pride and identity, and schools have their part to play in fostering the sports stars of tomorrow. It was also commonly assumed that sport and competition are synonymous, and since competition is a 'natural' part of life, it was nonsense to suggest that games could or should be made less competitive. Furthermore, it was argued that society is competitive, and sport is therefore a useful preparation for life. On the other hand, the agenda of the physical education teachers was, according to the critics, 'ideologically motivated' and teachers were pursuing idealistic and dangerously impractical egalitarian notions such as mixed sex and ability groupings that threatened to undermine standards and achievement. In the ultra-competitive world of international sport, and by implication international trade, 'quick bowlers' raised on stool-ball were unlikely to survive.

Inside the physical education profession, responses to this critique ranged from bewilderment to incredulity, and frustration to defiance. A number of teachers pointed out in letters to the press that competitiveness in sport had got out of hand, and that sport encouraged undesirable behaviour among pupils, parents and coaches, with 'schoolteachers, and more often, parents mindlessly bellowing at the touchlines until they are voiceless and crimson in the face becausing losing is the end of the world'.[19] One teacher pointed out that teachers were quickly blamed for the failures of international sports performers, but rarely ever congratulated when teams were successful. Others suggested that the obses-sion with winning was simply irrelevant to school physical education, and that boys and girls of all abilities deserved the teacher's attention, not just the talented few.[20] Several commentators claimed the allegation that team games were on the decline in schools was simply wrong. Hardy[21] cited the evidence of a number of surveys to show that, far from declining, participation in some team games had actually increased.[22] At the same time, he conceded there had been a change in teachers' attitudes, and they seemed to value competition and winning at all costs less than they might have done formerly, placing greater emphasis instead on 'self development' and 'wellness' of pupils. Low[23] concurred with Hardy's view that the decline in participation in games was a myth, and argued that where rates of participation may have varied in certain places, these variations were due to such factors as the teachers' industrial action, declining school roles and school closures and the merging of single sex institutions, rather than a spirit of animos-ity towards competition among physical educators. Some teachers argued in support of games, but felt they had to be modified to meet the needs of pupils.[24]

The Physical Education Association (PEA) was also stung into action, pub-lishing a statement late in 1986 denouncing the media for its determination to present a 'malicious, ill-informed, and one-sided viewpoint', and various other parties for the naked pursuit of their own self-interest. Their statement clarified the position of the physical education profession towards team games as positive and supportive, emphasizing the value of a 'balanced' programme in which pupils of all abilities, creeds and both sexes were to be given the opportunity to play, but called on the government and the national governing bodies of sport to do more to facilitate liaison between school programmes and adult sport.[25] They also published in March 1987 the report of their own *Commission of Enquiry into Physical Education in Schools*, which had been set up in October 1985. While the PEA may, as they claimed, have 'anticipated' the public debate by several months, the findings and recommendations of the report were nevertheless very much shaped and driven by it. The question of whether 'sport is declining in strength and further, if so, is that the fault of the schools?' was very much the leading concern.[26] The Commissioners sought to undermine physical education's critics by querying the assumption that it was the school's role to foster elite sports talent in the first place, but their investigation, which covered primary and secondary schools and involved consultation with a wide range of interested parties, continually returned to the question of the relationship between school physical education and sport, and particularly elite sport, in the broader community.

Their findings revealed 'confusion' among the interested parties over the proper aims and purposes of physical education; 'role conflict' among physical education teachers; 'constraints' in terms of time and facilities; the continuing domination of curriculum content by team games; an increased interest among teachers in health and fitness; and variable quality of teaching between the primary and secondary schools, with teaching in the former emerging as generally 'not satisfactory'. The Commission's recommendations ranged across the matters exposed by these findings, and focused on the urgent need for a clearly articulated philosophy for physical education, more consultation between governing groups, greater co-ordination of research and development activities, and tighter guidelines and increased supervision of young teachers. Indeed, young teachers were singled out as being in need of particular attention; 'we recommend that a careful check is kept to avoid the over-commitment of young teachers on peripheral tasks...there is a critical need, in our opinion, for in-service courses and supportive professional links, especially, perhaps, for young teachers'.[27] There was no indication in the Commissioners' Report, however, of what precisely constituted a 'peripheral task'. Indeed, since the term 'peripheral' implies a centre or core, and since the Commissioners had earlier indicated the lack of a 'clearly articulated philosophy' for physical education, the basis on which they were able to identify a 'peripheral task' needs to be questioned. This singling out of young teachers suggests that another, unarticulated agenda might have been operating here, perhaps not unrelated to fear of the so-called ideologically motivated young teachers Richard Lindley identified in the *Panorama* programme. Indeed, taken together, the Commission's solution to the problems allegedly besetting the physical education profession boiled down to more centralized control of teachers' work in which the PEA and other groups like the Sports Council, the CCPR and the Department of Education and Science (DES) provide 'guidelines', 'support' and the funding necessary to establish regular in-servicing of teachers.

The PEA Commission's assurances that all was basically well within physical education, apart from some isolated trouble-spots such as primary schools, school/club liaison and young teachers, which could be remedied by some high level consultations and pronouncements and increased surveillance, may on the surface have presented a broad support and defence of physical educators' activities in schools. But the fact that the PEA considered the issue of the purpose of school physical education to be in such urgent need of review at this time by a Commission of Enquiry, no less, merely seemed to confirm that physical education's critics had a point. The claim that the Commission anticipated the public debate by some months could be interpreted in any number of ways, but this anticipation did little to prevent the Commissioners' attention being transfixed by the agenda set by the critics, not by themselves.[28] In responding to the critics, the PEA could have marshalled the easily accessible evidence provided by independently conducted research which clearly showed the allegations that school sport was in decline to be false. Yet a Commission of Enquiry was established in preference to a less onerous course of action. What was so important about this issue that required elaborate refutation, reassurance and conciliation?

Physical Education Discourse: Alternatives and Continuities

The fact that the debate had become so public would, of course, have been sufficient reason for some urgent and overt action by the PEA. An additional problem, no doubt, was the uncomfortable fact that many of the critics were important and prominent public figures, and understandably the PEA would have wished to respond in a way that befitted the eminence of these critics. If the whole episode had simply been a matter of some ill-informed statements that could have been easily refuted, a Commission of Enquiry and all of the furore that did surround the debate would have been unnecessary. But this episode was not a simple matter of some misguided allegations; it was much more significantly a struggle over the symbolic terrain that team games in schools have come to occupy, a terrain littered with a range of political and cultural values that are of central importance to the workings of British society. It was not merely the alleged decline of team games, but the apparent threat to the values that had been invested in team games, that created this public debate. And the critics' aggression was entirely due to the perceived nature of this threat, caricatured as trendy but dangerous left-wing idealism. Indeed, the claims that 'progressivist' ideas had 'crept into' physical education programmes were not entirely without foundation. Hardy, as we saw earlier, acknowledged that there had been a shift in physical education teachers' ideas towards competition, and the PEA's Commission of Enquiry warmly supported the renewed interest of teachers in matters of health and fitness. Even Richard Lindley and *Panorama* seemed to be in favour of some of these new ideas about health. So even though games playing was not on the decline, it was the emergence of a new, alternative 'discourse' in physical education that lay behind the public debate.

Evans and Clarke argue that two innovations have made a significant impact on physical educators and in a relatively short space of time had achieved the status of the 'official discourse' in physical education. They suggest that this discourse consists of a 'set of ideas and rationales which not only define what the curriculum and teaching of PE ought to be, but also provide a philosophy of action, a way of thinking and talking about the place and purpose of the subject in the broader school curriculum'.[29] Evans and Clarke identify these new arrivals as 'teaching games for understanding' and 'health-related fitness'. While each innovation has emerged from separate origins and has been sponsored by different parties, Evans and Clarke claim that taken together they constitute an alternative way of thinking about physical education to the traditional approach, which has had at its centre competitive team games.

The 'teaching games for understanding' (TGFU) innovation originated in its present form in the work of Bunker and Thorpe and their colleagues.[30] TGFU begins with the claim that traditional games teaching methods have been largely ineffective, since they tend to produce good performers of physical skills but poor players, who understand little about the strategies of games. Bunker and Thorpe argue that too much emphasis has commonly been placed on the development of motor-skills and too little on players' awareness of game strategies and their decision-making capacities. Their solution is to begin all games teaching with a modifed form of the adult version of a game, and to teach what they have called 'enabling skills' only when the learner can appreciate the need for them in the game. At the centre of this approach is the notion of 'understanding'; the challenge Bunker and Thorpe lay down to conventional skill-led approaches to games teaching is to integrate the players' cognitive appreciation of the game with their physical skill development. Bunker and Thorpe also argue that through TGFU many more pupils gain a valuable experience from playing games. They suggest that since a modified version of the adult form of a game is an appropriate starting point for teaching, there is no necessity for all children to reach the level of the adult game before they can experience success and enjoyment. Within TGFU, pupils can play a successful game of tennis without having to play with adult-size racquets or on a full-size court. In conventional games teaching, the adult version of the game tends to be seen as the ultimate end-point of games teaching, notwithstanding the pupils' age, ability, and strength. Within TGFU on the other hand, the emphasis is placed on modifying the game to suit the learner.

Like TGFU, health-related fitness (HRF) began to attract the attention of British physical educators in the early 1980s. Many advocacies of HRF start with a critique of sedentary lifestyles and the relationship between sedentariness and health problems like obesity, coronary heart disease and stress. Protagonists argue that vigorous physical activity of sufficient intensity and regularily administered can play an important part in the prevention of these diseases, and suggest that traditional physical education programmes based on games are ineffective in combatting the effects of sedentariness. Although games and sports involve physical activity, supporters of HRF claim that this is neither regular nor vigorous enough to have a training effect. On top of this, because (they claim) so many children experience only failure and frustration within the traditional approach, they develop negative attitudes to all physical activity. Hence the widely reported rapid dropout rate from organized team sports in adolesence and adulthood. To remedy this problem, HRF programmes give prominence to vigorous physical activities that are usually non-competitive and place few demands on pupils for skilful performance. Many programmes also include diagnostic measurements of body fatness, physical work capacity, height and weight, and on the basis of the information teachers can tailor programmes of activity to the specific exercise needs of individual pupils. In order to run programmes that cater for individual differences, teachers need to allow pupils greater autonomy to work alone and without close supervision, suggesting an alternative form of pedagogy to the traditional teacher directed approach associated with team games. The overarching concerns of HRF are for physical fitness and well-being, for 'looking good and feeling good'. In communicating these concerns, much of the language and terminology of HRF borrows from medicine, social psychology and exercise science, and its proponents often cast themselves in a paramedical role, as 'fitness consultants' as well as 'health educators'. HRF practitioners claim to provide a service that is informed by scientifically-based knowledge, and stress the centrality of individual responsibility for the maintenance of health and fitness, demanding informed and responsible decision-making on the part of individual pupils.

Evans and Clarke have pointed out that these innovations share:

a number of common features and prescriptive themes. Both start from a critique of conventional practice in PE, both challenge the content of the curriculum, especially its emphasis on competitive games, and its authoritarian pedagogical mode. Both claim to offer a curriculum which is not only more beneficial but also more accessible to the majority of pupils.[31]

The emphasis within traditional programmes on a minority of elite performers at the expense of the majority of less talented pupils emerges as a key concern in TGFU and HRF, and each stresses the importance of meeting the needs of individual pupils rather than attempting to approximate the needs of the group. HRF in particular is characterized by an explicitly pupil-centred pedagogy in which the teacher aims to tailor programmes specifically to the requirements of each individual.[32] The modification of games in TGFU to suit the abilities and physical capacities of children reflects a similar concern, and through this claims to offer all children the opportunity to experience success, achievement and satisfaction. Given the focus on the individual pupil, both innovations highlight non-authoritarian roles for teachers and less didactic approaches to teaching, requiring teachers to develop alternative forms of pedagogy that complement the focus on individual needs. In summarizing these similarities and pointing to their broader significance, Evans and Clarke suggest that:

> Together these initiatives have in recent years vied for a place not simply within, but as 'the privileging text', the dominating curriculum in the official discourse of PE. Both carry an image of practice in which relationships between teachers and pupils and between pupils and knowledge are significantly altered. Emphasis is upon a negotiated curriculum, on less didactic modes of teaching, upon pupils creating for themselves a curriculum (new game form or personal HRF programmes) which is sensitive to individual interests, abilities and future life-styles. Theoretically at least these initiatives have the capacity radically to alter and challenge patterns of power and authority which have long featured in both the academic and physical curriculum of schooling.[33]

This is not to say that, as the 'official discourse' in physical education, these innovations have been implemented in all or even a majority of physical education programmes. It is, rather, the ideas and values each embodies that have had a notable impact on discourse in physical education, on the ways physical educators have been talking and thinking about their subject. At the same time, it is important not to overstate the significance of this alternative discourse, nor its alternativeness. For example, it would be possible for TGFU to be used, as part of a traditional approach to games teaching, as a technology for achieving more effective performances in games and sports at elite levels. While, as some commentators have suggested, there may indeed be some consistency between a 'physical education for all' philosophy and TGFU, it is questionable whether this slogan itself necessarily means abandoning elite sport. Indeed, it could be argued that the notion of 'physical education for all' implies the need for a broader base of participation which can support higher levels of achievement at elite levels. So while more people find success at 'their own levels' within TGFU, there is no radical challenge to the assumptions underlying traditional games teaching. Similarly, while HRF may represent a distinctly different way of thinking about physical education, few advocates have proposed that games should be left out of HRF programmes. And while HRF may encourage pupils to reflect on the part exercise plays in their lifestyles, it has recently been criticized for paying too little attention to the potential hazards of excessive exercising and over-dieting.[34] Indeed, as Evans and Clarke themselves have recognized, there are silences in this 'official discourse' that leave questions of gender and race, for example, un-answered. A number of recent studies of how teachers have interpreted and applied TGFU and HRF to their practice have confirmed that the effects of this discourse cannot be 'read-off' from the potentially radical features they may or may not contain.[35]

While these qualifications provide some balance to the extreme claims made by physical education's critics that an insidious left-wing idealism has been undermining 'traditional physical education' in state schools, this does not mean that the potentially alternative view of physical education these recent innova-tions represent is irrelevant, nor that the debate itself was a storm in a tea cup. The debate was not only about an alleged demise of competitive team games in physical education and the implications of this decline for British society more broadly; it was also, as Terry Williamson clearly perceived, a struggle over the *meaning* of physical education, in terms of its aims, content, and pedagogy. In an Editorial for the *Bulletin of Physical Education* in 1986, and referring to the media coverage of the debate, Williamson said:

> What *really* upset me was that articles such as these should appear in national newspapers at such a sensitive time, not just because teacher morale is low, but at a time when it is by no means certain where the 'seat of power' or control of the curriculum will finally rest. I am extremely concerned that a lobby such as this should be commanding such a high profile at this moment in time. It is a lobby that has to be admired for exercising their power in a persuasive and skilful manner, but it is a lobby which has only a limited interest in mind and one which is 'out of step' with the way many teachers, advisers and lecturers who are in touch with the day-to-day developments in our schools would consider to be in the best interests of our pupils. It is also a lobby whose definition of 'physical education' is, to say the least, questionable.[36]

Williamson's insight is an important and profound one. His comments suggest that the aims, content and pedagogy of the subject are not politically neutral, but on the contrary are in part constituted by the symbolic values attributed to physical education. The debate was not simply a wrangle over the actual num-bers of schools playing competitive team games, and those physical educators who attempted to wrestle with the issues at this empirical level alone were understandably bewildered and frustrated, since it could easily be shown that there was no substance, *in fact*, to the critics' allegations. It was, instead, about the kind of physical education that should be taught in schools, and *who* should have the right to define what this should be.

The issue of school sport and its relationship to physical education was important to this struggle only in so far as it possessed, as John Evans has pointed out, important 'representational qualities'.[37] The decline of competitive team games encapsulated and expressed a range of broader educational, cultural and political values that some parties felt to be under threat, and it was used as a *metaphor* for the perceived rise to prominence and power of oppositional values that threatened the interests of a coalition consisting largely of right wing politicians and their allies, and other groups with specific stakes in the fate of school sport such as journalists, professional sports administrators, and less visibly, the corporate sponsors and financiers of commercial sport. Evans has described some of these representational qualities that led physical education to be selected as the subject of the *Panorama* programme.

> It was largely because what was happening in physical education could be used to illustrate or signify much broader curricular or ideological trends in the educational system that PE came to be allocated such a prominent and public position...PE could be used to signify all else that was wrong with State secondary educational provision and to vilify and negate progressive elements in it. *Panorama* carried, both implicitly and very obviously, contrary or counter-positional images of how physical education in particular and education and schooling in general, should properly otherwise be. Indeed it is difficult if not fully impossible to understand the *Panorama* narrative without first having some broad knowledge of all else that had been said or claimed about the nature and state of educational practice, especially in the State comprehensive system in Britain by agents of the political right since the mid 1960s. In this respect we can see that their critique of PE arises not from the BBC programme makers' conscious or malicious endeavours to act against the interests of the PE profession, but out of a dominant political culture which they share.[38]

Evans' comments clearly locate the debate over the decline of competitive team games within some of the broader concerns that make the episode intelligible in the first place, and he places particular emphasis on the continuing assault on comprehensive schooling by the political right. At a time when the Educational Reform Bill and its policies for a national curriculum, extensive pupil and teacher assessment and the right of schools to 'opt out' of the state system were being promoted by the Thatcher government, the debate over physical education clearly served to assist the Conservatives to drive home their message that 'trendy ideas' like non-competitive activities in the curriculum were 'left-wing', 'unnatural', and actually harmful, and that such radical alternatives as those proposed by Secretary of State for Education Kenneth Baker were therefore necessary. Indeed, as I will go on to argue in the final chapter of this book, the Thatcher government were able to benefit from the debate over the alleged decline in school sport leading up to the 1987 General Election. I will suggest that the furore over physical education and school sport acted as a rallying call to the political right, who were at that time in severe danger of crumbling and dividing through conflict within the Conservative ranks, and that the school sport debate served as a useful, and appropriately emotive, issue which enabled the right to temporarily overlook its differences and present a united front.

There were other, older associations and emotions evoked in this debate as well that helped to give the critics' allegations such force and apparent credence, such as the use of sport as a means of promoting national pride and identity, the 'naturalness' of competition, and the feeling of uniting with cohesion and solidarity against a common foe. And while Evans is right to point out that this critique of school physical education was part of a larger scale attack on comprehensive schooling and its associated ideology in the present, we need to note that it would not have been possible to use physical education as a potent symbol of creeping left-wing progressivism had these other, older associations not been put in place well in advance of this episode. In this respect, physical education did not suddenly, over the period of several months in 1985 and 1986, become infused with a cluster of representational qualities that then incited a range of groups and individuals to engage in an acrimonious debate. Nor was 'physical education' a clearly articulated school subject, with broadly agreed aims, content and pedagogy, until this equilibrium was upset in the early 1980s by the arrival of TGFU and HRF. On the contrary, the *meaning* of physical education has been the source of contestation and debate for many, many years, and different groups both inside and outside the subject have held quite conflicting views on what physical education is and why it should be part of the school curriculum.

If we wish to understand why it was that physical education was vilified for trendy, left-wing progressivism in the second half of the 1980s in Britain, and why paradoxically this idea was a source of 'much amusement in staffrooms up and down the country',[39] we need to look in some detail at how contemporary discourse in physical education has been constructed. In order to do this, we need to turn our attention to the immediate postwar period in which the British people were busily engaged in a process of 'social reconstruction'. The period between 1945 to 1970, and especially the mid 1950s and early 1960s, are of particular importance to contemporary physical education in Britain, since it was during this period that physical education became established in the new secondary schools for the masses, created by the 1944 'Butler' Education Act in England and Wales and the 1946 Education Act in Scotland. This period represents a watershed in school physical education, since it marks the transition from physical training in the state elementary schools taught by generalist teachers, to the creation of a 'subject' taught by specialist secondary school teachers. The period also marks the collision of three separate traditions in physical education, and their incorporation into a single subject in the mass secondary schools; the competitive teams games of the boys' public and grammar schools, the Swedish gymnastics and games of the girls' private schools, and the physical drill of the state elementary schools, each of which embodied different and in some cases widely disparate ideologies.

I will argue in Chapter 7 that the intervening fifteen year period between 1970 and 1985 has seen no radically new additions to the trends set in motion during the immediate postwar years. Of course, there have been developments and elaborations of the themes that formed the substance of contemporary physical education discourse (up to 1985); but as I intend to demonstrate substantively through an investigation of the immediate post-war period in Chapters 4 to 6, the 1970s and early 1980s, in contrast to this period, formed a time of consolidation and realization, not radical change. I will go on to suggest in Chapter 7 that it is only with the recent debate in the mid 1980s that a new moment has been initiated in physical education discourse that marks the beginning of the formation of new structuring discourses that will take us into the next century.

Before going on to discuss in some detail the struggles to define physical education in the postwar period and the various competing discourses generated out of these struggles, the next chapter outlines some of the broader principles derived from other recent studies of the social construction of school knowledge and school subjects and sets out to explain some of the key ideas, such as 'discourse', which have framed this study.

Notes

1 Hendry, L. (1975) 'Survival in a marginal role: The professional identity of the physical education teacher', *British Journal of Sociology*, **26**(4), 465–476.
2 *Today* 'Barmy Britain', 11 July 1986.
3 *Panorama* 'Is Your Child Fit For Life?', March 1987.
4 See Whitty, G. (1985) *Sociology and School Knowledge: Curriculum Theory, Research and Politics*, London: Methuen, for an overview.
5 For example, Goodson, I. (1985) *Social Histories of the Secondary Curriculum* Lewes: Falmer Press; Popkewitz, T. (1987) *The Formation of School Subjects*, Lewes: Falmer Press.
6 See Evans, J. and Davies, B. (1986) 'Sociology, schooling and physical education', in Evans, J. (Ed.) *Physical Education, Sport and Schooling: Studies in the Sociology of Physical Education* Lewes: Falmer Press, pp. 11–37.
7 For example, see Connel, R.W., Ashenden, D., Kessler, S. and Dowsett, G. (1982) *Making the Difference: Schools, Families and Social Division* Sydney: George Allen and Unwin for a description of the 'competitive academic curriculum'.
8 Bunker, D. and Thorpe, R. (1982) 'A model for the teaching of games in secondary schools', *Bulletin of Physical Education*, **18**(1), 3–8; Kirk, D. (1982) 'Physical education, sport and education', *Bulletin of Physical Education*, **18**(3), 29–33; Whitehead, J. and Fox, K. (1983) 'Student centred physical education', *Bulletin of Physical Education*, **19**(2), 21–30.
9 'Worried Sports Chiefs Call for Games Policy' *TES* 13 December 1985, p. 5.
10 'Bottom of the class' *Observer*, 5 January 1986, p. 36; 'Pupils' view of sport sparks competitive games row' *TES* 21 January 1986, p. 14.
11 'Get in there and win' Editorial, *TES* 11 July 1986, p. 2 .
12 'Howell calls for sports re-think' *TES* 8 August 1986, p. 5.
13 Pollard, A. (1988) 'Physical education, competition and control in primary education', in Evans, J. (Ed.) *Teachers, Teaching and Control in Physical Education* Lewes: Falmer Press, pp. 109–123.
14 Lindley, R. 'Passing the fitness test?' *The Listener* 12 March 1987, p. 12.
15 *TES*, note 10.
16 Lindley, note 14, p. 13.
17 See Evans, J. (1988) Magic Moment or Radical Critique: The Rise and Rise of the New PE. Paper presented to the Conference on Leisure, Labour and Lifestyles, University of Sussex, July.
18 Evans, note 17, p. 3.
19 *TES* 1 August 1986, p. 13; *TES* 17 January 1986, p. 23.
20 *TES* 17 April 1987, p. 14.
21 Hardy, C. (1986) 'Competitive team sport and schools', *British Journal of Physical Education* (Health and Physical Education Newsletter), **17**(2), ix–x.
22 Also *TES* 5 February 1988, p. 16.
23 Low, G. 'Give a child a sporting chance', *Education* 8 August 1986, p. 130.
24 See Poynton, S. (1986) 'Games do have a place and value: They provide sportsmen and sportswomen', *British Journal of Physical Education*, **17**(5), 161–163;

Alexander-Hall, J. (1986) 'A case for the retention of team games in the second-ary school curriculum', *British Journal of Physical Education*, **17**(5), 163–164.

25 Physical Education Association, Executive Committee (1986) 'Sport education in schools', *British Journal of Physical Education*, **17**(6), 196.

26 Physical Education Association (1987) *Physical Education in Schools — Report of A Commission of Enquiry* London: PEA, p. 7.

27 PEA, note 26, pp. 53–54.

28 The original terms of the Enquiry make no mention of the sport/physical education link, yet as I noted earlier this was a leading and frequently recurring issue throughout the report; see the Enquiry remit note 26, p. 3.

29 Evans, J. and Clarke, G. (1988) 'Changing the face of physical education', in Evans, J. (Ed.) *Teachers, Teaching and Control in Physical Education* Lewes: Falmer Press, p. 126.

30 Bunker and Thorpe, note 8; and Spackman, L. (1983 Ed.) *Teaching Games for Understanding* Curriculum Development Centre, The College of St. Paul and St. Mary, Cheltenham.

31 Evans and Clarke, note 29, p. 128.

32 For example Whitehead and Fox, note 8.

33 Evans and Clarke, note 29, p. 129.

34 Tinning, R. (1985) 'Physical education and the cult of slenderness: A critique', *ACHPER National Journal*, **107**, 10–13; Colquhoun, D. (1989) Healthism and Health-Based Physical Education: A Critique. Unpublished PhD Thesis, University of Queensland, Australia.

35 Evans and Clarke, note 29; Pollard, note 13; Leaman, O. (1988) 'Competition, cooperation and control, in Evans, J. (Ed.) *Teachers, Teaching and Control in Physical Education* Lewes: Falmer, pp. 97–107; Sparkes, A. (1987) The Genesis of an Innovation: A Case Study of Emergent Concerns and Micro-Political Solutions. Unpublished PhD Thesis, Loughborough University; Kirk, D. (1986) Researching the Teacher's World: A Case Study of Teacher-Initiated Innovation. Unpublished PhD Thesis, Loughborough University.

36 Williamson, T. (1986) From the Editor. *Bulletin of Physical Education*, **22**(2), p. 6.

37 Evans, note 17, p. 5.

38 Evans, note 17, p. 6.

39 Leaman, note 35, p. 107.

Chapter 2

Curriculum History and
Physical Education as Discourse

The Australian journalist and social critic, Phillip Adams, recently wrote an article on Clive Wearing, the subject of a British television documentary called Prisoner of Consciousness. Wearing suffered from a condition brought about by the 'herpes simplex' virus which destroyed a large section of his brain. As a result, he suffered loss of long term memory, and apart from a miscellany of competancies, could not retain information for more than a few minutes. Inspired by the documentary, Adams drew an analogy between Wearing's condition and the state of consciousness in society at large in an age of mass media.

> There's a tendancy to live, more and more, in a world of vivid, lurid immediacy, a present tense made more tense by the magnifying glass of the media. A present so powerful that it obliterates the past. That's simply something to be plundered for counterfeit nostalgia — its nothing but a quarry for pastiche music and 'fashion'. 'Now' becomes NOW, a succession of over-bright, hyped presents, more like sequins than sequence...We are constantly confronted and astonished by events without precedent or context, yet imagine ourselves to be well-informed. That's how we buy tired, second-hand goods like the New Age or the New Right and imagine them to be revelations. Our lives are feverish, superficial and, for all our wondrous communications technologies, ignorant.[1]

Adams' comments could as easily have been motivated by the public debate in British physical education as the chronic amnesia of one unfortunate individual. The mere fact that contributors to the debate, both for the prosecution and the defence, could happily talk about 'traditional physical education' as if this was something that all sides acknowledged as a historical fact, was in itself revealing of our imprisonment in the lurid present. Team games were indeed traditional to physical education, but up until the end of the second world war only in the male and to a lesser extent female private schools of the upper classes, a group which constitutes a very small minority of the British population. Yet, in the space of a mere forty years, the appearance of potential alternatives to this form of physical education in state secondary schools is apparently sufficient cause to stimulate an outcry from a range of interested parties.

This apparent lack of a historical sensitivity can be particularly damaging in terms of responding to new developments and events. Indeed, Musgrave[2] has argued that the recent upsurge in interest in what he calls 'curriculum history' has been marked by a shift in motivations from a need to simply understand the past, to a desire to participate more effectively in complex practical situations in the present. This point has been made forcefully by Goodson in his critique of the ways in which History of Education had traditionally been done in Britain.[3] Goodson has suggested that while the institutionalized form of History of Education has been, like every other subject, far from monolithic, it has tended to retain what he calls an Acts and Facts flavour. In this form, History of Education deals mainly with institutionalized and formal 'developments' in education but rarely with the social detail of change, thus presenting historical information as at best a partial account of change, and at worst as inert and irrelevant to contemporary projects. The effect of this treatment of history in teacher education courses has been two-fold, first in terms of presenting history as of little concern to teachers' and schools' current needs, and second, by working back on the teaching of History of Education courses and resulting in their omission from teacher education because of this perceived irrelevance. Goodson has argued at some length to the contrary, that historical studies of the school curriculum form an essential component of any research effort that seeks to understand the ways in which contemporary efforts to bring about change can be accomplished, since without a detailed sensitivity to what he called the internal nature of schooling and its changing forms over time, attempts to effect change are likely to be unsuccessful.

Goodson has not been alone in his claim that curriculum history has immediate relevance to contemporary projects. In a recent and comprehensive review of curriculum history research, Seddon[4] remarked that, following a period of neglect by curriculum researchers in the 1950s and 1960s, studies of the history of school subjects and pedagogy, and of the curriculum field itself, have proliferated in the 1980s. She claims that despite a degree of unevenness across countries in terms of numbers of studies and active researchers, the sub-field of curriculum history has now reached a stage of self-conscious reflection, in which issues of purpose, method and theory have begun to be worked through by exponents. As a result of this reflective effort, Seddon has been able to map a number of key issues which she has proposed as an agenda for future curriculum history research. In particular, she claims (following Kliebard and Franklin) that the substantive focus of this sub-field 'centres curriculum in the selection, organization and distribution of *knowledge*; sited in *educational institutions* and hence, implying that curriculum is oriented to *learners*. Additionally, it indicates that curriculum is the consequence of people's activity which constitutes social and political processes over time, that is, there is a relationship between *people and things*'.[5] According to Seddon, this statement provides a useful means of identifying the central concerns of curriculum history as a sub-field of curriculum and educational research more broadly, though a number of other key issues continue to present themselves as in need of resolution by curriculum historians; she stresses especially the issues of the boundaries of curriculum history, the nature of historical research, and the place of theory in curriculum history as matters which are currently under debate by researchers in the field.[6] Despite varying opinions on these matters among curriculum researchers, a common thread running through most of this recent curriculum history work has been the explicit use of

history to inform contemporary projects for change, and thus an acknowledgement that curriculum research is, as Reid clearly indicated,[7] an inherently political
activity that is interwoven with the pragmatics and practicalities of educating and
schooling.

This more recent concern for the use of history to inform contemporary
action is in sharp contrast to the ways in which history has commonly been done
in physical education and sport. Most history in physical education has generally
taken the form of the production of chronologies and narratives, descriptive
accounts of events and the 'great men' behind them.[8] These factual, untheorized
chronological histories have brought to light much that is of importance and
interest to anyone concerned with social and educational change, and in this
respect, this work is valuable. However, John Evans and Brian Davies have
argued that this kind of historical work has tended to project an unproblematic
image of the development of school physical education as a single line of evolution from drill through physical training to the comprehensive programmes of
today. They also have suggested that 'conflict and disagreement within the ideas
and attitudes (towards physical activity, the body and sport) of middle class
males or females, and between their aspirations and other social and ethnic
groups', remain largely unexplored'.[9] Thus, when it comes to using this information in the context of contemporary curriculum debate, we are faced with a
number of difficulties. One of the most important is how we can make sense of
the process of change on the basis of this kind of historical evidence. What,
indeed, is this information evidence of? In order to answer this question, and to
render this information of some use to combatants in contemporary struggles,
we need to find a way of theorizing it, of making sense of the past in relation to
the present.

By this, I am not suggesting that we raid the past[10] in order to legitimate our
current activities and aspirations. One example of this use of history is occuring
in relation to the revitalised interest within the physical education profession in
matters of health and fitness discussed in the previous chapter. Contemporary
protagonists for a health-related orientation to the curriculum cite historical
precedent as a means of legitimating their current concerns; 'physical educators',
so the rhetoric runs, 'have since the earliest days of the subject's entry into the
curriculum, had a major concern for health and physical fitness'.[11] As I will point
out in Chapter 6, the dangers of such comparisons are that current social conditions and the interventive measures they inspire have changed a great deal since
the late nineteenth century. Physical activity at that time was viewed as a
response to fears for the physical deterioration of the race, and one component of
health alongside adequate food, clothing and fresh air. This was a therapeutic use
of exercise, an after-the-event cure, or at least treatment, for particular manifestations of poor health such as poor posture, pigeon chests and bad feet, created by
the conditions of that time. The contemporary rhetoric linking physical activity
and health is quite different. In the sedentary, consumer-oriented and leisured
present, the concern is for prevention rather than therapy. Exercise is no longer
seen as a compensatory treatment for illnesses brought on by deprivation, but
rather as an integral part of modern lifestyle, as an antidote to overconsumption
and its end-products. To cite one discourse in physical education as the precedent
for another, out of time and context, is wholly mistaken. The similarities are
noted without any acknowledgement of underlying differences.

The point of importance is that if information from the past is to be of service to our contemporary ruminations, then our interest must have a more or less explicitly stated purpose. In other words, as curriculum researchers our interest in the past is not what I would characterize as a disinterested antiquarianism, but is instead an integral part of our contemporary projects. Within such a view, the central focus of this study is not the history of physical education; it might be described, more appropriately, as a study of the process of change. By understanding how physical education has changed, and how these changes articulate with broader movements in society, we will be in a better position to pursue our contemporary projects with a greater chance of success. The motivation for studying the past is intimately bound up with our understanding of the present and our vision of what the future could hold, and it is to gain greater control over our current circumstances so that we may better influence those in the future.

Social Change and Physical Education as Discourse

It is not just the down-side of our mass communications technologies that are to blame for the ways in which participants in the 1985–1988 public debate conceptualized physical education in the lurid present. All of our experiences as students and teachers in educational institutions encourage us to view school subjects as stable, unchanging categories of knowledge. Indeed, the school day is built around periods of activities, each discrete, with its own beginning and end, and with its own characteristics. In the primary school these curriculum categories are already firmly established in broad groups, such as language arts, computation, creative activities, by the end of the infant stage. By the time we reach secondary school, they have become even more refined and established to the point that each has its own specialist teachers, who teach grouped in specific locations in the school. And colleges and universities take this process further still by building their entire organization and administration around particular sets of subjects or disciplines. It is not surprising that we tend to think of curriculum categories as fairly settled and established subjects. Indeed, challenging the idea that subjects are stable entities is much the same thing as questioning the way in which we construct our professional identities as students and teachers.[12]

These ideas about the instabilty of school subjects are not particularly new. Michael F D Young and some of the other contributors to *Knowledge and Control*,[13] published in 1971, are generally credited with introducing into contemporary educational discourse the idea that school knowledge is socially constructed, and moreover, while we are all implicated in this process, those people who have a disproportionately large impact on the construction of school knowledge are most often members of a group they characterize as the dominant class. Subjects are not rationally agreed bodies of established, neutral facts and ideas, but instead reflect the values and culture of, and disproportionately advantage, the people who create and perpetuate them. According to this New Directions view, this has effectively and practically meant failure at school for the majority of working class pupils, females and certain ethnic groups because school subjects are imbued with the values and culture of the white, Anglo-Saxon middle and upper classes, an influence which has marginalized and denigrated their own working class, feminine and ethnic cultures. Research by sociologists dating from the 1950s seemed to provide empirical support for this theory, revealing that despite more egalitarian approaches to the organization of educational systems, such as the introduction of comprehensive schools and the abandonment of selection exams, working class, female and certain ethnic groups of pupils still found less success at school than their middle class, male, white counterparts.

Part of the project of Young and his colleagues was to show that since subjects are not absolute and politically neutral categories of knowledge, then educational practitioners could play an important part in defining what is to count as worthwhile knowledge. Critics[14] argued, however, that their research failed to show how this might be possible, and their analyses offered only a naive possibilitarianism[15] that underestimated the power of vested interests to control knowledge production and legitimation through, for example, the examinations system and its use by the tertiary education sector and industry as a means of sifting and sorting pupils for the job market. One critic, Ivor Goodson,[16] has argued that Young and his colleagues failed to give names and faces to the dominant groups in society who are allegedly responsible for constructing school knowledge. This failure, by implication, leaves us none the wiser in terms of how we might overcome this domination.

Goodson's own work has attempted to remedy this shortcoming. He suggests that the focus of attention in understanding how school knowledge is constructed is to examine the actions of what he calls subject communities. These communities are not homogenous, but instead comprise amalgamations or coalitions of opposing and rival interest groups. Taking his lead from New Directions sociology of education, Goodson claims that school subjects are not monolithic, but instead consist of coalitions that are continuously shifting. The friction this movement creates among sub-groups within a subject community and between subject communities is motivated, according to Goodson, by the pursuit of material interests. He contends that there is a pattern in the evolution of a subject, through pedagogical and utilitarian concerns towards the ultimate achievement of academic status.

> The material interests of teachers — their pay, promotion and conditions — are broadly interlinked with the fate of other specialist subject communities. The 'academic' subject is placed at the top of the hierarchy of subjects because resource allocations take place on the basis of assumptions that such subjects are best suited for the able students who, it is further assumed, should receive favourable treatment.[17]

An important element in the achievement of academic status, which Goodson equates with acceptance into the structure of public examinations, is the establishment of a university discipline base. From this base, specialist teachers can be trained and deployed in schools to further consolidate the status of the subject.

In attempting to give names and faces to the so-called dominant groups who construct school knowledge, Goodson concentrates our attention on those actors most directly involved practically in the fate of particular bodies of knowledge. In the process, he supplies us with much that is of substantive interest in discovering how subjects in the secondary curriculum, in particular, come to be what they are. His work has also usefully illustrated the point that school subjects are not immutable, politically neutral bodies of knowledge, but are generated and take particular forms according to the practical interests of segments of the educational community. Goodson admits, however, that his concern for the activities of those involved practically and professionally in the development of school subjects has meant that he neglects in his own studies of Geography and Environmental Studies what he calls the structural origins of the climate of opinion that allows subject communities to get started in the first place. He makes the point that it is 'the structuring of material interest which provides the mediating mechanism between structural and interactional levels',[18] but this insight does not allow Goodson to reveal who does this structuring, how, and for what purpose. He concentrates on what Stephen Ball[19] has referred to as the 'relations of change', the actual activities that play a part in initiating change, and neglects to show how the 'conditions of change', the structural dimensions of society and of schooling create an appropriate climate of opinion that allows certain things to happen, to infuse and give form and substance to these relations.

Goodson claims that 'macro level changes may be actively reinterpreted at the micro level',[20] a comment which has led Kelly to point out that

> Goodson's approach interprets 'political' interests in terms of the mate-rial interests at stake in factional conflict. The idea that knowledge is 'socially constructed', for Goodson, seems to refer to the fact that it is the product of social interaction. A more critical interpretation is re-quired which sees the 'social' construction of knowledge in terms of the political interests of a particular social order. This demarcation lies in Goodson's interpretation of 'vested interests' as *material* interests of fac-tion members, without accounting for socio-cultural interests along ideological lines.[21]

Kelly claims that the within subject focus of Goodson's work, and his preoccupa-tion with material interests, lead him to neglect the ways in which broader socio-cultural forces intersect with the struggles of coalitions in particula sites, and so render him unable to explain the actions of individuals and groups which, on the face of it, seem to work against their own interests. Hence, Kelly claims, Goodson is unable to account for protagonists' actions which are underwritten by forces or motives other than the pursuit of material self-interest. He suggests that this neglect can be overcome to a degree by incorporating the notion of 'hege-mony' into Goodson's analysis of inter-factional conflict.[22] Kelly argues that this notion supplies a means of thinking about how the willing compliance of sub-ordinate groups in their own oppression is won and inequitable power relations sustained, and so provides a dimension that is missing from Goodson's approach.

I agree with the general thrust of Kelly's claim that Goodson's concern to portray the relations of change within and between subject communities tends to focus his attention too exclusively on the interactional dimensions of power struggles, and in so doing leads him to understate the structured relations of power, even though I think his critique fails in places to do justice to the depth and innovativeness of much of Goodson's work. Goodson has attempted in his more recent work to answer some of the questions these objections raise, which he considers in terms of what he sees as the internal and external forces acting on coalitions' actions.[23] This characterization of internal and external forces does broaden the focus of Goodson's work, and moves some way towards resolving the underlying problem which preoccupied Young and his colleagues in *Knowledge and Control*, which was to account for the ways in which the structure of knowledge in the school curriculum played a part in creating disproportionate levels of success achieved by middle over working class pupils (and we might now add, by boys over girls, and whites over blacks). But it still does not quite adequately provide a way of approaching this problem in the terms it has been characterized recently by some social theorists, who suggest that the process of change, the question of vested interests, and the nature of domination and subordination are immensely complex, contradictory and indeterminate,[24] or as one theorist puts it, power is generated 'with no-one directing it and everyone increasingly emeshed in it, (where the) only end is the increase of power and order itself'.[25] This does not mean that Goodson's stress on the pursuit of self-interest is irrelevant to accounts of power, but that merely to attempt to integrate micro and macro forces cannot do justice to the dynamic and convoluted nature of the operation of power in the process of social change.

However, this underlying problem in social research is not confined to Goodson's work or the field of curriculum history, but has since the early 1960s preoccupied social researchers in a range of fields including education. Evans and Davies suggest that the proliferation of theoretical approaches in the sociology of education following *Knowledge and Control* has led to appeals for 'some form of a synthesis in theory...or method...capable of making the connections between consciousness, human agency, cultures and social structure'.[26] Attempts to achieve this synthesis have been far from simple or trouble free, since factionalism among social researchers has tended to exacerbate differences in emphases and to establish these differences as polarities in terms, for example, of macro *versus* micro, interpretivist *versus* structuralist paradigms, or of studies of the production of social relations *versus* the production of individual subjectivity.[27] While real differences of point of view do exist among researchers, it would be fair to say that many of the current binary oppositions in social theory which appear to be fixed are, in fact, analytical conveniences which are themselves socially constructed.[28] This being the case, these apparent polarities are open to reconstruction, and the coherence of any new theoretical construct viewed as a matter of its usefulness for the particular purposes the researcher has in mind.

The purpose of this study is to build on the key insight produced by the work of Goodson and others, that change in the curriculum is the product of struggle and contestation between rival groups, and to apply this insight to explain recent conflict over the aims, content and pedagogy of physical education in schools. In undertaking such a study, I have tried to accomodate the notion that the interests of these rival groups are constitutive of and constituted by prevailing socio-cultural conditions, by instituttionalized practices organized around such characteristics of society as gender, race, and social class, and that the achievement of society — the capacity of individuals to live collectively as populations — is only possible by the convoluted circulations of power and its manifestation in instituionalized social relations.[29] The study is centrally concerned with the social production of physical education as a field of knowledge in schools, and with the ways in which the whole range of social practices this field embraces, such as sport and games playing, exercising, dancing and so on, are represented by physical educators (and others with interests in physical education) to other members of society as coherent, meaningful and significant aspects of culture. More broadly, the study attempts to explore the part played by this field of knowledge and the meanings generated by and around it in the ordering and achievement of society, centred on the events surrounding the 1987 General Election outlined in detail in Chapter 1 and revisited in Chapter 7.

In order to examine how the meaning of physical education has been constructed in Britain during the postwar period, I have focused on the ways in which vying individuals and groups have represented their understandings of physical education. The consequence of such a focus has been to treat the actions of these parties as discursive formations, as linguistic systems which express their attempts to make sense of physical education.[30] Consequently, the notion of discourse is a key concept in this study. In its most basic sense, discourse refers to the ways in which people communicate their understanding of their own and others' activities, and of events in the world around them. In other words, it refers to the ways in which they speak about, in this case, school physical education, not only through what they say verbally, but through what they write and what they do; and also through the gaps or silences in their discourses, what they *don't* say, write or do. The notion of discourse allows ideologies, which circumscribe the activities of particular individuals and groups, to be explored, revealing on the one hand the extent to which broader social forces have made an impression on their consciousness, and at the same time indicating the ways in which these forces have been appropriated and put to use in practical situations. The focal point of this study is a range of discourses in physical education which communicate something of the meaning of physical education for the speakers of these discourses. The notion of discourse is, therefore, central to a study of the social construction of school knowledge, since discourses in themselves embody *definitions* of their subject, in this case school physical education.[31]

This way of viewing the actions of vying groups as discursive formations precisely locates such notions as ideology and hegemony as 'frameworks of thinking and calculation about the world'.[32] Hall argues that ideologies appear in language, in 'the domain of meaning and representation', and in 'the rituals and practices of social action or behaviour which always occur in social sites'. He goes on to suggest that 'every social practice is constituted within the interplay of meaning and representation and can itself be represented. In other words, there is no social practice outside of ideology. However, this does not mean that, because all social practices are within the discursive, there is nothing to social practice *but* discourse...it does not follow that because all practices are *in* ideology, or inscribed by ideology, all practices are *nothing but* ideology'.[33] Hall's point is that all attempts to make sense of the world utilize language or language-like systems of signs, (in addition to written and spoken languages, music and mathematics would be two other commonplace examples), and so an analysis of social practices as discursive systems reveal the attempts to create meaning that are inscribed within them. At the same time, there are limits to this process. Every attempt to examine social processes, including this study, utilizes the same systems of representation it analyses, which means that *all* social analyses are in this sense ideological. Moreover, society cannot be understood by examining discursive formations alone, since social life has objective dimensions that exist beyond individual or collective comprehension; each person and each social group have, at any one time, only a partial knowledge of the world in which they live.[34]

Discursive formations are generated out of social practices carried out in particular sites, in the case of this study, practices centred around the teaching of physical education in schools. However, these formations are neither uniform nor necessarily internally consistent. Hall points out that ideologies are systems of representation which 'operate in discursive chains, in clusters, in semantic fields', and that the fixing, or what he calls articulation, of one system to another is determined by prevailing conditions in any specific place and at any given time;[35] for instance, in Chapter 5, I will explore the process whereby one system of representation expressed by the notion of the games ethic was articulated with a number of other systems, one of which was the problem of teenage delinquency, another, national identity, (and etc.) to comprise the discursive formation of 'traditional physical education'.

Hall notes, in addition, that the existence of these chains of significations which make up discursive formations make it simplistic to talk about *the* dominant ideology. He stresses that there is interplay between chains, that they contest each other, they draw on common concepts, but then rearticulate and disarticulate them in specific sites and use them for specific, sometimes contrary, purposes. The concept of ideological hegemony, as it is worked through in the writings of the Italian Marxist Antonio Gramsci,[36] provides a useful means of expressing this contingent, contested and constant process of struggle to utilise discursive formations to win consent from competing groups for social practices which advantage some factions of society over others. Gramsci's use of the notion of hegemony as co-extensive with the entire social process marked a significant break with previous uses of the term, and with static notions of particular ideologies linked too firmly to particular social class groups.[37] He suggests that in advanced capitalist democracies, inequitable power relations are not maintained in the main by brute force or coercion, but instead by the willing compliance of the oppressed in their own subordination. This compliance is achieved by the appearance of inequalities as part of the natural order of things, as fixed and unproblematic. Gramsci argues that in the complex process of negotiation and compromise that characterizes democratic class societies, hegemony is never total or absolute, and indeed the existence of oppositional or alternative discursive formations plays an active and constitutive part in the process. In this Gramscian sense of hegemony, Raymond Williams has pointed out that structured power relations and the inequalities that derive from these form part of people's consciousness at the level of commonsense and the everyday, and so are co-extensive with culture. For Williams

> Hegemony...is a whole body of practices and expectations, over the whole of living: our senses and assignments of energy, our shaping perceptions of ourselves and our world. It is a lived system of meaning and values — constitutive and constituting — which as they are experienced as practices appear as reciprocally confirming. It thus constitutes a sense of reality for most people in the society, a sense of absolute but experienced reality beyond which it is very difficult for most members of the society to move, in most areas of their lives. It is, that is to say, in

the strongest sense a 'culture', but a culture which has also to be seen as the lived dominance and subordination of particular classes.[38]

Through this notion of hegemony, Williams is suggesting that power relations are manifest and expressed in and through social interaction, but not always and sometimes never at the level of conscious awareness and deliberate strategy. Furthermore, the contingent and processual nature of the hegemonic, as a constitutive part of the ongoing flow of everyday life, denies the possibility of a *dominant* ideology associated with a particular social group. As Hall suggests, the *actual* dominant groups in society utilise a range of ideologies to advance their own positions, but the chains of ideas and images which make up these ideologies are most often in general circulation in a society, and are reassembled by different fractions of society for different purposes. At the same time, as Hall stresses, the contingent nature of this process of fixing chains of ideas to each other to form discursive formations does not imply that there are no determining principles in the distribution of power and privilege. Social formations are, as he suggests, a structure in dominance,[39] with distinct tendencies and a certain configuration; power is perpetuated through generations and some social groups do, consistently, disproportionately occupy positions of privilege and influence over others. The precise nature of this structure in dominance is a matter for investigation, however, not reductive determination, since the distribution of power is dependent on a whole range of prevailing conditions and circumstances in any specific location at any given time.

Defining Physical Education: the Social Construction of a School Subject

The act of defining physical education is a social process, one which involves drawing on ideas in general circulation, and fixing these ideas in a meaningful configuration. This fixing, as an instrinsic part of defining the subject, is no arbitrary process. As I aim to show in this study, particular definitions of physical education have gained acceptance as the orthodox version of the subject, and these definitions have advantaged certain social groups over others at particular times in history. In the final chapter of this book, for example, I will try to show how the crisis surrounding physical education at the time of the 1987 General Election was able to be turned to the advantage of the Thatcher government and a number of other social groups. In this respect, no definition of physical education is politically, socially or culturally neutral. Every attempt to define the aims, content and pedagogy of the subject involves making sense, which in turn involves a selection and articulation of particular sets of ideas.

At the same time, there is no suggestion that this process is conspiratorial, or that some hidden hand is at work. I plan to show in the following chapters that no definition is ever uncontested, no matter how widely accepted and staunchly defended, nor entirely consistent in its outcomes or implications, no matter how carefully thought out. As Gramsci's notion of the hegemonic suggests, the presence of alternative and oppositional discursive formations to the orthodoxies of the day plays a constructive role in reformulating future definitions, even though their radical potency may be absorbed, fragmented or dissipated in the process.

Some groups may indeed consciously conspire to bring about certain ends, and these actions, as Goodson's work so clearly demonstrates, form an important consideration in understanding the social construction of physical education. But their plans can never anticipate and account for all circumstances and conditions they will encounter in the future, and it is with this process, of constant adjustment, struggle and *re*-presentation that this study is centrally concerned.

The book is organized around four chapters which draw on historical material, one chapter sketching some dimensions of British political, cultural and educational life in the postwar period which are of particular importance to physical education, and three chapters dealing in much greater detail and depth with specific aspects of physical education discourse. I have not attempted to undertake an exhaustive study of the entire postwar period for a number of reasons, one of which is that I do not believe the documentation of every fact and event, relevant or not, to be necessary to make the point the book is written to make. I have also tended to concentrate attention unevenly across the period for much the same reason, concentrating most often on the 1950s. While the text is constructed around chronological events for the most part, this was done for the sake of readability and coherence more than any slavish belief on the immutability of temporal sequencing. At the same time, each of the three chapters on physical education discourse deals with broadly overlapping waves of events and activities that flow from the early part of the postwar period, from the mid 1940s to the early 1950s in Chapter 4, through the middle part, from the early to late 1950s in Chapter 5, and on to the later part, from the late 1950s to the late 1960s in Chapter 6. In Chapter 7, I overview briefly the consolidation and elaboration of these themes during the 1970s and early 1980s, thus returning the analysis to the second half of the 1980s and a discussion of the new forces that are likely to be unleashed as a result of the recent public debate over school physical education.

As I have previously remarked, the major purpose of this book is to work through in substantive terms the social construction of physical education during this period, and to identify the emerging discourses that have come to form the underpinning structure of contemporary physical education programmes. In the process, I attempt to show that the activities and subject matter contained in these discourses are by no means neutral, self-evident or natural. The physical education programmes in place in the school curriculum today are the outcome of contestation and struggle between a range of competing groups' attempts to define the subject. In the process, the activities that make up programmes, the ways in which they are taught, and the reasons that are preferred for teaching them all contain the residue of these struggles, and reflect the interests of the contesting parties. These interests are not reflected in an equitable manner, however, since some parties, as we will see, have been able to mobilise resources which have not been available to others. Since physical education programmes in schools advantage some parties more than others, some children who experience these programmes in schools are, often unjustly, disadvantaged. Indeed, it is this problem that has concerned some sociologists of school knowledge since the publication of *Knowledge and Control*,[40] and has been at the root of the more recent debate over physical education, since some physical educators have begun to recognize that their programmes may be relevant to only a small proportion of their pupils.

Of the three chapters which focus on physical education discourse, two deal with the more readily recognizable aspects of the contemporary debate, competitive team games and the health and fitness orientation, while the third, Chapter 4, explores a transitional phase in school physical education during the 1940s and 1950s centering on the demise of gymnastics as the core of physical education. This chapter outlines the factors and circumstances surrounding this decline in influence in gymnastics, and the concomitant decline of a distinctly female influence in physical education. The debate over gymnastics reveals a fundamental rift within the physical education profession between female and male physical educators, a rift which has had lasting influence, and competing definitions of physical education associated with each party. The females championed educational gymnastics, which embodied a form of child-centred progressivism, while the males supported competitive gymnastics, which was embedded in the logic of scientific functionalism and drew on the new knowledge of skill development, biomechanics and exercise physiology. Chapter 5 shows how the male physical educators also promoted scientific functionalism in relation to competitive team games in the new mass secondary schools after the war, and investigates the installation of team games at the heart of male, and later female, physical education programmes. The invention of 'traditional physical education', with competitive team games at its core, took place during the 1950s as games superceded gymnastics and the influence of the male physical educators overcame that of the females. It was at this point, during the 1950s, that the most far-reaching reconstruction of the meaning of physical education took place. The dominance of the male influence was further consolidated in relation to the redefinition of the link between physical education and health, and elaboration of this issue forms the substance of Chapter 6. The new view of this relationship was encapsulated in the notion of physical fitness, which was constructed around the scientific knowledge of exercise.

Woven through the substantive concerns of these chapters are a number of other themes which were part of political, cultural and educational life in postwar Britain, and played an important role in shaping the form and content of these discourses in physical education. These themes are sketched broadly in the next chapter, and relate to issues such as the rise of mass secondary schooling, social class and egalitarianism, affluence and mass consumerism, and teenage delinquency, youth culture and the erosion of traditional values. These issues saturated popular consciousness and everyday concerns in a myriad of different and diffuse ways, and Chapter 3 is a selective attempt to highlight the major factors which appeared to have a decisive impact on physical education discourse. The values and expectations created during the social reconstruction of Britain after the second world war have had continued relevance for contemporary social life, and the account in Chapter 3 may provide readers with some useful points of orientation in terms of understanding the ways in which current political, cultural and educational trends are shaping physical education discourse now.

Notes

1 *The Australian Weekend*, August 19–20, 1989.
2 Musgrave, P.W. (1988) 'Curriculum history: past, present and future', *History of Education Review*, **17**(2), 1–13.

3 Goodson, I. (1988) *The Making of Curriculum: Collected Essays*, Lewes: Falmer Press.

4 Seddon, T. (1989) 'Curriculum history: A map of key issues', *Curriculum Perspectives*, **9**(4), 1–16.

5 I have made a similar point about curriculum research more generally in Kirk, D. (1989) 'Curriculum research and educational praxis', *Curriculum Perspectives*, **9**(4), 41–50; although in the case of curriculum history *per se*, Seddon is stressing the temporal dimensions of this process of the social construction of knowledge.

6 See for example Goodson, note 1, and Musgrave, note 2, for two informative discussions of these issues.

7 Reid, W.A. (1978) *Thinking About the Curriculum: The Nature and Treatment of Curriculum Problems* London: Routledge and Kegan Paul, p. 98.

8 With a number of notable exceptions in the work of for example Mangan, J.A. (1981) *Athleticism in the Victorian and Edwardian Public School*, Cambridge University Press; Fletcher, S. (1984) *Women First: The Female Tradition in English Physical Education, 1880–1980*, London: Althone Press; Hargreaves, J. (1986) *Sport, Power and Culture: A Social and Historical Analysis of Popular Sport in Britain*, Cambridge: Polity Press.

9 Evans, J. and Davies, B. (1986) 'Sociology, schooling and physical education', in Evans, J. (Ed.) *Physical Education, Sport and Schooling: Studies in the Sociology of Physical Education*, Lewes: Falmer Press, pp. 11–37.

10 Young, M.F.D. (1975) 'Curriculum change: Limits and possibilities', *Educational Studies*, **1**(2), 129–138.

11 See Anne Williams' historiography, Williams, A. (1988) 'The historiography of health and fitness in physical education', *PEA Research Supplement*, **3**, 1–4.

12 See for example Bernstein, B. (1971) 'On the classification and framing of educational knowledge', in Young, M.F.D. (Ed.) *Knowledge and Control: New Directions for the Sociology of Education*, London: Collier-MacMillan, pp. 47–69; Bucher, R. and Strauss, A. (1976) 'Professions in process', in Hammersley, M. and Woods, P. (Eds) *The Process of Schooling* London: Routledge and Kegan Paul/Open University Press, pp. 19–26.

13 Young, M.F.D. (1971 Ed.) *Knowledge and Control: New Directions for the Sociology of Education*, London: Collier-MacMillan.

14 Bates, R. (1981) 'What can the new sociology of education do for teachers?' *Discourse*, **1**(2), 41–53; Demaine, J. (1981) *Contemporary Theories in the Sociology of Education*, London: MacMillan.

15 Whitty, G. (1985) *Sociology and School Knowledge: Curriculum Theory, Research and Politics*, London: Methuen.

16 Goodson, I. (1987) *School Subjects and Curriculum Change* Lewes: Falmer Press; Goodson, I. (1984) 'Subjects for study: Towards a social history of curriculum', in Goodson, I. and Ball, S. (Eds) *Defining the Curriculum: Histories and Ethnographies* Lewes: Falmer Press, pp. 25–44, Goodson, I. (1985 Ed.) *Social Histories of the Secondary Curriculum: Subjects for Study* Lewes: Falmer Press; Goodson, I. (1988) *The Making of Curriculum: Collected Essays* Lewes: Falmer Press.

17 Goodson (1985), note 16, p. 360.

18 Goodson (1984), note 16, p. 43.

19 Ball, S.J. (1985) 'English for the English since 1906', in Goodson, I. (1985 Ed.) *Social Histories of the Secondary Curriculum: Subjects for Study* Lewes: Falmer Press, pp. 53–88.

20 Goodson (1983), note 16, p. 3.

21 Kelly, N. (1988) Redefining Socio-Historical Analyses of School Subjects: An Appraisal and Extension of Ivor Goodson's Approach. Mimeo, University of Queensland, p. 7.

22 See the exposition of hegemony below.

23   See Goodson, I. (1988) *The Making Curriculum: Collected Essays* Lewes: Falmer Press, especially pp. 7–11.

24   Hall, S. (1985) 'Signification, representation, ideology: Althusser and the post-structuralist debates', *Critical Studies in Mass Communication*, **2**(2), 91–114.

25   In Dreyfus, H.L. and Rainbow, P. (1982) *Michel Foucault: Beyond Structuralism and Hermeneutics* Brighton: The Harvester Press, p. xxii.

26   Evans and Davies, note 9, p. 29.

27   See, respectively, Hargreaves, A. (1985) 'The macro/micro problem in the sociology of education', in Burgess, R. (Ed.) *Issues in Educational Research: Qualitative Methods* Lewes: Falmer Press; Evans and Davies, note 9; Hall, note 24.

28   Fitzclarence, L. 'Media, Physical Education and the Problem of Binary Associations', Seminar, Deakin University, May 1990.

29   Turner, B. (1984) *The Body and Society: Explorations in Social Theory* Oxford: Blackwell.

30   Hall, note 24.

31   The methodological implications of the use of this notion of discourse as a focal point of the study have meant a heavy reliance on written and other documentary evidence in the form of scholarly articles, research reports, personal accounts and anecdotes, films and novels and a range of other records such as official statistics and secondary accounts such as historical analyses. No piece of evidence is treated simply, at face value, but is analyzed to yield its reflexive meanings. In other words, each source of information not only tells about something in particular, an event for example, but also reveals something about itself, its relationship to other accounts of the same event, the political persuasions of its author perhaps, or the intended impression the account is meant to convey. In this respect, each element in a discursive formation is analyzed in relation to other discursive formations in order to yield accounts that are thoroughly contextualized and so intelligible interpretations of the construction of physical education discourse in the postwar years.

32   Hall, note 24, pp. 99–100.

33   Hall, note 24, p. 103.

34   See, for a detailed social phenomenological account of the partiality of knowledge, Schutz, A. (1962) *Collected Papers Vol 1* The Hague: Martinus Nijhoff. See also Anthony Giddens (1979) *Central Problems in Social Theory* London: MacMillan, pp. 72–73 for an elaboration of this notion, in particular where he notes that individual consciousness is bounded in specifiable ways and that awareness 'shades off' beyond day-to-day activities. Giddens suggests that all social actors have 'some degree of penetration of...social forms'; however, he makes a useful distinction between discursive and practical consciousness, and argues that while people commonly know how to be competant social actors at the level of practical consciousness, they may be quite unable to express this understanding linguistically, an inability that in no way undermines their social competancies. This study is most concerned with the discursive dimension of consciousness, though it should be noted that there is no hard and fast division between discursive and practical, and that the act of committing thoughts, opinions and ideas to the written word contains both elements.

35   Hall, note 24, p. 104.

36   Gramsci, A. (1971) *Selections From the Prison Notebooks* London: Lawerence and Wishart.

37   Williams, R. (1977) *Marxism and Literature* Oxford University Press.

38   Williams, note 37, p. 110.

39   Hall, note 24, p. 91.

40   See Whitty, G. (1985) *Sociology and School Knowledge: Curriculum Theory, Research and Politics* London: Methuen.

Chapter 3

Politics, Culture and Education in Postwar Britain

The twenty-five year period that followed the end of the second world war was marked by a number of paradoxes in British political and cultural life. One of the most prominent messages running through all aspects of social life was the notion that Britain had emerged from the destruction and austerity of the war years as a stable, conflict-free society in which consensus and convergence were the key themes. The invention of mass secondary schooling did much to both reflect and confirm this view, encapsulating many of the postwar hopes and ideals for a more egalitarian and prosperous future, one in which the bourgeois ideology of meritocracy — just reward for hard work and talent — dominated political and educational policies and commonsense perspectives on life more generally. Yet beneath these hopes and ideals and the conviction that the British people had earned *their* just reward, were signs that bode ill for the future. Britain had indeed produced more wealth in the immediate postwar years but very soon after began to fall behind the productivity of its rivals in the international market-place. And while some sections of the population became more prosperous, there was in fact little change in the overall distribution of wealth and privilege. In the social and cultural sphere, there was a popular conception of the 1950s as an era of moral deterioration and rising teenage violence and crime, through which rebellious youth threatened disruption of the social order. As we will see later in this chapter, it has been argued by some analysts of this period that in reality, this culture of rebellion was inflated to displace and contain the threat of any genuine social unrest, and the values and social mores of the majority of the population changed far less rapidly and dramatically than was popularly portrayed at the time.

The introduction of mass secondary schooling was of as much symbolic as practical significance in this era of paradoxes, and embodied many paradoxical features in its own right. During the war, free secondary education for all was projected as a central element in postwar 'social reconstruction'. Much of the agitation for this innovation had come from socialist reformers in the 1930s, and mass secondary schooling carried with it many of their values as it developed into the 1950s. From the start, however, the egalitarian project of the socialists was undermined by the structuring of the new system along selective lines, and even though comprehensive schooling (with its slogan 'equality of opportunity') became a metaphor for an equal society in the late 1950s and early 1960s, it was never able to rid itself of the meritocratic ideology of the selective system, which was in itself a reflection of the socially stratified, consumption driven and materialistic society that Britain became during the postwar years.

The purpose of this chapter is to outline briefly some of the key features of the political, cultural and educational contexts in which physical education discourse was located and developed in the postwar era. It explores, firstly, the major features of party-politics in the aftermath of the second world war, a period in which the policies of both Conservative and Labour parties underwent transformations as Britian emerged after 1945 into the new world system of international capitalism and the 'cold war'. The theme of consensus which dominated political life also infused social and cultural life, and the second section of the chapter outlines some of the main aspects of everyday life and its representation in film, literature and television. The third and final section locates educational discourse of the time within this nexus of politics and culture, and identifies the key issues that circumscribed educational practice throughout the period.

Consensus in British Postwar Politics

The two major parties in British political life experienced mixed fortunes following the end of the second world war, with Labour governments in the late 1940s and the early 1960s forming bookends to a prolonged period of Conservative domination through the 1950s. Labour's early period in government was marked by austerity in the years immediately following the cessation of hostilities, but also with the hope and promise of better times to come, with Labour riding high on the ideals of 'social reconstruction' after the physical and spiritual devastation of the war. When prosperity arrived under the Conservatives during the 1950s, it seemed as if those hopes had been realized. The Tories won three successive elections through the 1950s and captured the high ground of social imagery, as the government for an affluent society. This period of prosperity was relatively shortlived, with the sterling crisis of 1961 marking the beginning of the end, both for the Conservatives' run in government and the heady optimism of the immediate postwar era. Yet despite the varying fortunes of each party in government and their respective associations with austerity and prosperity, the outstanding feature of political life in the postwar era was the degree of consensus among protagonists of the apparently opposing policies of the Conservative and Labour parties. Indeed, there was widespread acceptance across the political spectrum of the 1955 General Election message that British society was conflict-free. Behind this consensus, the policies of each of these political parties was in the process of being redefined as their proponents struggled to make sense of the new balance of economic and military power in the postwar world.

Labour came to government in 1945 with its largest ever majority (before or since); of the number who voted (some seventy-three per cent of the population), forty-eight per cent voted Labour. In some respects, Labour's success at the election was a reflection of the feeling at the time of the need for change. Soldiers coming back from the war were determined that victory should not be marred by a return to the Depression years, where unemployment had stood at around one and three-quarter million in 1921 and at over two million throughout the 1930s. The election of a Labour government, with its package of welfare policies, seemed to represent the radical break with the past that was needed to ensure that the future had been worth fighting for.[1] The phrase 'welfare state' had been coined in the 1930s, and was in widespread use during the war in pointed contrast to Hitler's 'warfare state'. While the phrase has come to be used in a variety of ways since, it generally referred to the policies and schemes through which central and local government intervened in the management of a range of social problems.[2] In the years leading up to the end of the war, a cluster of policies were devised and enacted that were explicitly aimed at what was described at the time as 'social reconstruction'. The major priorities were unemployment, housing and health care, and the policies developed in these areas formed the beginnings of the contemporary system of social security, the large local authority controlled housing estates, and the National Health Service. Other areas of life also felt the benefits of this era of reconstruction, particularly education, but also child-care, the Arts, and the environment.

Full employment was a particular goal of this and subsequent governments, and this need was met in the initial postwar years through the massive expansion of building programmes, especially new houses and factories in the blitzed areas (the first 'new towns' date from the period between 1945 and 1950), with the creation of new schools, colleges and hospitals to house the rapidly expanding medical and educational services. The war had also provided a stimulus to science and technology, and indeed for many members of the political left, the twin forces of science (harnessed to peaceful use) and socialist democracy marked the beginning of a new age of enlightenment.[3] New industries, particularly electronics and optics, grew directly out of the broader application of technology beyond purely military purposes. Employment was created out of the commercial development of nuclear power to generate electricity, and the wider applications of artificial fibres and pesticides. People also benefitted more generally from the civilian development of such inventions as radar, radio isotopes in medicine, and from the widespread use of penicillin.

Despite the radical changes that were proposed and brought into being during this period — free medical care, subsidized housing, financial provision for the unemployed, sick and elderly, free secondary schooling — there was, on the surface at least, a degree of consensus among the rival political parties. This was due in part to the fact that irrespective of which party gained power in 1945, each would have faced the same problems, of restoring full employment and extending social services to meet the needs of social reconstruction. Thus, when the Labour government finally ceded power to the Conservatives in 1951, there was little change in the overall direction of policy. Labour had expected Tory retrenchment and an overturning of the war-time commitments to the welfare state, but apart from some de-nationalization the 'New Conservatism' stood by the welfare state and accepted the necessity of state intervention in managing the economy. There were, certainly, differences of opinion between the rival factions, particularly as we will see in relation to education.[4] The Suez crisis of 1956, where the Conservative Prime Minister Anthony Eden attempted through the use of 'gun-boat diplomacy' to depose the Egyptian President Nasser, sharply divided the country along party lines. The issue of defence focused around the nuclear question was in the late 1950s to draw an even more marked divide between Labour and Conservative, and 1959 marked a highspot in the career of the Campaign for Nuclear Disarmament (CND) which was supported by a broad range of left wing organizations. It is significant to note in this context that neither education nor defence were important election issues for either party until the beginning of the 1960s.

However, the political consensus of the immediate postwar years can also be explained by the fact that many of Labour's policies were less radical than they seemed. A case in point was the nationalization of the coal industry in the late 1940s. Many of the miners at first believed that the ownership and running of the mines would be passed on to the workers. Instead, the same managers and supervisors from the more efficients pits were retained to do the job they had done previously under private ownership.[5] There was little change for the miners in any practical sense. The ideal of a free health service provides another example of a potentially radical innovation that was subsequently watered-down. Ironically, the first move away from this ideal was made by the Labour government which, as part of its rearmament policy at the outbreak of the Korean war, sought to raise funds by imposing a charge on health service prescriptions. In education, the adoption of the 'tripartite system' for the reorganization of secondary schooling, while it was not without its critics within the Labour party,[6] was another example of the psuedo-radicalism of the time.[7] Thus, while the Labour-sponsored welfare programme seemed to be radical, optimistic and ambitious, in reality the Labour government did little to upset the balance of power during its term of office between 1945 and 1951. The Labour leaders who came to power in 1945, such as Hugh Dalton, Sir Stafford Cripps and the Prime Minister Clement Atlee belonged firmly to the upper classes. Indeed, social surveys conducted at the time revealed that while there was a fair amount of upward and downward movement within and between classes, the British public were under no illusions that they belonged to a classless society, and invariably differentiated between three broad levels of upper, middle and working classes. Other institutions had also weathered the war years, such as the nation's professed loyalty to the monarchy, and marriage, which maintained its popularity after a peak of 60,000 divorces in 1947, six times the pre-war average.[8]

After the Conservative victory in 1951, the basis for political consensus altered. The Conservatives, as I have already suggested, carried on with the welfare initiatives set in motion by Labour. But as the 1950s progressed, it was the Labour party which developed an identity crisis that forced it towards policies that were in some cases barely distinguishable from those of their Tory rivals. Even though Labour lost the General Election of 1951, it still polled more votes than the Conservatives with just under fourteen million compared with the Tories' thirteen and a half million. The Conservatives won 321 seats to Labour's 295 due to the disproportionately large majorities of Labour's wins in some of its traditional strongholds. But because of the nature of this result, Labour politicians did not regard their defeat as indicative of a loss of faith among their traditional supporters. The 1955 election was a different matter however, with Labour losing an estimated one and a half million votes, despite the fact that there were more voters, electorates and no unopposed seats.[9] Voter apathy was blamed for the overall downturn in voting, but it was Labour which bore the brunt of the losses. For the first time, Labour politicians began to harbour serious misgivings over the continuing loyalty of their traditional base of support and, more generally, their public image.

The successive Conservative victories thus caused Labour to revise some of its key policies and principles. Above all, after 1955 the Tories were able to discredit Labour's claim that Conservatism brought 1930s-style unemployment, and forced Labour on to the back-foot with the Tories' powerful self-imagery as the party of prosperity. Labour had no alternative imagery to offer, and as one commentator has argued, 'by a process of inversion, the reasons for Tory success became the causes of Labour decline'.[10] The Labour response to Conservative monopoly was to abandon the traditional class-based analysis of capitalism. Their alternative was a revisionist policy that saw full employment, welfare and the erosion of poverty as no longer dependent on nationalization, a policy which shared the Tory diagnosis that these goals could be achieved within a mixed economy. As working class affluence followed postwar austerity, the Labour vote fell absolutely and proportionately with each election. Some sections of the Labour Party believed they saw in this decline the traditional working class base of support being steadily eroded. Doris Lessing's *Pursuit of the Working Class*, for instance, led her to the conclusion that 'the entire working-class of Britain has become tainted by capitalism or has lost its teeth. It is petit bourgeois to a man'.[11] Mark Abrams, commissioned after Labour's third successive election defeat in October 1959 to discover what image of Labour was held by different groups of voters, confirmed the conviction on both sides of the political divide that the Labour Party was increasingly associated with the working-class and the poor, and that it was 'obsolete in terms of contemporary Britain'.[12] Affluence was believed to have dismantled old class barriers, and the working class were becoming embourgeoisified by rising living standards and middle class values.

In the run-up to the 1959 election, the Conservatives attempted to repair their dented image after the Suez fiasco and Eden's resignation early in 1957, by constructing a campaign based entirely on this social imagery of themselves as the party of prosperity. They reportedly spent up to £468,000 on advertising between June 1957 and September 1959, and were now able to build on the contemporary social experience of higher wages, full employment, and more material possessions. One poster in the campaign showed a cloth-capped worker with a plump, prosperous looking face and a caption which read:

> Six Conservative years have brought big improvements all round. Life's better in every way than it was. He and his wife are both clear about that. So many more things to buy in the shops. More money to buy them with too. The kids are coming along well at school. In fact in his view a pretty encouraging outlook for all of them. Well what's so special about that? Aren't there millions these days who are just as well fixed?[13]

Ownership of a television, car, washing-machine and refrigerator were celebrated by the Conservatives as the material symbols of progress and the good life, and in this they were once again able to wrong-foot Labour, since any oppositional rhetoric from them could so easily have been interpreted as opposition to prosperity. Nevertheless, Labour party policy had undergone considerable revision since the 1955 election, and in 1959 the party approached the campaign with a measure of confidence. In the event, the 1959 election witnessed the fourth successive rise in the Conservative majority and a further erosion of Labour's proportion of the poll, with Labour's third election defeat of the decade being read by some as a sign of the demise of Labour as a party that could govern.

Even the New Left, who virtually stood alone in challenging what later came to be revealed as the 'myth of affluence', had to concede in the late 1950s that something had changed in relation to the prosperity of the British working class.[14]

However, fortunes were soon to change. During the early 1960s the Conservatives found it increasingly difficult to maintain their image as the party of prosperity. After the war, exports were revealed as the Achilles' heel of the British economy, and between 1954 and the end of 1960, Britain's share of world manufacturing exports decreased from around twenty per cent to below fifteen and a half percent, while Germany, France, Italy and Japan increased either the percentage or the rate of growth of their exports at levels significantly higher than Britain's. In addition, Britain's role as 'central banker' for sterling in the international market placed it in the precarious position of having assests that fell far short of the potential claims of creditors.[15] These factors indicated a deep-seated problem that, despite regular fluctuations, was representative of a long term downward trend.

> British capitalism faced increasing competition in world markets: it was continuously losing part of its share of world output and exports. Its level of investment and economic growth was low by international standards. This lack of competitiveness, combined with unwillingness to devalue the exchange rate, led to repeated crises in the balance of payments which were always answered by restrictions on home demand, thus further checking the rate of growth.[16]

This downward cycle in the economy was exacerbated by the Conservatives' reluctance to acknowledge Britain's changing role in the world system, and while the country's economic growth could still look impressive in isolation, compared to its international competitors it was dropping behind. The Conservative leadership changed hands in 1963, but the anachronistic figure of the new Prime Minister Lord Home offered little hope of a realignment in Conservative attitude to Britain's declining role as a world power. Meanwhile, the Labour party's policy during this period has been described as the social-democratic variant of the Conservatives' consensus policy,[17] and the installation of Harold Wilson as Labour leader early in 1963 saw a dramatic recovery of Labour's fortunes. No longer burdened by its traditional associations with the poor and the working classes, Labour approached the 1964 election on a platform of 'youth, dynamism and progress',[18] and while the Wilson Labour government that came to power later that year brought a social-democratic flavour to policy in a range of spheres, the ideals that underpinned these initiatives had much in common with Conservative policy of the time.

Consensus was, then, the overwhelming feature of political life in postwar Britain. While there were, certainly, major points of disagreement between the Conservatives and Labour on specific issues during the postwar years, and also divisions within the ranks of each parliamentary party, these rivalries were over-shadowed by the widespread feeling abroad at the time, that after the deprivation and hardship of the war and its aftermath, the British people 'had entered into their just inheritance'.[19] A number of other forces were at work too. There was a common agreement between the two major political parties over the problems that needed to be tackled in the effort to rebuild the country, and until the mid 1950s, in the transition from austerity to affluence, the Conservatives did little to upset the democratic charter for social reconstruction that had been earlier championed by Labour. And later, in the late 1950s and early 1960s, when it began to become clear that continuing prosperity depended on the rearticulation of Britain's role in the world system, the rival parties differed little in terms of how such a task should be undertaken. There was, too, a continuity in British society that worked, in Marwick's words through 'complacency, parochialism, and lack of serious structural change' to undermine and subvert the potential radicalism of the initial postwar years. This consensus betrayed the fact that while the appearence and ethos of change was abroad, there was at the same time a structured conservatism in British political life that lay beneath noisy euphoria and heady optimism. And while there was a general agreement from most points on the political spectrum that the lot of the British worker had improved to some degree, there was also considerable concern over the social and cultural conse-quences of affluence, and the suggestion by some commentators that this pro-gress had brought with it attendant 'cultural dangers'.[20]

Social and Cultural Life: Change and Continuity

Consensus may have been the chief characteristic of political life in postwar Britain, but this era has also been portrayed as one of acute and rapid social change. There were, in the initial postwar years, many changes and disjunctions that were due directly to the disruption of the war itself, such as the breakup of families and the destruction of homes, factories and hospitals. In the face of these upheavals and the euphoria that accompanied victory, the idea gained a degree of credibility that a genuine break from what had gone before might be possible. But euphoria lasted only for a short while, and many of the potentially radical ideals of the immediate postwar era were quickly to be watered–down, over-turned, or as in some cases of educational policy, undermined from the start. And in some cases, such as the social class divisions in society, it has been suggested that very little changed at all. Despite the apparent transition from austerity to affluence in the 1950s, the relative distribution of wealth and privilege remaining fairly constant with pre-war levels.[21] Indeed, as one historian has argued, the question 'What Went Wrong?' is a particularly apt epitath to this period for it reveals an ethos of optimism abroad in many sections of society in the 1940s and 1950s that was subsequently to turn to a disappointment which was being openly acknowledged by the end of the 1960s.[22] The postwar period was characterized by a number of contrasting features in social life: optimism and an almost unbridled confidence in the creation of a prosperous future for all; an austerity that stemmed directly from the effects of the deprivations of war and that lasted for many people until the mid 1950s; and, as we have seen, a degree of apparent consensus in politics that stood in stark contrast to the disturbing underswells of class conflict during the Depression years of the 1930s.

The optimistic view that a better society was on the way needs to be set in the prevailing austerity of the late 1940s and early 1950s. There were widespread shortages of the most basic necessities in life, and for the masses rationing did not completely end until the early 1950s.[23] The shortages also extended to building materials, and many of the Labour government's good intentions were frustrated on this point. There was an acute shortfall in housing and it was common for newly married couples to spend the first few months, or even years, of married life in one of their parents' homes, or else to emigrate only to find the same problems elsewhere.[24] There was a feeling among some who identified themselves as working class that living conditions were improving for them during the life-time of the Labour government (1945–51). Marwick has argued, however, that 'the basic fact remained; to be working class meant performing manual work, most usually under arduous, uncongenial, or just plain boring circum-stances'.[25] On the other hand, there was little evidence of aspiration to middle class status among many of the working classes. The use of education as a means of social mobility had long been understood, but agitation for the common school remained the work of a minority of the politically motivated. 'Individual members might move upwards, but conditions within the working class, not excluding working class attitudes themselves, discouraged educational aspiration'.[26] As restrictions on lifestyle were eased, however, and the material conditions of existence improved, it is easy to imagine that this 'progress', relative to the deprivations of the war years, confirmed the feeling that the British people were on the threshold of a better life.

While working class occupations may have remained arduous and uncon-genial, the nature of the work itself was nevertheless changing through the 1950s. Figures show that there was an important decrease in what was classed as 'unskilled labour' between 1931–61, and an increase in all other categories of work, the largest increases being in the 'semi-skilled' and 'technical' groups.[27] These figures bear witness to the ongoing decline over this period of the tradi-tional heavy industries and the ascendency in the new lighter industries, based on the recent technological advances, in which women workers played a key role. By the end of the 1950s, the idea was already abroad that this rapid advance of technology required each new generation to have 'more' education, meaning longer periods at school and in special training courses. People in education and industry began to talk of the 'knowledge explosion',[28] the need for a technologi-cally proficient work-force and more scientists and technicians to improve in-dustrial productivity. For the first time scientists began to appear on the boards of multi-national conglomerates like Unilever.

The rapid advance of technology hand-in-hand with increasing affluence had its most profound impact, not in the workplace, but in the home. Over a relatively short period of time people's day-to-day lives were profoundly affected by devices like washing-machines and vacuum-cleaners, by motor-cars, and by television. As the consumer society began to take off, the role of women became more important as they were targeted by advertisers as the likely purchasers, or at least users, of their appliances. Women were also going out to work in greater numbers as their (alleged) dexterity with intricate tasks was used in industries like electronics. The impact of technological advance at this level cannot be over-emphasized, because it brought changes to the fabric of people's everyday lives, and had a crucial impact at the subconscious level of value and assumption. Scientific advances were made somewhere 'out there', in the laboratories of universities and research institutes that few undoubtedly ever stopped to think of or consider, but the results of this work were nevertheless felt directly and personally by people throughout society. Marwick has commented that:

in the sixties there evolved a technological civilization of a sort not previously seen in Britain...now the concept of one unified technology, based on what its apostles termed 'the systems approach', was beginning to influence every aspect of social organization.[29]

In train with growing affluence and prosperity came mass consumerism, and working class youth became an important target group for the advertising and sale of mass cultural products. Indeed, the 1950s was the decade in which 'youth' attracted enormous attention and gained a distinctive cultural status. The 'teenager' was invented in the United States in the 1940s, the term coined by American market researchers who wished to describe young people with money to spend on consumer goods, and imported along with the pop culture of rock 'n' roll music and the phenomenon of the 'teenage idol'. These idols, like Elvis Presley, Cliff Richard, and James Dean, were all young people. They were also highly 'successful' and gave prominence and legitimacy to youthful values that never before had commanded such prestige and power and such an influence on their adolescent fans. The 'affluent teenager' became something of a metaphor for the decade, representing the cutting edge of social change. As Hill has argued, 'central to the imagery of the 'affluent teenager' was the idea of a dissolution of old class barriers and the construction of a new collective identity based on teenage values'.[30] At the same time, this new society of classless, affluent youth exposed the dark underside of the new Britain, in which traditional values good and bad were to be cast aside in the hedonistic rush towards the good life, and the teenager soon came to be associated with the extremes of affluence and the debasement of working class culture.[31] By the end of the 1950s, the idea of the menacing teenager had, allegedly, 'stirred up panic' among some sections of the adult community, and the question of social control became a public issue, stimulating government action[32] and official reports on youth.[33] However, in a retrospective analysis of the moral panic generated around the ideas of the violent teenage gang and promiscuity among youth, Montgomery argued that these allegations had been grossly inflated by the media and other agencies. Although teenage convictions did increase during the 1950s, they peaked at only twenty-one per thousand in 1958, and only a small proportion of these convictions were for violent crime.[34] The notion of the classless teenager was also a myth. The 'Teddyboy' culture was confined almost exclusively to working class youth, and teenage consumerism was also a working class, rather than middle class, phenomenon.

The Arts, and in particular cinema and television, played a crucial role in the postwar period not only for their portrayal of contemporary cultural concerns, but also for their part in working back on their audiences to form, and provide a means of expression of, particular cultural attitudes. According to John Hill, the smugness and complacency of the British intelligentsia was shattered in 1956 following the Royal Court's production of John Osborne's *Look Back in Anger*, which had antecedents in new poetry and writing in the early 1950s.[35] In British cinema, the demise in the quality of films being produced at the Ealing Studios in the late 1940s was followed by a genre of 'new wave' cinema, which was marked by its attempts to portray social and cultural issues in a realistic form. A cluster of 'social problem' films emerged, with issues like juvenile delinquency, prostitution, homosexuality and race becoming standard preoccupations. *The Blue Lamp*

(1950),[36] *Violent Playground* (1957) and *Spare the Rod* (1961) were just three of the films that dealt with the problem of youth, while race was the subject of films like *Sapphire* (1959) and *Wind of Change* (1961). *To Sir With Love* was just one of the several films of the time that utilised educational settings and issues to confront broader cultural concerns. Hill has commented that the film, though made in the 1960s:

> nonetheless looks back to the 1950s...in the organization of its assumptions...it involves a new recruit to the teaching profession confronted by a hostile and threatening classroom...Thackery (Sidney Poitier) abandons the school curriculum (throwing the set books into the waste bin) and ultimately succeeds in winning over the pupils. His educational philosophy, however, is entirely middle-class in its attitudes, consisting primarily of 'suburban formality' (addressing the girls as 'Miss') and 'culture for the masses' (a trip to the museum). The role performed by Poitier, in this respect, is eloquent. He is both like the kids but not, a 'toff' yet at the same time ordinary. An immigrant from the colonies, with a background of poverty and manual labour, he functions as a mediator between what the kids currently are and what they might yet become. 'If you're prepared to work hard, you can do almost anything, you can get any job you want', he explains (a statement which is ridiculous even in the film's own terms since he himself is unable to get a job as an engineer).[37]

There were also important portrayals of working class life in both cinema and literature. Indeed, many of the films that were most strongly representative of working class life, such as *Room at the Top* (1959), *Saturday Night and Sunday Morning* (1960), *The Loneliness of the Long Distance Runner* (1962) and *A Kind of Loving* (1962), began life as novels. Their authors were soon to be labelled collectively as 'angry young men' by the press, along with the novels' and films' leading characters. Indeed, while Stuart Laing has argued that this stereotyping was at times quite inaccurate,[38] he has suggested that there was a direct link through from Kingsley Amis' *Lucky Jim* (1954), and *Look Back in Anger* and *Room at the Top*, to the 1960s novels of Sillitoe, Storey and Barstow, in terms of 'the young male hero on the make in the fluid social situation of the new Britain'.[39] The 'angry young man' was portrayed in many of these literary and cinematographic creations as in some respects a brutal and uncultivated intellectual, who was at the same time fatally attractive to the more culturally sophisticated but physically and emotionally vulnerable middle class female, a relationship which intentionally or not had symbolic significance for the workings of society more generally, and which was most explicitly and vividly drawn out in John Fowles' *The Collector* (1963). In this novel, Fowles' working class butterfly collector-come-antihero imprisons ('collects') and is eventually responsible for the death of an attractive and bright middle class female art student. Fowles' message about the changes being wrought on working class culture through consumerism had much in common with one of the central arguments in Richard Hoggart's critique of mass culture in *The Uses of Literacy* (1958). Hoggart argued that mass consumerism had begun to debase the older values of working class culture, where in a 'throwaway society' the act of buying and consuming becomes paramount over owning and cherishing, and this debasement can be seen in Fowles' character's desire to simply collect, possess and then dispose of objects. A less socio-pathological representation of working class life that had a much broader popular impact than these films or novels, however, was conveyed through television, which by the end of the 1960s had become a major leisure-time pursuit of a huge cross-section of the population. Hoggart's evocation of working class life was also an important stimulus to the immensely popular television series *Coronation Street* which first went to air in 1960, and which, according to Richard Dyer, continually reproduced Hoggart's four key elements of 'traditional working class life' — 'common sense, the absense of work and politics, the stress on women and the strength of women, and the perspective of nostalgia'.[40]

Despite this stress on working class life and the difference and diversity of the working classes in relation to other class cultures in Britain, the dominant social and cultural themes of the period were consensus, conformity and progress in a conflict-free environment. Hill suggests that the film *Left, Right and Centre* (1959), a political comedy centering on an election campaign in an old London seat, stands out as an eloquent statement of these assumptions.

> Affluence, consensus, political convergence, mass culture and the posi-
> tion of women are neatly intertwined in (the film's) comic treatment of
> a Westminster by-election. The changes wrought by affluence and the
> advent of mass culture have irrevocably transformed the social order.
> The old aristocratic seat of Wilcot Priory has been 'handed over' to the
> masses who now flock to enjoy its rich variety of amusements (every-
> thing from fruit machines to 'sex in 3-D'). Lord Wilcot (Alistair Sim)
> has accomodated to this new order by an adoption of political 'neutral-
> ity', supporting his nephew's selection for a Tory candidature only in so
> far as it serves his 'sordid financial' ends. But if Wilcot Priory signifies a
> Tory adjustment to the postwar settlement, so this new social order has
> also rendered redundant the traditional rhetoric of socialism. 'Toryism
> means unemployment, poverty, destitution, starvation, despair', ex-
> claims a Labour Party supporter. The camera meantime reveals a row of
> rooftops, a TV ariel attached to each chimney. The result for politics is a
> complete absence of distinctions in policy. A Tory MP (one of the party
> 'intellectuals') mistakenly addresses a Labour Party rally, only to enjoy
> the same rousing reception he subsequently receives from a Tory meet-
> ing for exactly the same speech. As one elector sums up to a TV
> reporter, the result 'don't make no odds either way'.[41]

At one level, this view of British society in the postwar era as conflict-free contradicted the volume of representations of working class life through various media, and the statistical evidence that showed continuing inequities in the distribution of wealth and privilege. At another, though, it revealed a general willingness on the part of many people to accept the message that they had 'never had it so good', despite the obvious cultural differences that they were acutely aware of in their own daily lives. Dissent and other forms of opposition to this notion were then conveniently located within particular sub-cultural groups such as 'youth' and later 'immigrants', thus helping to sustain the collectively created myth of postwar Britain as in the main an equal, classless and conflict-free society, apart from particular abberations like juvenile delinquency. Just as accounts of teenager violence and promiscuity had been inflated, so were claims that social values and norms were breaking down among some groups. Surveys conducted in the 1950s and early 1960s suggest that this picture was, too, invariably exaggerated, especially in terms of social relations. Marriage and monogamous relationships were still valued and practiced by people at different social class levels, and only a minority ever indulged in the widely publicized pursuits of wine-drinking, drug-taking and free-love. At the same time, there were some important changes in attitudes towards homosexuality, censorship, and illegitimacy, and 1960s saw the introduction of the Abortion Bill, the more widespread use of the birth-control pill, and the abolition of corporal punishment.[42]

While there may have been 'a new hedonism abroad in the land' in the late 1950s and early 1960s, this was tempered by complacency generated by a growing prosperity and the continuation of traditional institutions. Marwick points out that even though prices were on average sixty-three per cent higher in 1969 than 1955, there was a real increase in average weekly earnings of thirty-two per cent between 1955 and 1960, and one hundred and thirty per cent between 1955 and 1969. In addition, when the Labour government came to power in 1964, there had been little change in the constitution of the political power-brokers; of the Wilson Labour cabinet, six members were the products of the most exclusive public schools, and only two had graduated from universities other than Oxford. Marwick also suggests that popular views on social class divisions in the mid 1960s were similar to those of the 1940s and 1950s. The blue-collar worker may in some cases have been in a position to make higher earnings than his white-collar counterpart, but 'to be working class in the sixties ...despite the occasional instance of rapid upward mobility, meant a 'life sentence' of hard manual work where, by an implicit irony, the attainment of middle class living standards was only possible through expending, on overtime, even more excessive amounts of energy in a traditional working class way'.[43]

Educational Discourse: Myths and Disenchantments

Education was a key component of social reconstruction at the end of the war and the expansion of the secondary school system was widely supported by politicians of all shades, to the extent that the rival parties did not see the need for their own policies on this subject until the beginning of the 1960s. More than any of the other changes of the postwar era, mass secondary schooling embodied the hopes and ideals for a stable and prosperous future society.[44] At the same time, the prospect of secondary schooling for all was a new event, and so its planning and structuring went beyond the experience of all who had a hand in its adminis-tration. For everyone involved, mass secondary schooling was from the begin-ning an experiment. But its success or failure as an experiment from the start could never have been judged impartially, since popular education was infused with so many of the key social ideals of the time. Its fate was similar to that of many of the other potentially radical initiatives of this postwar period. It began as a medium for social reform, became a metaphor for a just and progressive society, and was exposed by the end of the 1970s as a means of working class repression and social control and of maintaining the status quo. A number of key notions existed in tension with each other within the discourse on education — selection versus equal opportunity, enlightenment versus the need for skilled technicians, emancipation versus repression — and these were played out with only minimal resolution in the debates that grew in prominence and significance towards the end of the 1950s.

The Emergence of Mass Secondary Schooling: 1945–1957

The 1944 Education Act (in England and Wales — similar legislation was passed in Scotland in 1946), known as the 'Butler Act', was the product of a wartime coalition government. The Act had been part of a self-conscious attempt early in the war at 'social-reconstruction' in Britain, which itself was part of the effort to look beyond the war to a better world and in the process help boost morale.[45] The key notions the Act enshrined were that the length of schooling should be extended, in the first instance from fourteen to fifteen, but as soon as practically possible to sixteen (this in fact did not happen until 1973), and that this secondary education should be free to everyone. Although post-elementary education up to the age of fourteen had been available since the Fisher Act of 1921, the provision of free secondary education for all represented a shift in thinking from this idea of an add-on to elementary, to the notion that all children should experience secondary education as a continuing, but at the same time distinctively different, stage of their educational development. Indeed, as Wardle has suggested:

> until the very end of the nineteenth century there was absolutely no idea of continuity between primary and secondary schools in the modern sense; in fact the word 'primary' was not used, and 'secondary' had a very different meaning from modern usage. The assumption was that the great bulk of the population had no use for secondary education — however it might be defined, and would be unable to afford it even if they desired it.[46]

The creation of the mass secondary school system thus represented a substantial rearticulation of the purpose of working class schooling and the relationship between both phases.

The idea of a 'common school' for all children had been around in socialist politics for a long time, and it was the lobbying of left wing pressure groups that was in large part responsible for the introduction of mass secondary schooling.[47] However, when the Labour government came to office in 1945, the structure for secondary school reorganization they adopted was the 'tripartite system' advocated in the Norwood Report of 1943.[48] The proposed tripartite system was to consist of three types of schools, grammar, technical, and modern, to cater for three types of pupil, and each school was intended to enjoy 'parity of esteem'. The key device for allocating pupils to the correct school was the 11-plus (in Scotland the 'qualifying exam', taken at age 12), which consisted of an IQ test and tests in English and Maths. In practice, few technical schools were ever set up, and the system was tripartite in name only. It became in reality a bipartite system of secondary modern schools for the 11–15 age range, and the grammar schools catering for the 11–18 age range. Only the grammar schools, in the beginning, could provide the courses leading to the qualifications that secured a place in a university or in the professions. A succession of Labour and then Conservative Education Ministers (later called Secretaries of State for Education) firmly supported this selective system. Ellen Wilkinson, the first postwar Labour Minister, claimed that since the grammar schools no longer charged fees, there was nothing to prevent those pupils with ability from gaining a place in one. She felt that individual 'merit' was the correct criterion for selection. Her successor, George Tomlinson, who had a working class background and wide experience of working in LEA administration before entering politics, was a wholehearted supporter of this meritocratic ideal, and was firmly convinced of the superiority of the hierarchical and elitist British system. At the same time, Fenwick[49] has argued that neither the Labour nor the Conservative party had anything resembling a policy for education when the General Election came around in 1945, and indeed this situation was to continue until well into the 1950s. Even then, education did not become an election issue until much later. This apparent ambivalence to education and unquestioning acceptance of popular wisdom on the part of the majority of the population, including Education Ministers, helps explain in part why the idea of a selective tripartite system was so readily supported.

There were other factors that encouraged the incorporation of this model into policy. At a practical level, the reorganization of schools had to be accomplished with existing resources, in terms of buildings and staff. Just as the shortages of materials affected the building of houses and hospitals, so too they affected the building of new schools. While the government did embark on a massive programme of building and training of the extra teachers needed to run the system, these things took time to organize.[50] At least as influential, though much more difficult to assess in its effects, was the pernicious testimony of the educational psychologist who claimed there were three types of mind, the academic, the technical, and the ordinary, which suggested in turn three types of educational provision in the form of grammar, technical and modern schools. While talk of free and extended secondary schooling had dominated much of the pre-war debate in education, it was this much narrower issue of fitting particular types of pupil to appropriate types of schools that came to dominate subsequent discussions in the postwar period.[51] This psychologistic discourse played a key role in legitimating the selective system. The tripartite structure had the support of the neutrality and factuality of science, and on top of this, mental measurement had been used with apparent success in contributing to the war victory.[52]

This is not to say that the tripartite system went entirely uncontested,[53] though it was not until the early 1950s that critiques of the psychologistic foundations of the system began to emerge. The main criticism of intelligence testing was based on its claim, firmly accepted in the 1930s and 1940s, to be able to measure intelligence divorced from social determinants. Proponents of IQ testing like Cyril Burt had claimed that:

> by intelligence the psychologist understands in born, all-round intellectual ability. It is inherited, or at least innate, not due to teaching or training; it is intellectual, not emotional or moral, and remains unin-

fluenced by industry or zeal; it is general, not specific, i.e. it is not limited to any particular kind of work, but enters into all we do or say or think. Of all our mental qualities, it is the most far-reaching; fortunately it can be measured with accuracy and ease.[54]

In response to such claims, uncertainty about intelligence and environmental factors was being expressed in the 1940s, and Brian Simon's work in the 1950s was the first to bring these doubts over validity and accuracy together, claiming that environment and social class in particular had a profound effect on educational attainment, a point that was soon to be supported by the findings of sociological research.[55]

There was also some criticism of the tripartite system from the Conservatives at their party conference in 1951. They condemned IQ tests for allowing 'smart Alecs' with little 'character' or 'perseverance' through the system, and called for wider criteria in assessment of pupils. A little paradoxically, they also claimed that there had been an overall deterioration in educational standards caused by an over-emphasis on 'self-expression' rather than 'examination as a measure of ability, industry and character'.[56] This reference to 'self-expression' was provoked by the growing adoption by teachers of some of the ideas of 'progressive education', such as centering the curriculum on the individual pupil's needs, especially in the primary school. Later the Conservatives were to defend tripartism and selection with growing vigour against the 'triumph of mediocrity' they took progressivism to represent. There was, at the same time, growing pressure from left wing groups for the establishment of non-selective comprehensive schools. However, Conservative hostility to the idea of comprehensive schooling was influenced by its association with the radical left, whose Marxism and Soviet orientation of the 1930s and 1940s was out of step with the anti-communist paranoia of the cold war in the 1950s.[57] In the immediate postwar years though, the logic of differentiation based on 'merit' dominated, and formed the popular as well as the official view of how secondary schooling should be organized.

Meanwhile, it was 'teachers within the Labour movement and others committed to radical educational change (who) can claim to have kept the case for the comprehensive school alive, despite the Labour government's opposition, and to have achieved a precarious ascendency during the first year after Labour's fall from national power'.[58] While tripartism was official government policy throughout the late 1940s and 1950s regardless of the party in power, there was some freedom within the Education Acts, on the part of local education authorities, to modify this policy. Scotland rejected the tripartite system in 1947, with the comment that 'the whole scheme rests on the assumption that teacher and psychologist alike must challenge — that children of twelve sort themselves out neatly into three categories to which these three types of schools correspond'.[59] In England, the (then) London City Council had set up three comprehensive schools by 1954, and other LEA's followed in Coventry and Leicester. These schools were only approved if it could be shown that they would not be competing with already existing grammar schools, and so tended to appear first of all in those areas with Labour controlled councils and in places which had to be rebuilt following the wartime bombings. By 1957 there were thirty-two comprehensives in England and by 1962, one hundred and fifty-two.[60] Such was the apparent 'success' of the shift towards comprehensive schools that right wing teacher associations were beginning to realize by the mid 1950s that what had started as 'experiments' in comprehensive schooling were now beginning to challenge the grammar schools in practice.[61] Since the GCE had been introduced in England in 1951, pupils from secondary modern as well as comprehensive schools had begun to record increasing examination successes; Rubinstein and Simon claimed that these results questioned the whole basis of tripartism and the validity of the 11-plus, and lent support to the increased provision of comprehensives.[62]

The Conservative response at the time lacked organization and clear direction, and had little impact on the momentum the comprehensive rollercoaster was beginning to gain. But the right wing critique, in the form in which it had begun to be articulated at the 1951 conference, exposed some of the internal contradictions in radical thinking that were to come home to roost in the 1960s, finding a soft underbelly in the slogans of progressivism and the ideal of equality of opportunity. In the optimistic years of the 1950s, when the British people had 'never had it so good', and in the context of the cold-war with the USSR, there was a pull towards the consensual middle ground in educational matters as in other areas of political policy-making. Anything left of centre was, in the words of Stuart Hall, 'in imminent danger of falling off the edge of the world into the clutches of the Kremlin'. It would appear to be something of a contradiction, then, that notions of equality of opportunity, comprehensive schools and progressive education were on the ascendency in the latter half of the 1950s, running as they apparently did against the prevailing consensual politics of the time. However, by the time these notions had achieved offical policy status with the restoration of the Labour government under Wilson in 1964, their early radical intent had long been washed out by a profoundly materialist conception of education that infected left party-political educational thinking and was nurtured in the first blossomings of the affluent consumerism of the 1950s and early 1960s.

Education and Consumer-Orientated Materialism: 1957–70

By the late 1950s the tripartite system was coming under increasing attack. While there may have been good pragmatic reasons for adopting this form of organization in the austerity of the 1940s, a decade-and-a-half later and in a time of relative affluence, tripartism was leaning more and more heavily on the crutch of psychologistic theory. The problem was, this theory was also crumbling under sustained criticisms from outside and inside psychology itself. There were at least three major sources of critique; the evidence of examination results from secondary modern schools and already existing comprehensives, concerns over the role of education in economic productivity and the wastage of so much potential talent through the influence of the selective system, and the growing influence of sociological analysis.

In the case of the first criticism, throughout the 1950s left wing reformers such as Brian Simon had been pointing to the increasing successes of secondary modern and comprehensive school pupils in the GCE exams, and took this to be evidence of the questionable validity of the 11-plus and the psychological theory of innate intelligence that supported it. Much discussion centred around the degree of error that was acceptable in the matching of pupils and schools, and of how more 'reliable' methods could be found for predicting educational attainment (as measured by examination results). Some argued that the successes of sixteen year-olds in the GCE who had originally failed the 11-plus showed how unfair and innaccurate this method of selection really was, and so questioned the need for separate schools from age eleven. Others replied that combining the grammar and secondary modern schools and so turning them into all-through comprehensives would lead to the steady lowering of academic standards and the celebration of mediocrity. They pointed out, with some justification, that the already existing comprehensive schools invariably practised some form of differentiation of pupils, either streaming or setting them according to ability across or within subjects. This claim lead others to respond that at least the selection process could be deferred through this method until age fourteen or fifteen, by which time pupils would have had a chance to settle in to secondary education and their performances could then provide more reliable indicators of their academic potential. The fact that these or similar arguments continued to be rehearsed by rival factions throughout the 1960s and 1970s provides a sense of the inconclusiveness of these discussions. However, the criticisms of tripartism from this source were enough in the 1960s to encourage the Wilson government in the belief that the secondary modern schools held untapped talent, and lead to an attempt to set up comprehensive schools and abolish the 11-plus. But at the same time it is significant to note that fundamental meritocratic notions underlying selective schooling were never seriously questioned by Labour, an issue I will return to shortly.

Another important factor in the critique of a selective secondary school system was the emergence of educational sociology and its usurping psychology as the major scientific research instrument of educational policy. The studies of Floud, Halsey, and Douglas all revealed that the 1944 Act and the provision of free grammar school places for the academically able had done little to alter the social class mix of these schools.[63] The places were invariably filled by middle class pupils, while the secondary modern schools had an almost exclusively working class clientele. These findings probably surprised few people at the time, despite the fact that they contradicted the popular meritocratic rhetoric that passed for educational policy. What they did show, however, was that intellectual ability and hard work were to a large extent determined, and more than this defined, by the individual's social class location. They were also circumscribed by class culture. Young and Wilmott's study of *Family and Kinship in East London*, published in 1957, revealed the strong pressure not to take advantage of a grammar school education from within working class communities themselves, and the subsequent ostracization and class dislocation of many of those who did.[64] Moreover, the upwardly mobile working class person (usually male) who had in previous decades been presented as proof that the meritocratic ideal was well founded, was now being revealed in his true light, it was claimed, not as the confirming instance of the rule, but as the exception.[65]

While this research challenged the psychologistic theory that failure was the result of pathological factors located in the individual and shifted the focus to factors within the class structure of society, it failed to fully comprehend the significance of its findings. So did the Labour policy makers who, with an interesting twist of logic, concluded that when all secondary schools became comprehensive schools functioning like grammar schools, then the large un-tapped potential of talent among the working classes could be put to use by British industry. In 1965, the Labour government put this logic into practice when it issued a circular that instructed all local authorities to reorganize their secondary schools along comprehensive lines. The vision of universal secondary education modelled on the middle class values of the grammar school, and the belief that education was an investment in the 'human capital' that would meet the needs of the economy was well illustrated in Harold Wilson's much quoted speech to the Labour party conference the year before Labour regained office.

> But to train the scientists we are going to need will mean a revolution in our attitude to education, not only higher education, but at every level...As socialists, Democrats, we oppose this system of educational appartheid, because we believe in equality of opportunity. But that is not all. We simply cannot afford to neglect the educational development of a single boy or girl. We cannot afford to cut off three-quarters or more of our children from virtually any chance of higher education.[66]

The CCCS writers[67] suggest that this speech displayed the duality of the left's attitudes towards education, at least in terms of its party-political strain, juxtaposing as it did an emotive rhetoric of equality of opportunity with a concern for economic efficiency, and thoroughly embued with the logic of meritocracy. Indeed, the ideal of equality of opportunity in education was by the late 1950s becoming more clearly articulated as a metaphor of, and as a means towards, a more equal society. Many of the notions of progressive education, particularly its child-centredness and its emphasis on meeting the needs of indi-vidual pupils, had had a profound influence on the practices of many teachers in the primary sector by this time. Both progressivism and equality had become closely and significantly linked in radical socialist thinking about education since at least the 1920s. Both became part of the official policy of the Labour Party in the late 1950s, and central planks in their vision of initiating social change through education.

However, Jones in his book *Beyond Progressive Education*[68] has argued that the radical intent contained in these notions had been fatally subverted long before they became enshrined in the received wisdom of party policy. In the case of progressivism, he has suggested that what it was or could be was rarely expressed coherently in policy terms, and meaning shifted depending on who was using the term. Much of the thinking that was gathered under the pro-gressive banner was indeed critical of existing orthodoxies, and progressives were often child-centred, preaching humanitarian and anti-industrial messages. However, even by the early 1950s, some of these progressive ideas were being used as an apology for apparent lack of academic ability. Secondary modern schools, according to Rubinstein and Simon, 'were to base their curricula on the immediate experiences and interests of the children who, it was held, gained more from practical activities than from abstract thinking and analysis'.[69] Jones argues that as the process of incorporation and assimilation of progressivism into established educational structures continued, many of its ideas came to be associ-ated with second-rate education and so were systematically discredited. Of those progressive ideals that did survive and maintain credibility many, like individualism, were de-radicalised by their fusion with other bourgeois definitions of such notions.

The ideal of 'equality of opportunity' revealed even more clearly the undermining of the radical socialist intent behind mass secondary schooling and the duality of Labour Party thinking about education. Bennett has argued that there had been at least two important views of education within radical and working class thought, and he suggested that both had their genesis in the nineteenth century. The first was a view of education as 'a means by which working people could 'improve' themselves through personal enrichment and the acquisition of liberal culture'.[70] This was, he suggested, a collective exercise, a matter of creating class consciousness and contributing to the common good of the working community. The second view positioned education as just one means (among others) of social mobility, where 'quick wits' and ability could be exchanged for personal reward, a view that was, essentially, individualistic. Bennett commented that while these views were apparently contradictory, both had existed in socialist thinking about education, not separately, but together in tension.

It was clearly a version of this second view of education that lay at the root of the tripartite system put in place by Labour in 1945, and it was this same view that infused the official Labour government policy of the early 1960s which had the notion of equality of opportunity at its heart. Bennett has made this point explicitly.

> This doctrine of equality of opportunity had enormous implications for education itself. First, it assumed that the purpose of the education system was simply personal advancement in material terms. Above all, it endorsed the principle that education, like society itself, is a competition, a process that produces winners and losers. The purpose of the policy is to ensure that the rules of this competition are fair — that everyone has an equal chance.[71]

Whether the former view of education in socialist thinking had ever been mooted in the relatively pure form in which it was expressed by Bennett is arguable, implying as it does a revolutionary form of collective consciousness, and embodying the contradictory notion of the need to draw on middle and upper class culture as a means of raising working class consciousness. It could be argued that it was a version of this notion that underwrote the early calls for a common school in the 1930s and 1940s, though these are difficult and problematic notions that defy statement in this simplistic form. Nevertheless, Bennett's claim that the postwar version of equality of opportunity was saturated by the materialism of a fast expanding consumerism is supported by other evidence and commentaries. For instance, writers like Rubinstein and Simon, whose support for comprehensive schools was clearly in evidence, saw working class pupils' performances in examinations as a legitimate indicator of educational attainment and as a major function of the secondary school. In Jones' analysis of the limits of Labour's reformist educational policies he too suggests that there was never an attempt within official Labour party circles to interrogate the capitalist logic of the education/economy relationship, particularly in terms of the stratification and division of labour, the development of critical consciousness among the working classes, or the fostering of a radical pedagogy in the teaching force.

The writers from the CCCS lend further support to this analysis in their claim that Labour's concept of an equal society was a thoroughly materialistic one, entirely dominated by the logic of capitalist production and the technological efficiency of systems management. Labour's was a one dimensional conception of class as 'quantitative' (and not cultural), and on the basis of this thinking inequality could be eliminated through the redistribution of goods.[72] As they put it 'class was not about social relations, or power, but about degrees of social difference or distance, and the degrees of 'resentment' or contentment that followed'.[73] This lead to a view of education 'as a consumer good, a mark of status and a means to personal social mobility. The problem with education lay not so much in what it was, or what it did, but in how it was distributed. In this view, all sense of education as a lived process (occuring in and out of schools) was completely lost'.[74]

Given the consensual politics of the period, it is perhaps unremarkable that the dominant view of education within the Labour Party should have so closely resembled the logic of mass consumerism that circumscribed the context in which political policy-making took place.[75] At the same time, this same relatively uncritical acceptance of consumerism and the idea of the stability of society had much to do with the profound indifference of the majority of the working classes to the role of education in making a better future. When the Labour government introduced means tested 'National Assistance' in 1946, many people in need and who were entitled to benefits did not apply. According to Marwick, this was due to the way in which the system and its impersonal bureaucracy intimidated and humiliated the intended beneficiaries; it was a 'failure to understand how ordinary, bemused, ill-educated people react, rather than one of deliberate harshness; it was, indeed, a failure very much in keeping with the consensus that had developed during the war between upper class politicians, upper class civil servants, and self-educated working class representatives of lofty vision'.[76] This statement captures something of the working class experience of the welfare state generally, and of state education in particular — impersonally administered through a large professional bureaucracy, intimidating, patronising, and for many, distinctly unpleasant. It also suggests that while the left's policies, encapsulated in the slogan that 'equality of opportunity' became, seemed to be designed specifically for the benefit and to the advantage of the working class population, these policies were not a form of socialism, but an ideology of professional politicians. It was, as the CCCS writers have noted, a view from the outside and above.[77]

Conclusion

Lawson and Silver[78] have cautioned that judging the precise impact of educational discourse on the lives and experiences of children at school is incredibly complex. They suggest, by way of example, that one of the most important but underplayed issues in this respect is regional differences, and the widely disparate conditions in some regions compared to others, particularly north to south, and urban to suburban and rural. We can add to this the national cultural differences between England and Wales, Scotland, and Ireland. With this sobering qualification in mind, I suggest this chapter has done little more than map the contours of the political, cultural and educational preoccupations of the period, and identified some of the key themes and events. It can, however, help us to locate physical education within this dense matrix of cultural life of postwar Britain. Three themes in particular can be identified as being of special significance to our explorations of physical education discourse in the next three chapters.

The first of these themes is the ideal of egalitarianism, which as we have seen in this chapter was closely associated within educational discourse with some of the ideas central to progressivism, such as responding to the needs of pupils, permitting learning to be led by the child's own interests, and respecting the dignity of the individual. Competitive team games and eventually a range of other sports came to hold important symbolic significance for interested parties such as politicians, educational administrators and physical educators, as a medium through which egalitarian ideals could be realized, as aspects of mass culture. Sport was portrayed as a 'language' that people of all social classes and nationalities could 'speak', as a 'common denominator' between political and cultural divisions. Linked to egalitarianism, progressivism was an important force, promoting the 'relevance' of school activities in relation to an individual's cultural background. Games and sports were also seen to facilitate the realization of a second cultural theme, which was the notion of a conflict-free society. Proponents of this view argued that competition on the games field redirected potentially aggressive impulses that could otherwise lead to delinquent be-haviour. Physical education was awarded the task of fostering the idea of a stable society, and providing a socially desirable alternative to youth culture. Moreover, physical educationists themselves took this idea of a conflict-free society to heart in their approach to developing 'scientific physical education' in the 1950s, by adopting the tenets of 'objective' experimental science and applying them to their research. And a third and related theme of specific relevance to physical education discourse was the notion that school physical education could channel the social cohesiveness allegedly promoted by games playing to the good of the nation, thereby assisting Britain in the highly competitive international trade market. In this respect, physical education in schools came to be viewed as an important site for the production of national pride and identity, as the beginning point in the creation of champion sports performers, and at the same time a means of imbuing nationalism in all children, stars or otherwise.

Just as this two decade period was characterized by a number of striking paradoxes that ran through many aspects of society, so do these paradoxes appear, in their own substantive form, in physical education discourse. As we will see from the chapters that follow, school physical education was, like the rest of postwar society, reconstructed and transformed in ways that marked a distinc-tive break with what had gone before, but at the same time it carried forward older ideas into new and quite different political and social circumstances. Physic-al education discourse was not merely underwritten by the wider social forces discussed in this chapter; it was also an important site for the production and legitimation of these forces, and for their absorption into the cultural life of the groups of children who experienced physical education programmes. As such, the themes of egalitarianism and social cohesion, consensus and nationalism, were reworked and remade within physical education discourse, and re-entered the endless cycle of cultural production to be appropriated by particular coalitions and interests and utilised in the public sphere for their own purposes, before entering physical education in an altered form to be reworked once again. In the chapters that follow, it is important to bear in mind not only Lawson and Silvers' sound advice about time-lag in relation to regional and sub-cultural variations, but also the point that this cycle of cultural production is uneven and highly complex. What follows, then, is in itself a reconstruction of physical education discourse in the postwar period, an abstracted account of ideas and events.

Notes

1 'The people's flag', Channel 4 TV, November, 1987.
2 Marwick, A. (1982) *British Society Since 1945*, Harmondsworth: Penguin, p. 50.
3 Centre for Contemporary Cultural Studies (1981) *Unpopular Education: Schooling and Social Democracy in England Since 1944*, London: Hutchinson, pp. 68–69.
4 Though see Stuart Laing for a detailed analysis of the election strategies and counter-strategies of each party, in Laing, S. (1986) *Representations of Working-Class Life 1957–1964*, London: MacMillan, pp. 4–6; and Marwick, note 2, pp. 102–111.
5 'The peoples' flag', Channel Four TV, November, 1987.
6 McCulloch, G. (1988) 'The Norwood Report and the secondary school curriculum', *History of Education Review*, **17**(2), 30–45.
7 With respect to education, Chitty argues that the 1944 Act had a 'number of serious weaknesses and shortcomings which effectively undermined its good intentions', in Chitty, C. (1988) Central control of the school curriculum, 1944–87, *History of Education*, **17**(4), p. 321.
8 Marwick, note 2, pp. 42–48.
9 Laing, note 4, p. 6.
10 Hill, J. (1986) *Sex, Class and Realism: British Cinema 1956–1963*, London: British Film Institute Books, p. 6.
11 Lessing, D. (1960) *In Pursuit of the English* London: Granda, p. 11.
12 Abrams, M., Rose, R. and Hinden, M. (1960) *Must Labour Lose?* Harmondsworth: Penguin.
13 Butler, D.E. and Rose, R. (1959) *British General Election of 1959*, London: MacMillan, p. 136 facing.
14 Hall, S. (1960) 'The supply of demand', in Thompson, E.P. (Ed.) *Out of Apathy*, London: Stevens; Rowntree and Lavers surveyed York in 1950 to reveal how far social welfare policies set in motion since 1936 'had succeeded in reducing poverty'. Rowntree's previous surveys in 1900 and 1936 provided comparative yardsticks. Using updated but similar criteria, the study concluded that those 'living in poverty' had been reduced from 31.1 per cent in 1936 to 2.7 per cent in 1950, and this would have been 22.8 per cent if not for legislation introduced after the war. See Seebohm Rowntree, B. and Lavers, R.G. (1951) *Poverty and the Welfare State* London.
15 Shanks, M. (1961) *The Stagnant Society*, Harmondsworth: Penguin, p. 198.
16 Glyn, A. and Sutcliffe, B. (1972) *British Capitalism, Workers and the Profits Squeeze*, Harmondsworth: Penguin, p. 38.
17 Hall, S., Critcher, C., Jefferson, T., Clarke, J. and Roberts, B. (1978) *Policing the Crisis*, London: MacMillan, p. 235.
18 Laing, note 4, p. 21.
19 Marwick, note 2, p. 107.
20 Hoggart, R. (1958) *The Uses of Literacy*, Harmondsworth: Penguin, p. 318.
21 Hill, note 10, pp. 8–10.
22 Marwick, note 2.
23 Marwick, note 2.

24 As contemporary writers of the time like Doris Lessing tell us; Lessing, D. (1969) 'A home for the highland cattle', in *Five* London: Grafton (First published in 1953), pp. 68.
25 Marwick, note 2, p. 47.
26 Marwick, note 2, p. 47. This is a particularly important point concerning the gap between popular awareness of educational issues and the ideals of socialist reformers that I will return to a little later in the discussion; see also Hoggart's discussion of the 'earnest minority' of upwardly mobile working class people who experienced dislocation and a heightened awareness of class distinctions and class-based issues, in Hoggart, note 20, p. 22.
27 Rubinstein, D. and Simon, B. (1966) *The Evolution of the Comprehensive School 1922–1966* London: Routledge and Kegan Paul, pp. 52–54.
28 Hutchins, R.M. (1968) *The Learning Society*, Harmondsworth: Penguin.
29 Marwick, note 2, p. 114.
30 Hill, note 10, p. 11.
31 See Hoggart, note 20; Young, M. and Wilmott, P. (1957) *Family and Kinship in East London* Harmondsworth: Penguin.
32 For example, in the form of the Butler White Paper of January 1959, intended to introduce a programme of prison-building for young offenders and the administration of a 'short, sharp, shock'.
33 Albermarle Report (1960) *The Youth Service in England and Wales* London: HMSO; Wolfenden Report (1960) *Sport and the Community* London: Central Council for Physical Recreation.
34 Montgomery, J. (1965) *The Fifties* London: Allen and Unwin, pp. 173–174.
35 Bradbury, M. (1987) *No, Not Bloomsbury*, London: Arena, pp. 101–102.
36 See Hill, note 10, pp. 180–222 for brief details and descriptions of these films.
37 Hill, note 10, p. 112.
38 Laing, note 4, p. 62.
39 Laing, note 4, p. 61. This notion of the author as 'angry young man', with attendant working class, North of England origins and scholarship/grammar school and redbrick university education, has become part of the folklore of the literary scene in Britain, caricatured in the novels of Malcolm Bradbury and David Lodge; Bradbury, M. (1965) *Stepping Westward*, Secker and Warburg; Lodge, D. (1984) *Small World*, Harmondsworth: Penguin.
40 In Laing, note 4, p. 184.
41 Hill, note 10, p. 145.
42 Marwick, note 2, Chapter 9.
43 Marwick, note 2, p. 161–2.
44 'The educational reforms which were to take effect from 1945 were intended to remove some of the stigmas attached to lower-class education, provide a new pattern of opportunity, and to set education in a framework of improved welfare and social justice'. Lawson, J. and Silver, H. (1973) *A Social History of Education in England*, London: Methuen, p. 421.
45 The Act was begun in 1942 and presented as a Bill in 1943, see Lawson and Silver, note 44, p. 417.
46 Wardle, D. (1970) *English Popular Education 1780–1970* Cambridge University Press, p. 116.
47 CCCS, note 3, pp. 60–61; Rubinstein and Simon, note 27, pp. 40–41.
48 The Norwood Report had been much vilified by both the left and the right for its recommendations that set up the 'tripartite' notion. Norwood himself played a not entirely distinguished roll in pushing through his own elitest 'Christian and Platonic prejudices' — see McCulloch, note 6.
49 Fenwick, I.G.K. (1976) *The Comprehensive School 1944–1970: The Politics of Secondary School Reorganisation*, London: Methuen.

50 Fenwick, note 49, p. 44.
51 CCCS, note 3, pp. 58–59.
52 The CCCS authors suggest that 'assessment and differentiation in the service of some greater good was a proposition not easily challenged in the absence of any adequate contemporary critique'; CCCS, note 3, p. 61.
53 See McCulloch, note 6.
54 Burt, C. (1934 Ed.) *How the Mind Works* London: Allen and Unwin, pp. 28–9. A similar kind of thinking lay beneath the desire of the scientific functionalist's view of physical capacity and their concerns for measurements of strength and endurance, see Chapter 5.
55 Lawson and Silver, note 44, p. 424; See Simon, B. (1953) *Intelligence, Psychology and Education: A Marxist Critique*, London: Lawrence and Wishart; and Young, M. (1958) *The Rise of the Meritocracy 1870–2033: An Essay on Education and Equality*, Harmondsworth: Penguin.
56 In Fenwick, note 49, p. 64.
57 CCCS, note 3.
58 Fenwick, note 49, p. 81.
59 In Rubinstein and Simon, note 27, p. 48.
60 Rubinstein and Simon, note 27.
61 This concern coincided with teachers' disgruntlement with the outpacing of salaries by price rises and the rapid increases in workers' wages against their own. They began to express their resentment, contrasting their lower-middle class poverty with the new working class affluence, through increasing militancy between 1954–1956; see Lawson and Silver, note 44, p. 427–8.
62 Rubinstein and Simon, note 27, pp. 54–56.
63 Floud, J., Halsey, A. and Martin, F. (1956) *Social Class and Educational Opportunity*, London: Heinemann demonstrated how class affected the chances of gaining a grammar-school education; see also Lawson and Silver, note 44, pp. 422–426.
64 Young and Wilmot, note 31, pp. 174–185: see also note 26.
65 CCCS, note 3; and Hamish Paterson on the Scottish experience in Paterson, H.M. (1983) 'Incubus and ideology: The development of secondary schooling in Scotland, 1900–1939', in Humes, W.M. and Paterson, H.M. (Eds) *Scottish Culture and Scottish Education, 1800–1980* Edinburgh: James Donald, pp. 197–215.
66 Harold Wilson, quoted in Fenwick, note 49, p. 128.
67 CCCS, note 3, p. 96.
68 Jones, K. (1983) *Beyond Progressive Education* London: MacMillan.
69 Rubinstein and Simon, note 27, p. 54.
70 Bennett, D. (1982) 'Education: Back to the drawing board', in Smith, R. (1985) *The Inequalities Debate: An Interpretive Essay* Geelong: Deakin University Press, p. 91.
71 Bennett, note 70, p. 95.
72 'The economic and social trends of the 1950s were of immediate relevance to education. Full employment, social security and economic growth had all contributed to generally higher standards, in what became labelled at the end of the 1950s 'the affluent society'. It was also to an increasing extent a consumer society, at all levels'; Lawson and Silver, note 44, pp. 426–7.
73 CCCS, note 3, p. 73.
74 CCCS, note 3, p. 72.
75 'Although investigations in the 1960s were to upset some of the complacency about the affluent society, the predominant view of the society in the 1950s was moulded by memories of the pre-war world'; Lawson and Silver, note 44, p. 427.
76 Marwick, note 2, p. 53.
77 CCCS, note 3, p. 74.
78 Lawson and Silver, note 44, pp. 447–466.

Chapter 4

Gymnastics and Gender: Contesting the Meaning of Physical Education

At the end of the second world war, gymnastics formed the basis of school physical education programmes, to such an extent, in fact, that gymnastics and physical education were virtually synonymous. However, before the introduction of mass secondary schooling through the 1944 Education Act (in England and Wales), there had been a growing feeling among certain sections of the physical education profession that physical education was broader than gymnastics, and the 1933 Syllabus[1] reflected this view with its inclusion of games, swimming and athletics. The circumstances after the war were markedly different to those in which the 1933 Syllabus was written though, since it had been prepared with mainly elementary school pupils in mind. The new secondary schools, on the other hand, catered for older children and so presented the added difficulty of an unknown quantity in the shape of the fifteen year old when the school leaving age was raised in 1947. The problem for the profession was the extent to which gymnastics was likely to be able to hold the interest of these older pupils, and the fact that the maturer physique of the adolescent created new possibilities for the kinds of activities, some demanding strength and speed, that could be offered.

With the arrival of mass secondary schooling the demand for teachers grew, and after 1945 men began to enter the physical education profession in large numbers for the first time. Very soon, battle lines were drawn over which form of gymnastics should be taught in school programmes, and the two sides in the contest were distinguished almost entirely on the basis of gender, with the females preferring the new, 'progressive' educational gymnastics and the males, a form of competitive gymnastics. What was significant about the vitriolic debate that ensued over the next decade and a half was not so much the issue of what form of gymnastics should be taught but, rather, how physical education more generally should be defined. Since at this time gymnastics and physical education were regarded as almost synonymous by both the females and the males, this struggle struck at the very heart of the meaning of the subject in the new secondary schools, and had ramifications for teaching methods, content, assessment and many other pedagogical issues. The fact that gender was one of the main dividing lines between the opposing groups is particularly important in light of recent feminist critiques of physical education and sport as a male preserve,[2] a factor that is made all the more significant in that it was the formerly dominant female physical educators who found themselves and their definition of the subject under siege after the war. The male discourse that emerged in opposition to the female perspective is also revealing, since the debate provided a context in which the new doctrine of scientific functionalism, fostered by male physical educators during the postwar period, could be developed and refined.

The chapter begins with a description of three versions of gymnastics that were competing for curriculum time in British schools at the end of the second world war. From there, the demise of the formally dominant Swedish system is discussed briefly as a way of previewing two new discourses, one represented by the female educational gymnasts and the other by the predominately male scientific functionalists. We then turn to the debate that followed the male critique of educational gymnastics, which revolved around the notions of transfer of training in relation to skill learning, and the issue of competition. Finally, I will attempt to show how the conditions under which each discourse was nurtured and developed also set limits on the potential for progress of these versions of gymnastics, and of physical education as a school subject more broadly.

Three Versions of Gymnastics

By the end of the second world war, three distinct versions of gymnastics were competing for teaching time in school physical education programmes. The first of these, Swedish (or Ling) gymnastics, had been the hallmark of the professional female physical educator between the late 1890s to the 1930s, and the version of physical education officially approved by the then Board of Education for use in its elementary schools. The Swedish system was invented by Per Henrick Ling in the early decades of the nineteenth century and consolidated into a system of physical training at the Central Gymnastic Institute in Stockholm which he founded. It involved mostly free-standing exercises set out in tables that sought to systematically exercise each part of the body through increasingly intricate flexions and extensions. It also involved some apparatus work such as vaulting. Teaching within the Ling system was highly formalised and in the beginning especially, movements were performed to militaristic commands such as 'at the double!' and 'fall in!', and was easily practised with large groups in confined spaces. The Swedish system was boosted in Britain in the 1880s through the work of Swedish gymnasts appointed by the Board of Education to organize physical education in its elementary schools. One of these organizers was Madam Bergman-Osterberg, who in 1885 formed her own college of physical training for women.[3] Swedish gymnastics formed the foundation of the women's professional training, which was supplemented by massage, remedial exercises and games. Its main focus was the physical and physiological effects of exercise, and the entire system was based in an extensive body of 'scientific knowledge'[4] of functional anatomy and physiology.

The second form of gymnastics, which was witnessed in its modern form for the first time by British physical educators at the 1948 London Olympic Games, was German or Olympic gymnastics. German gymnastics had been around at least as long as Ling's system, and involved work on apparatus such as the rings, parallel bars and pummel horse. At the beginning of the twentieth century it had vied with the Swedish system for selection as the official system of physical training by the Interdepartmental Committee set up by the Royal Commission on Physical Training (1903) to produce a Syllabus of Physical Exercises for British schools. It lost that contest, and suffered the stigma of its German origins after the first world war to be neglected by all but a handful of enthusiasts in Britain until the 1940s. After the boost given by the 1948 Olympics, however, which presented gymnastics as a competitive sport made up of the six activities of floor-work, vaulting, rings, bars, beam and pommel horse, there was an increasing level of interest in this version of gymnastics with a growing number of advocacies for its inclusion in school programmes from the early 1950s.[5]

The third form was educational gymnastics, and it had made a rapid and dramatic impact on female physical education from the first appearance of Laban's ideas on movement and dance in Britain in the 1930s. Modern Dance was built on a radical critique of 'unnatural' movement patterns in industrial society that had, in Laban's opinion, much to do with the presence of mental illness and other personality disorders. In the spirit of other pyschoanalytic critiques of contemporary industrial society by writers and therapists like Wilhelm Reich, Laban's philosophy argued for the release of dangerously pent up and inhibited energies through free, spontaneous movement. Although Laban's main concerns were focused on the theatre and industry, his ideas were very quickly applied to gymnastics by female physical educators during the late 1930s and through the war years. Educational gymnastics borrowed from modern dance a concern for the qualitative dimensions of movement experience and selectively adopted some of the rhetoric and ideas of the fast growing and fashionable child-centred progressivism in British educational circles of the time, particularly those associated with humanistic liberal individualism.[6]

The Demise of Swedish Gymnastics

By the end of the second world war, Swedish gymnastics was under siege on several sides. In the climate of national optimism that followed the war, the work of the Swedish gymnast seemed to have little place. In the decade preceding the war, there had developed two mass movements created for and run by women, the 'Keep Fit' movement in the North of England and the Women's 'League of Health and Beauty' in the South.[7] Although the Central Council for Recreative Physical Training (later the Central Council for Physical Recreation) was formed through the collaboration of the Ling Association with the National Association of Organizers and Lecturers in Physical Education in 1935 in order to co-ordinate the work of these and other popular physical recreation groups, the Ling Association's formal involvement in these activities appears to have been limited to the participation of individual members. Indeed, as McIntosh[8] has noted, their under-representation on the various organizing committees that resulted from the Government's White Paper on *Physical Training and Recreation* in 1937 was attributed to a public image that associated them with 'knee bending and arm swinging'. Needless to say, this view was not shared by members of the profession themselves, who were inclined to lay the blame for their stereotyped image at the door of others, particularly the press. For instance, commenting on a tour by gymnasts from Sweden lead by Maja Carlquist, the Editor of *The Leaflet* complained 'it also dawned on a number of them (the press), as they gazed at the packed theatre, that there is a large section of the public interested in serious physical education...and that physical education is *not* 'pt'. Such thoughts among the press are long overdue.'[9] Notwithstanding this point of view, the Swedish gymnasts failed to improve either the popularity or public image of their version of 'serious physical education', and had little success in attracting the attention of the press in the decade following the war.[10]

Their fall from grace began in the 1930s, at a time when Swedish gymnastics was firmly established as the basis for the professional training of female physical educators, and had begun to play the same role in the new specialist colleges for men which appeared during the 1930s at Glasgow, Leeds and Loughborough. There had been earlier challenges from inside the subject itself, through the introduction of musical accompaniments to exercises by Irene Marsh, an innovation resisted staunchly by the Ling Association for many years,[11] and the modification of exercises by Elli Bjorksten in Finland and Elin Falk in Sweden to include rhythmic activities.[12] But these had done very little to challenge the firmly rooted orthodoxies of the system.

However, criticisms of the formality and functionality of the Swedish system, and especially its unsuitability for young children, began to gain ground towards the end of the 1930s. One reason for this was a reaction to the mass, command-style teaching method of Swedish gymnastics, partly due to the uncomfortably close association of these methods with the mass exercising of the Fascist and Nazi Youth Movements and with militarism. In addition to this, the arrival of Rudolf Laban in Britain in the late 1930s fuelled the already existing interest in his ideas on movement which had preceded him, and the female physical educators very quickly came to see Laban's work as a genuine alternative to Swedish gymnastics. Criticism from within the education profession also became more frequent. Addressing the Educational Association in London towards the end of the war, one distinguished speaker claimed that in the Swedish gymnastics lesson, pupils 'are treated like robots or marionettes and are made to perform agility movements according to the string-pulling of the instructor'.[13] Writing two years later, one of Her Majesty's Inspectors, Marion Wardle, caricatured the Swedish gymnastics lesson thus:

One can have the type of lesson in which the children come into the gymnasium and go straight to their lines, where they either stand or sit cross legged, waiting for the teacher's directions. An introductory activity may be given, probably in a set formation, such as a ring or a double ring. Then back to files where they perform a series of static exercises. Then to their section places for the 'heave' where they sit cross legged while the apparatus is brought out. When this is ready four, or possibly eight children stand and begin work at the teachers' command. This is followed by a 'balance' organized in the same way using either beams or forms — never both! After this back to files (or possibly wallbars) for abdominal and lateral exercises. Finally, section work, where the children again sit cross legged until the apparatus is ready, when the first four children begin to work at the teacher's or the leader's command. Throughout the whole period the children have had no single opportunity for moving freely and naturally and each individual has probably spent 10 to 15 minutes sitting cross legged on the floor.[14]

By the end of the war, an alternative form of gymnastics, drawing on Laban's principles of movement and already dubbed 'educational gymnastics', had made its mark among the female physical educators. In a series of articles that appeared in the *Journal of Physical Education* in 1945 and early 1946, it is clear that the Swedish gymnasts were by that time fighting a rearguard action. The articles attempted to defend what one author called 'formal movements, or gymnastics movements proper' from a number of challenges. These centred around the claim that Swedish gymnastics involved formal, mechanical and therefore 'unnatural' movements, and that these were 'non-creative and dull, merely a sequence of unnatural movements put together without meaning'.[15] The responses to this criticism reveal some of the assumptions the Swedish gymnasts made about their version of physical education. According to M E Squire, Principal of Anstey Physical Training College, it

is the only form of physical education which systematically attempts to affect bodily structure and to remedy possible defects of posture; therefore it should be the basis of all physical education in that it prepares a sound movable instrument upon which all other forms of physical education should play harmoniously.[16]

This statement conveys with certainty and conviction the idea that formal gymnastics was, for the Swedish gymnast, the fundamental form of human movement training. Another author, discussing the role of vaulting and agility work within the Swedish system communicates the same notion of the fundamentality of formal exercises in saying that 'the relationship of free standing exercises to vaulting and agilities is as grammar is to composition'.[17] The use of a descriptor like 'systematic' betrays something of the Swedish gymnasts' concerns for precision, physicality and for the functionality of movement. Similarly, their stress on harmony and their close attention to posture confirmed the importance of intervention in the physical development process, while the conviction of their statements suggested something approaching an absolute belief in themselves as a professional group and their system.

Given this view of themselves and their subject, the criticisms of the educational gymnasts, which was criticism from within their own ranks, must have been deeply unsettling. Those who wished to hold on to the Swedish system and its traditional values were unimpressed by the Laban-inspired educational gymnasts' criticism of formal exercises. Squire conveys something of the frustration that must have been felt by many of the Swedish gymnasts at this time when, in the final paragraph of her 1945 article, she fired this exasperated broadside.

If we only move in the natural directions with natural co-ordination there is a danger of working various sets of muscles only in one direction and range, and lessening the power of the individual to respond alertly to unexpected demands. If we never hold the body in a straight line or shew a precise position we shall lose much that is of value in self discipline, and this I think is the real danger in the modern gymnastic work. There is too much 'Do as you please as long as you move', too much so-called experimental work and no real training value...Can we not get back a little more discipline both mental and physical and keep our aim of achieving easy poise in movement on the most perfect possible structural foundation?[18]

The criticism of the lack of discipline and precision in educational gymnastics was to resurface time and again in future years from a variety of other sources. However well founded though, it was too late to save Swedish gymnastics, and over the next decade it was to disappear completely from the curriculum of the specialist training colleges.[19] Well before its eventual demise in the 1950s, a number of alternative versions of gymnastics were already waiting in the wings to take its place. Even though the Swedish system had been the hallmark of the female physical educator up until the 1930s, it had as I have already mentioned been taken on enthusiastically in the early days of the specialist colleges for males.[20] After the second world war however, the meaning of gymnastics would depend, as one contemporary commentator noted, 'on the sex of the individual'.[21]

The Female Creed: Educational Gymnastics and Child-Centred Progressivism

The female physical educators had begun, as early as the 1930s and still within the confines of the Swedish system, to critique the negative influence of modern industrial society on the quality of human life.[22] Maja Carlquist, a Swede who had worked closely with Ellen Falk in the 1920s and 1930s, argued that rhythm was an essential quality in movement that 'through civilization with its industrialization, mechanization and technology...has become more and more dulled...Look at the people in the streets; stiff feet — stiff restricted movements — stiff expressions on their faces...Here one can truthfully talk of the melody which was lost'.[23] This comment could easily have been made by a Laban-inspired educational gymnast. Laban himself did not commit his ideas on the place of movement education in wider society until 1948, when he published *Modern Educational Dance*. He had by then carried out research in industry, and had become convinced of the detrimental effects of simple, repetitive movement sequences of many factory-based occupations on the worker's emotional and intellectual health.[24] These ideas were eventually to find their way, in largely unaltered form, into the discourse of the educational gymnasts.[25]

This critique of modern industrial civilization was in tune with the popular educational discourse of child-centred progressivism in the 1940s and 1950s, particularly in the primary sector, though also in some of the new secondary modern schools.[26] As Hamilton has noted, the progressive movement in Britain from its inception in the late 1890s was constituted by a number of factions who were divided mainly by their views on the most effective way to change the social order, either by intervention at the level of institutions or by fostering individual growth. Hamilton argued that these factions were never clearly distinguishable however, and that their projects had considerable areas of overlap. It was this ongoing cycle of melding and disintegrating of the progressives' position that underpinned the notorious ambiguity of the notion of 'progressivism' by the 1950s and 1960s.[27] In the 1930s, some of the key features of child–centred progressivism had been set out for the first time in official policy; the idea, for instance, that the primary school curriculum should be 'thought of in terms of activity and experience rather than knowledge to be acquired and facts to be stored'.[28] Twenty years on, such ideas had become part of the official orthodoxy in the primary school, and while critics complained that progressivism displayed a chameleon–like ability to fit a diverse range of political ideologies and policy initiatives, it was most clearly seen to 'touch on issues of discipline, curriculum content and pedagogy; it (wa)s understood to be critical of authoritarianism, committed to the development of the 'whole person' and attentive to the psychology of learning'.[29]

The wide currency and official acceptance of these ideas in the primary school was entirely consistent with the Swedish gymnasts' embryonic critique of industrial civilization as it had been expressed by Carlquist, and so it is no surprise that Laban's ideas found fertile ground during the war years. Indeed, Fletcher has suggested that Laban's views on movement and dance added a dimension to the educational gymnasts' version of child–centredness that increased its intensity; 'to move away from directed work and learning based on imitation, to teach the children rather than the subject, had become a broadly accepted goal; but could the history or mathematics teacher draw on such a radical ideology as the concept of movement developed by Laban?'.[30] There can be little doubt that in contrast to the previous form of physical education in the old elementary schools, consisting mainly of a repressive mixture of Swedish gymnastics and military drill,[31] educational gymnastics was indeed 'radical'. The virtues of these progressive ideas and practices were particularly favoured for younger children. In one report on developments in Infants' education, it was noted that 'the abandonment of formal physical exercises and the adoption of the freedom of the newer exercises with the gradual effacement of the teacher are in complete agreement with the approach now accepted for reading and writing in nursery and infants' classes'.[32] Another commentator suggested 'it cannot too often be reported that it is 'the physical and mental and social child' who goes to school, and that any adequate and balanced scheme of education must cater for the whole child'.[33] Significantly, this radical new approach to physical education in the primary school received support from the Inspectorate. One Inspector described the benefits of the new methods.

> The semi-specialist tackles informal work more confidently because the informal approach plays a large part in modern teaching methods for the general subjects in which she has also been trained. Among the non-specialist teachers it has also been interesting to discover how readily they have taken to the freer methods, and what much higher standards of physical proficiency their children have attained since working on these lines. And I am thinking now of the supplementary teachers, the uncertificated teachers, the trained certificated assistants and heads, whose work I have seen both on the old formal lines and since their conversion to freer methods.[34]

This official patronage and enthusiastic endorsement by the Inspectorate and LEA Advisors gave the educational gymnasts' cause a tremendous boost, and resulted in the publication of the two curriculum guides *Moving and Growing* and *Planning the Programme*[35] by the then Ministry of Education in England. These guides appeared in 1952 and 1953, and were intended to replace the 1933 Syllabus for primary school physical education. As McIntosh has suggested, 'Movement' had come to express the official Ministry position on physical education in the 1950s in the same way that 'Posture' had done in the 1930s.[36] Neither of the guides mentioned Laban explicitly, but both were clearly and strongly influenced by his ideas and the work of the educational gymnasts. Given the fact that Laban himself only set out his ideas in written form as late as 1948, the guides represented the first authoritative statement of the educational gymnasts' creed.

While both *Moving and Growing* and *Planning the Programme* were reasonably well received within the physical education profession,[37] the achievement they represented for the educational gymnasts was not exactly celebrated by a heightened public awareness or appreciation. A report on the new guides in the *TES* in September 1953 reflects the very tenuous nature of the progress the educational gymnasts had made; 'from old-fashioned gym, P.T. or physical jerks to the modern concept of physical education, the transition has been rapid and is not yet complete'.[38] The *TES* report suggested that there was a lack of uniformity in physical education at this time, a problem it acknowledged could be addressed in part by the new publications. It is clear, though, that while the educational gymnasts had made rapid progress in some sectors of physical education, they had done little by this stage to dispel the popular elementary school stereotype of the 'drill teacher', or to communicate their ideas to a wider audience.[39] With the publication of these guides, they had achieved official recognition for their work. But this recognition was almost exclusively within the rarified environment of primary generalist teachers and female physical educators in schools, colleges and the Inspectorate.[40] This apparent indifference on the part of the wider teaching profession, never mind the general public, was to have a detrimental influence on the continuing progress of the educational gymnasts.

Nevertheless, in all of this support for the newer methods, the feeling emerges clearly from the female physical educators that they were finally up to date and in step with the most recent developments in education. Moreover, the days of 'knee bending and arm swinging', and the doubtful relevance of this version of their subject to the effort of rebuilding Britain after the devastations of the war, seemed to be over. Physical education had, in less than a decade it seemed, hauled itself up by the bootstraps to take a place at the cutting edge of educational policy and practice. But the apparent radicalness and intensity of this new version of gymnastics did not involve a gentle transformation of teachers' practices, nor did it seem able to be taken on in half measure. Marion Wardle's use of the term 'conversion' in a passage quoted earlier was not without significance.

It would not be unfair to say that many of the women who practised educational gymnastics in the 1940s through to the 1960s did so with a high level of conviction and emotional intensity. It is not uncommon to find them being referred to as 'devotees' or 'disciples', 'a mystic cult of female groupies' idolising Laban and accepting his ideas indiscriminately and uncritically.[41] Marjorie Swain, who returned to England from Australia on a visit in 1953 after an absence of almost twenty years, commented after attending one of Laban's classes, 'there was said to be something mystic about movement, which has to be experienced to be understood, and it does seem as if a mystic cult of initiates is growing up with a jargon all its own'.[42] Christine Roberts, who had used Laban's principles of movement in dance, wrote 'some of us view with alarm the tendency to claim too much for Movement Training: indeed in certain quarters it is rapidly becoming a 'way of life' and the unconverted are viewed with a certain degree of suspicion'.[43] Some of these features of the female creed may indeed have had their source in the charismatic power of Rudolf Laban; but many were also inherited.

Like their predecessors the Swedish gymnasts, many of the educational gymnasts continued to work in the insular and elite circles of their female colleges and girls' grammar schools, displaying that 'curious blend of therapeutic, upper-crust and feminine values' associated with the tradition set in motion in the 1880s by Madame Bergman-Osterberg.[44] This tradition was centred around 'The Ling Association of Teachers of Swedish Gymnastics', which had strict standards of membership that effectively prevented men from entering in large numbers, since there were few training courses acceptable to the Association that men could undertake. The Ling Association had had only three secretaries between 1900 and 1949, a factor that the Association's historian Yvonne Moyse claimed had done much to contribute to the stability and continuity of the gymnasts' work.[45] Whatever the benefits of such continuity, it was an important factor in carrying forward values that had underpinned the establishment of the female tradition at the end of the nineteenth century on into the very different world of the mid twentieth century. These were the values of the Victorian bourgeois class which, despite their concessions to female emancipation, were strongly framed by patriarchal concerns. As Jennifer Hargreaves has observed,[46] these concerns manifested themselves within a female version of Victorian familism, that required hierarchy, obedience to hierarchical authority, and absolute loyalty to the group. The significance of this for the educational gymnasts was that they inherited many of the qualities and the foibles of their predecessors, a factor that as we will see was to have dire consequences for the further expansion of their version of physical education. While their tradition was a source of sustenance and continuity, it was also a conservative force, making adaptation to new conditions and circumstances difficult. Their views on the new, up-and-coming sport of Olympic gymnastics was an ominous case in point; commenting on the Olympic gymnastics competition at the 1948 London Olympics, the Editor of *The Leaflet* (the mouthpiece of the Ling Association) remarked 'of competitive gymnastics, the least said the better. On this note of significant silence, we will close'.[47]

The Old and The New: Pleas for Moderation

If the educational gymnasts were less than successful in gaining recognition for their achievements from the general public, the intensity, assuredness and accompanying zealousness with which they adopted what was characterized among the female physical educators as 'the new' approach, had an unfailing capacity to provoke strong emotional reactions from within the profession. In the beginning, these reactions came, as we saw, from the 'old guard' Swedish gymnasts who were understandably unwilling to abandon overnight a lifetime's work in favour of an untried and radically different system. As early as 1947, Marion Wardle, a supporter of educational gymnastics, was able to caricature the excesses of the new approach as she had done for the old. Such classes, she said, involved

> a period of chaotic activity, in which children rush wildly about at their individual and group practices without apparently the faintest hope or intention of achieving good performances, and maintaining for most of the time a sort of monkey-house chatter.[48]

A decade later, another writer was to remark that 'the aim of the physical education teacher should be to find out what children would do if left to their own devices, and then make a career out of it!'.[49]

However, it was the intensity and assurance of the educational gymnasts that provoked most pleas for proportion in the profession in the late 1940s and early 1950s. Most of these calls for moderation were stimulated by what their authors saw as excessive zeal in following through the tenets of movement education. One writer, in an open letter in the Journal of Physical Education, decried the imposition of problem-solving on all children.

> We have, at the moment, I think, in the field of physical education, a tendency to force originality and initiative from children beyond what is right and proper — to lose, in fact, our sense of proportion about it... Do we not, perhaps, in our phobia against 'Teacher Direction' (which some of us seem to regard as the ultimate heresy) urge originality and experimentation in the physical sphere upon the child whose medium of expression may be the writing of verse or the painting of a picture?[50]

This letter prompted a string of responses supporting the plea for moderation, one of which highlighted the problem of balancing inventiveness and discovery in and through movement with the consolidation of skills.

> There seems to be too much emphasis on variety in the 'new' way and the child executes many beautiful movements which can never become known to him because he does not repeat them sufficiently. The children become absorbed in thought rather than in the quality of their efforts and the mechanics of the movements. Consequently, it seems doubtful whether they will absorb the same principles concerning movement as quickly as children under the 'old' way.[51]

This criticism of the lack of specificity and practice within educational gymnastics was to become a popular stick with which to beat the Laban-orientated women in subsequent years, and a key issue in the debate between the female and male sections of the profession that was to erupt later. In the meantime, debates over the relative merits of 'the old' and 'the new' continued unabated well into the

1950s, and showed that not all of the female physical educators had been seduced by Laban's ideas. Besides the pleas for proportion and moderation, the most common complaints about 'the new' gymnastics harked back to the guiding ideas of previous decades. One was that educational gymnastics paid too little attention to posture.[52] Another, as we have seen, was a concern for control, or rather loss of it, in 'the new' approach.

How 'radical' the educational gymnasts were in this respect is open to question though. Certainly, the idea of children moving on their own initiative would appear to have been anathema to the Swedish gymnasts. However, in a revealing debate at a Ling Association Conference on 'Gymnastics for Secondary School Girls' held in 1952, the radicalness of the educational gymnasts' child-centredness is brought into question. In summing up the debate, on whether 'the old' or 'the new' approaches better prepared girls for healthy living, the chair-woman wrote

> In order to say whether new or old methods made a difference, it was felt necessary to define the new and the old more particularly. In trying to do this, it was decided that the method in the end came back to the teacher, and if the teacher sincerely believed in what she was teaching, the results regarding healthy living would be the same.[53]

The notion of the teacher 'teaching what she believes in, and believing what she teaches' recurs frequently in the discourse of the female physical educators, and this implicit and unquestioning belief in the teacher's centrality to successful learning on the part of the pupils could almost be described as a 'cult of personality'. At least, both the new and the old guard shared a profound belief that the quality of the teacher was the single most important factor in successful teaching. It also suggests that while the educational gymnasts 'excesses' may have appeared outrageous to the old guard, the extent to which they had been able to break with the concerns of their predecessors may have been limited. Rather than displaying features of a radical child-centredness, this belief in the teacher, irrespective of subject matter, locates the female physical educators, old and new, firmly in a teacher-centred mode. Indeed, the dissenting voices among the female physical educators at this time showed as much concern for the effects of 'the new' approach on teachers as students. Much of this concern was directed at the de-skilling effect of the 'new' approach. One commentator noted that some generalist primary school teachers were:

> Conscious of the fact that there have been great changes in physical education since they trained, and being unable to get a clear overall picture of these changes, try to adopt what they think are the new methods, without properly understanding or believing them. Their lack of conviction gets through to the class with unfortunate results...Many of them would have continued to do excellent work along the lines of their training and convictions, but they are afraid of being considered old-fashioned by their HMI. Just how much ministerial pressure really exists I found it impossible to estimate, but evening and vacation courses contain many mature teachers who feel that their promotion and future

success depend on their mastery of the Art of Movement as interpreted by Laban.[54]

Another wrote that:

> There seems to be considerable anxiety among many members of our profession. Some are caused distress by feeling that they are hopelessly (through lack of experience and time to gain that experience) divorced from new trends which are apparently receiving so much official approval. Others fail to understand the new approach and consequently resent it. Those who do understand it preach it with a fervency which might be more helpfully put into print. Teaching, whatever subject it may be, depends upon personal conviction, understanding and sincerity. The lack of confidence in their methods among people in our profession today is a very unhappy state of affairs.[55]

These comments reflect not only the conflict that was occurring within the female tradition in physical education, but also the uncertainties and pressures produced by rapid changes in other spheres of life. Away from the gymnastics debate, the whole conception of physical education had been widening considerably,[56] an issue that will be examined in detail in the next chapter. The Ling Association itself, for so long a bastion of female supremacy in physical education, was also changing. In the Editorial of *The Leaflet* in August 1954, the editor acknowledged that the Ling system 'had gone' and that the scope and membership of the Ling Association had broadened. In the same issue, the President Muriel Webster suggested in an open letter that the name 'Ling' lead others to think in stereotypical terms of the Association as concerned only with Swedish gymnastics, which she conceded was something narrower than 'physical education'. In July 1955, *The Leaflet* announced the appointment of a new General Secretary, Peter Sebastian, who was the first male ever to hold this position, and six months later, in December 1955 the Association changed its name to the Physical Education Association of Great Britain and Northern Ireland, thereby formally severing ties with the exclusive female tradition.

While the debate raged among the female physical educators over the relative merits of 'the old' and 'the new' gymnastics, Swedish and educational respectively, another challenge was beginning to emerge that was to generate much more acrimony and emotion, and to have a more profound effect on the future of physical education. This challenge did not lie in a return to the 'old way', but in the new knowledge derived from scientific measurement that was being produced in the university departments of physical education. It was at this point, in the early 1950s, and perhaps not coincidentally at a time when the educational gymnasts had received official approval of their work from the Ministry, that a distinctively male perspective began to emerge.

Scientific Measurement and the Male Perspective

Before the 1940s, physical education had not presented itself to men as an attractive career in the way that it had for women. Part of the reason for this was the association of the field with militarism, and the fact that the earliest physical education teachers in the elementary schools provided by the government for the masses were former army non-commissioned officers. These men were generally regarded by teachers as their social inferiors, a label that stuck with male physical educators for many years.[57] When the unsuitablity of ex-army personnel for teaching young children was finally recognized and the drill teachers removed, there were few institutions that offered courses in physical education for men. This situation persisted until the 1930s, when specialist colleges for men were established at Jordanhill in Glasgow (1932), in Leeds (1933) and Loughborough (1935).[58] The stigma of the social inferiority of the male physical educator in relation to their female counter-parts remained, however, until well into the 1960s when the private female colleges had been dissolved into other larger, mixed-sex institutions.[59]

With the massive expansion of the secondary school system after the war, the projected 'baby boom' and the raising of the school leaving age to fifteen in 1947[60] teachers in every subject were in short supply, but this was particularly true for male physical education teachers since a 'system' of training had hardly existed before this time. So great was the demand that men were being 'qualified' to teach after undertaking courses of only short duration. This situation produced some anxiety among Ling Association members. One male member wrote to *The Leaflet* to express his concern that men were being appointed to teaching positions who

> When questioned, prove to have no theoretical knowledge of the sub-ject, but merely a rudimentary collection of games and movements...It is high time the gymnastics profession made a stand against this present-day attempt of short-course trained men to masquerade as qualified instructors...The fully qualified gymnast has as much to lose by quack-ery as the fully qualified doctor, and it would seem advisable to voice a protest without delay.[61]

Given the inferior status of males in the profession, this sort of comment was not good for male physical educators. Despite this influx of allegedly under-trained teachers though, men very quickly made headway in respect of their status problem. In December 1945, thirty male and twenty female physical education teachers were appointed to the promoted positions of 'Principal Teacher' in Senior Secondary Schools in Glasgow for the first time, and this was acknowledged as a major breakthrough since it offered male and female physical education teachers the same prospects for advancement and salary that teachers of other subjects enjoyed.[62] A decade later, the *TES* reported on the all-male Carnegie College, Leeds' twenty-first aniversary, pointing out that its graduates occupied promoted positions in University and University College Departments of Physical Education such as Birmingham, Bristol, Durham, Exeter, Hull, Leeds and Liverpool. In the intervening period, men had clearly become more influential in the physical education profession, and this was in part due to the mere fact of larger numbers which had allowed them to begin to catch up on the women.[63] There were two main paths males could follow to become qualified physical education teachers, a two year general teacher training at a training college to be followed by a supplementary year at a specialist college, or a three year university degree in Arts or Science followed by a specialist supplementary year at college. In Scotland, in contrast, male teachers could become qualified by undertaking a three year diploma course specializing entirely in physical education.[64] However, the male teachers who were degree qualified had a head-start on their male and female sub-degree qualified colleagues in terms of promotion and access to advanced study even though they had at least two years less training in physical education, a factor that may explain the apparent success of Carnegie students in gaining promoted positions in the university departments.

Nevertheless, throughout this period, the male physical education teacher was valued more for his sound character and practical ability than his intellectual capacity. In a conference address in 1958, Mr Hugh Brown, Director of the all-male Scottish School of Physical Education (SSPE), claimed that in selecting candidates 'attention is paid to natural strength, speed, flexibility and co-ordination'.[65] Even though there continued to be a shortage of male teachers, the SSPE regularly found only one third of its applicants to be acceptable. In addition to physical proficiency, prospective students had to meet academic standards that were only 'slightly below Scottish University entrance standards'. More importantly though, they had to be of sound character; 'it is most unlikely that a lad with an unsatisfactory record of behaviour and attitude will find a locker in our dressing rooms'.[66] Underpinning each of these criteria, Brown affirmed that the emphasis at the SSPE was 'first, last and all the time, on *teaching*', and that it was a particular strength of character that lay at the heart of good physical education teaching. In this, Brown was articulating a male version of the females' 'cult of personality'.

> I believe...(that) the force of example in teachers is all important. In such things as speech, dress, personal cleanliness we are constantly under the keen scrutiny of that hypercritical section of the community — the school boy...Constantly I am reminding myself that we are charged with the task of training *men* to teach *boys*. This is a purely masculine sphere. Training *must* at all times be strong, must be virile.[67]

The strength of conviction in Brown's statement is the equal of the female physical educators' assuredness and intensity, but it is here that the similarity ends. His view of the type of personality appropriate to teaching physical education to boys, 'masculine, strong, virile', makes no attempt at convergence or conciliation with the female physical educators. On the contrary, it can be read as an attempt to make clear and explicit the view that there is a difference between male and female physical education and that this is entirely right and proper. The fact that male and female physical educators trained in single-sex institutions or courses would certainly have done nothing to discourage this view of 'natural' gender-based differences, and while perhaps not all of the male physical educators who began to flood the profession in large numbers in the postwar period would have agreed whole-heartedly with Brown's sentiments, it is likely that few would have contradicted the main thrust of them.[68] Needless to say, the philosophy elaborated by Brown that lay behind the preparation of male teachers was bluntly at odds with the new ideas that had swept aside Swedish gymnastics.

The male physical educators were attracted to quite a different set of ideas.

One of these was their view of the central importance of competitive games and sports in physical education programmes. Another was the new scientific knowledge that was beginning to emerge, particularly knowledge relating to the development of physical fitness and to the acquisition of physical skills. Both of these matters are treated in detail in subsequent chapters, but both are relevant to the gymnastics debate in relation to the rise of Olympic gymnastic activities as a competitive sport and the associated issue of how to develop gymnastics skills. At the end of the war, a Ling Association Easter Holiday gymnastics course for males drew on activities outlined in the 1933 Syllabus, consisting mainly of free standing and bench exercises done in groups and some vaulting and agility work; in short, a form of Swedish gymnastics.[69] By 1954, some six years after Olympic gymnastics had been witnessed for the first time at the 1948 London Olympics by many of the current generation of male teachers, courses in 'apparatus gymnastics' were being run for males by the CCPR and the Amateur Gymnastics Association. This shift by the males towards a form of gymnastics in schools that resembled Olympic gymnastics was as much a reaction to the female sponsored educational gymnastics as it was an attraction for Olympic gymnastics as a competitive sport. Drawing on the logic of competitive sport and the new scientific knowledge of physical activity, the male physical educators began to crystallize their own perspective in direct opposition to the educational gymnasts'.

The open opposition of male physical educators to educational gymnastics became apparent when their criticisms began to enter the public sphere in the mid 1950s. As a result of a National Conference on Physical Education held in Edinburgh in 1954 involving both male and female physical educators and which was expressly concerned with the problem of gymnastics, the organizers set up a special committee to carry out an investigation into the content of the gymnastic lesson for boys. The dispute revolved around which of the three versions of gymnastics should be taught in Scottish schools.[69] After four one day meetings, the committee decided to support traditional Swedish gymnastics which had had a strong foothold in the Scottish School of Physical Education, the male college, since its establishment in 1932. What was interesting about this decision was the rejection of educational gymnastics on the grounds that it would undermine the traditionally high standards of gymnastic skill at the SSPE, an issue that was to form the corner-stone of the male critique of educational gymnastics.

Meanwhile, south of the border, David Munrow's influential *Pure and Applied Gymnastics* was published in 1955, and this book became the mouthpiece of male opposition to the progressive trend in physical education.[71] The book was significant not only for the distinctly alternative position it stated in relation to the educational gymnasts' and thus its representation of the male philosophy, but also by virtue of the fact that it was read by many of the educational gymnasts and so formed one of the few avenues of communication between the rival parties.[72] Munrow eloquently articulated the views of the coming force of scientific measurement, and how this new knowledge could be applied to physical education. Gymnastics, for Munrow, involved exercises designed to have particular effects on the body, and while his definition actually excluded many of the activities that made up Olympic gymnastics, we will see that the logic underlying his view supported this version of gymnastics over educational gymnastics. Munrow questioned whether the way forward for physical education lay with any single 'system' of gymnastics at all, which he considered to be subservient to the broader notion of 'physical activities and their related skills'.[73]

The new knowledge derived from scientific measurement was being produced in the university departments of physical education that had been established at Edinburgh, Liverpool, Manchester, Birmingham and Leeds during the 1930s. Their initial role was to provide recreational programmes for the students, but they soon added to this a research function.[74] In 1949, physical education became an option within the BA degree at Birmingham, and this institution along with Leeds in particular appointed staff with research orientations. Many of these staff were male, and as we saw earlier all of the Directors of the university physical education departments were male. In adopting the perspective and discourse of scientific measurement, the university physical education departments were following another trend in postwar British society in the same way that the educational gymnasts had fallen in with the progressive movement.

There is no doubt that the second world war gave the technology of fitness development and the acquisition of skill[75] a boost comparable to other technological developments described in Chapter 2, such as the use of radar in commercial aviation, radio isotopes in medicine and the widespread use of penicillin.[76] Certain techniques like circuit training[77] had been shown to be an effective way of improving troops' physical fitness for warfare. But more significantly, the whole of British culture was suffused with enthusiasm for the power of science to bring about change for the better. The effects of scientific research could be seen everywhere, in all aspects of people's lives. The rapid advance of technology hand-in-hand with increasing affluence after the austerity of the immediate postwar years had its most profound impact in the home. The educational sector was strongly implicated in the 1950s in the rise of technology to these new levels of influence. Schools were soon to become, in the 1960s, a corner-stone in Britain's survival as a major industrial power, and a technologically-orientated curriculum was the way this was to be achieved.[78] The so-called systems approach began to be adopted by curriculum developers keen to promote educational innovations in schools. As we saw in Chapter 3, science also played an important part in sustaining and legitimating the new selective tripartite system of secondary schooling instituted by the 1944 Education Act, through the mental measurement school of educational psychology and its construction of IQ tests for the 11-plus exam. And it was in this wider social and political context that the male physical educators began to see their subject as being scientifically-based.

Munrow had argued that the university departments of physical education had an important role to play in the production of scientific knowledge of 'the body's mechanical and psycho-physiological behaviour in acquiring and performing intricate physical skills' since this was 'an area not being fully tackled by any other branch of learning'.[79] On the basis of this view, he argued that 'the men could not at the moment subscribe to a general account of movement training' and 'doubted if movement training was capable of refining physical techniques'.[80] By the middle of the 1950s, the stage was set for a debate between male and female physical educators over the nature of gymnastics which, in effect, was a debate over the definition of physical education writ large.

Inside the Debate

There were two major issues which help to focus the debate that developed through the 1950s and 1960s in the wake of the demise of the Swedish system, between the female educational gymnasts and the males with their functional scientific perspective. The first was the controversy surrounding the level of specificity required for skill development and the problem of transfer of training. The second related closely to this first matter, and concerned the application of objective standards to gymnastic performance and the place of competition in the gym. Both issues revealed the essential nature of the differences between the female and male discourses.

In *Pure and Applied Gymnastics*, Munrow presented a definition of gymnastics that was narrowly physical and functional. He argued that physical educators had in the past placed too strong an emphasis on Swedish gymnastics skills, and had neglected skills in other sports and games. This emphasis was doubly misplaced, he claimed, since these formal gymnastics exercises had a very high skill threshold level before competent performance became possible. In moving away from the Swedish system after the second world war, he suggested that male and female physical educators had reacted in different ways to this problem.

> The men have made overt acknowledgement that other skills are as important and have 'diluted' the gymnastic skill content of gymnasium-work so that now boys may be seen practising basket-ball shots and manoeuvres, carrying out heading practices or practising sprint starting.[81]

Munrow's definition limited gymnastics to the exercises which were designed solely for their 'effect on particular parts of the body'. These effects were the development of strength, suppleness, stamina and skill; the muscles, joints, heart and lungs, and nervous system being the parts of the body affected. Skill could be developed through simplified skill drills which Munrow regarded as a form of gymnastic exercise. This sort of work had been growing in popularity with male teachers for some time,[82] and involved breaking down complex physical skills, like shot putting or serving in tennis, into smaller sequences of movement and practicing these as drills in the gymnasium. Munrow went on to contrast the male response to the female reaction

> The women, in the main, have... 'diluted' the traditional gymnastic skills by a quite different device. They have ceased both to name and to teach them. Instead, a description is given, in general terms, of a task-involving apparatus and individual solutions are encouraged. A much wider range of solutions is thus possible; some may include traditional skills but many will not.[83]

The problem with the female alternative to the Swedish system, as Munrow saw it, was that pupils rarely had the chance to consolidate their skills. The educational gymnasts' response to Munrow's challenge appeared in an article by Marjorie Randall in 1956, in which she attempted to clarify the movement approach in light of Munrow's critique.[84] However, this 1956 response was rather muted in comparison to a maturer expression of her position that appeared six years later in 1961 in a book, *Basic Movement*. In the opening chapter of the book, Randall immediately went on the offensive to contest Munrow's functional definition of gymnastics, suggesting that 'the masculine approach...has become largely outmoded so far as women's work is concerned'. She claimed that 'women's gymnastics...have been emancipated from the restricted practices of stereotyped patterns of movements based upon anatomical classification. The physiological and anatomical ends..are incidentally served'.[85] The major aim was the achievement of what Randall called body awareness, which included (merely physiological) nervous control combined with a higher level kinaesthetic awareness that could be developed through experience into an intuitive control of movement. She added to this a concern to engage the child cognitively in contrast to the male approach which she accused of stressing only the physical effects of exercise, and consequently regarding the intellect as out of range. She claimed:

> The masculine approach to gymnastics...separates content from method. Munrow's gymnastics exercises can be directly and formally taken or informally taken. Movement gymnastics requires the intelligent co-operation of the child, rendering command-response methods obsolete...this represents a big break-away from the traditional approach of the 'see this' and 'do it this way' school of thought.[86]

Randall's response showed that behind the less formal methods of educational gymnastics lay an attempt to treat the pupil wholistically, encouraging the concurrent development of intellectual and creative abilities in a movement medium, and relegating the physical effect of movement to a level of lesser importance. However, the notion of body awareness which lay at the centre of this scheme embodied claims for learning which ran directly counter to the new knowledge being produced by motor learning theorists. The educational gymnasts claimed, in much the same way as the Swedish gymnasts had before them, that the movement experience they had to offer was a general foundation upon which more specific skills could be built.[87] The notion of body awareness expressed this idea of a generalized kinaesthetic control. As early as 1949, however, members of the Birmingham University staff including Peter McIntosh and David Munrow, questioned whether there was such a thing as generalized skill training.[88] Joining this debate in 1953, another Birmingham staff member, Christine Roberts, argued that:

> 'the mingling of the general character of a movement with the necessarily limited mechanics of a movement is surely going to produce a false situation in relation to certain skills...as a basis for actual learning it seems to me to be too wide to produce the precision required in specific skills'.[89]

This view was supported by an extensive literature on training and skill development which had accumulated by the late 1950s.[90] On the basis of this evidence, Barbara Knapp, yet another Birmingham University staff member, argued that transfer of training was most likely to occur when the tasks in questions were similar, and so the best way to learn a specific action was to perform that action repeatedly over a period of time.[91] Commenting specifically on this issue of transfer of training in the context of the gymnastics debate, she wrote

> It often appears to be assumed that what is learned in the gymnasium will be transferred elsewhere...There is no experimental evidence as yet to support the assumption that a training in movement will enable every individual to deal with situations in which movement is involved more satisfactorily than those who have had other types of training.[92]

The logic of experimental science, and its cannons of truth and proof feature strongly in Knapp's views on the educational gymnasts' claims.

> It cannot be claimed that educational gymnastics develops a central factor of physical activity for many attempts have been made to isolate a general motor factor but without success. Suggestions that it develops 'body awareness' or 'kinaesthetic sensitivity' should also be accepted with caution for proof of the existence of one such factor common to all motor skills is still awaited...Even if there is such a factor common to all motor skills its effect appears to be infinitesimal compared with other factors specific to any particular motor skill. Research indicates that skills are highly specific...and similar skills which are not identical can interfere with one another.[93]

The crux of the motor learning theorists' critique, which the male physical educators championed vigorously, was that skill learning is specific. Thus, the best way to master any physical activity was to practise that particular activity repeatedly until it had been learned. The male physical educators took this principle to heart and developed an approach to teaching skills that consisted of reducing a skill to its component parts, and learning these parts separately, before re-assembling them gradually until the entire skill had been learned. All of this appeared to make nonsense of the females' claim that it was possible, indeed preferable, to develop a general body awareness as a foundation on which to build more specific learning. Indeed, as if to emphasize the chasm this placed between them and the female gymnasts, the males blissfully adopted cybernetic and mechanistc analogies of the skill learning process, and talked of 'effector mechanisms' and 'feed-back loops',[94] analogies that were not only antithetical but also offensive to the educational gymnasts, since this reduction of human activity to mechnanistic processes through industrialization and factory work had been from the 1930s, as we saw earlier, an issue of central concern.

A second objection to the educational gymnasts' position related to the place of standards and competition in the gym. From the male perspective, it seemed unlikely that the educational gymnasts' child-centred approach could continue to stimulate pupils beyond the early stages of learning, and indeed many male physical educators were prepared to concede that educational gymnastics might be permissible if confined only to Infants. However, Munrow argued that it could not challenge older boys or girls and it was for this reason, as a stimulant or incentive, that competitive activity was essential. In *Pure and Applied Gymnastics* he complained

> Allied to a teaching philosophy which seeks actively to avoid confront-
> ing less able children with failure, is the belief that the child's own
> solution to the problem being always valid and right. This makes more
> sense with young children than with older boys and girls and with first
> efforts at a skill rather than with later ones...to leave children flounder-
> ing to evolve their own technique when we could guide them is a
> neglect of our professional duties.[95]

The child's own imagination and creativity set the limits on what could be
achieved, because intervention by the teacher was interpreted by the educational
gymnast as an imposition that not only set a standard against which the pupils'
success could be measured, but also where their failures and inadequacies could
be revealed. In Munrow's view, this double edged quality to objectively set
standards was unavoidable. 'If we attempt too much to shield the child from
failure we shall also shield him from real success. For success that all can have for
the asking is not worth having'.

In response to Munrow's view that standards were a necessary and important means of challenging pupils to strive for excellence, Randall suggested that
girls, particularly in adolescence, had quite different needs to boys. She argued
that the growing boy 'derives considerable prestige and social prominence
through physical advantage in competitive games which his increase in height,
weight and strength gives him'. Girls, on the other hand, may have little to gain
from competitive sport during the adolescent period, and so:

> In the gymnastic lesson let her be free from all this competition and let
> her progress at her own rate and find joy and satisfaction in the slow but
> sure progress of controlling her body. Through her pride in the mastery
> of her body in the gymnasium will grow a certain independence, secur-
> ity and emotional stability.

and:

> Teaching must be geared to the individual; it must be flexible and
> tolerant of a wide range in aptitude...no longer is her worth in the
> gymnasium measured by whether she can get over the box in long fly or
> whether she can put her head on her knees keeping her legs straight; but
> rather can she work to surpass her own standards without being har-
> rassed or harried because she cannot conform to a common one.[96]

The aims of independence, security and emotional stability contrast sharply
with the desire to develop strength, endurance, flexibility, and particular skills,
and to use these attributes in competitive situations. These contrasts reveal
starkly the contested issues that divided the male and female physical educators.
Munrow saw the educational gymnasts' apparent lack of standards as an arroga-
tion of the teacher's responsibilities, a refusal to take an active role in pupil's
learning.[97] Randall, on the other hand, argued that the incentive to improve did
not come from comparisons with other pupils. Indeed, she claimed that competition was likely to inhibit performance particularly among adolescent girls, and
comes instead from within each individual. What these contrasting views of the

issues of transfer of training and competition in gymnastics indicate are not simply different points of view, but different views of the nature of the entire educational process, including what it means to teach, what it means to learn, and more fundamentally, what the term physical education itself means. The two rival factions were not simply subscribing to different points of view on the same set of issue, but rather were operating on the basis of quite different agendas. There is a sense, then, in which Munrow and Randall, as two representative figures in this debate did not talk to each other, but talked past each other. Not only did they use languages that were foreign to each other ('the whole child'/ 'effector mechanism'), but the terms of the debate were themselves quite different for each group. For the educational gymnasts, movement was primarily a means of personal growth and self-realization, whereas for the male functionalists the central concern was the development of physical skills.

The Aftermath of the Debate

By the early 1960s, it was regarded as old-fashioned to think of gymnastics as the core of physical education as the subject expanded to include, as a matter of course, a wide range of other physical activities, particularly team and individual games, and outdoor pursuits. Indeed, as we will see in the next chapter, games were increasingly from the mid 1950s to become for the professional physical educator what gymnastics had been between 1890 and 1950. For this reason, Olympic gymnastics was never to occupy the role that Swedish gymnastics had done for females and males before 1940 or that educational gymnastics had for the females between 1940 and 1960. Indeed, the form of gymnastics advocated by Munrow in *Pure and Applied Gymnastics*, consisting of parts of skills that could be learned and practised in the gym in isolation from the whole activity, had as much application to games and other sports as it had to Olympic gymnastics.

And what of Olympic gymnastics? Little has been said about this version of gymnastics up to this point, and this is for the reason that it was not so overtly or obviously aligned with the male perspective as educational gymnastics was with the female. However, while as many women as men did participate in this sport as its popularity grew through the 1960s,[98] the new knowledge that sustained it owed little to the educational gymnasts or the female tradition. As we will see in Chapter 6, the males' focus on the development of physical fitness fitted them well for the task of preparing elite sport performers. This version of gymnastics was an international competitive sport that demanded exactly what the male physical educators could provide — knowledge of how to develop strength, muscular endurance, agility and high levels of precision skills. Thus, Olympic gymnastics was fostered within the emerging discourse of scientific functionalism, even though many females actively participated in the sport. Educational gymnastics continued to be fostered and developed predominately by female physical educators throughout the 1960s, but its influence was limited to primary schools and girls' physical education in secondary schools. While some males did teach educational gymnastics, they were few in number,[99] and as the scope of physical education programmes expanded in schools through the late 1950s and 1960s, the role and significance of educational gymnastics within the female tradition was also eroded, so that it became, like Olympic gymnastics, just one of the many forms of physical activity to be found in school physical education.

The importance of this debate goes far beyond the fate of the various forms of gymnastics themselves, however. This episode of contestation and conflict over the version of gymnastics to be taught in schools may in itself have become a non-issue by the beginning of 1960s, but its effects were to spill over into every other aspect of physical education in the two decades which followed. More to the point, the fact that the lines of conflict were drawn by gender is a matter of crucial importance, since this fact in itself challenged the notion, much touted throughout the postwar period, that knowledge was a neutral commodity untainted by the wider social, political and cultural divisions that mark society. By the end of the 1960s, and no doubt wearied by almost two decades of conflict, the females and males had adopted a stand-off position, most in effect agreeing to disagree. Some sought refuge in simplified rationalizations of the divide between the males and females; 'although there is undoubted intellectual content in physical education, it is not so clearly defined as in other subjects...there are two aspects to consider; the skill and the scientific on one hand and the fine arts on the other'.[100] Others by this time were even prepared to make admissions of culpability for earlier follies. Muriel Webster, a former Principal of Anstey College, one of the oldest women's colleges, commented that 'in the past we have done irrevocable damage by over-claiming' and admitted that the females could be justly accused of 'underestimating the place of specific skills; playing down the importance of physical strength, mobility and good poise; (and) throwing overboard the whole subject of health as an important aspect of the subject'. She also conceded that 'we are so often asked for proof of what we say and do and, perhaps unwisely, retaliate by questioning the value of some of the things that can be measured'.[101] Some of the men, too, were prepared to shift. Both RE Morgan (of Circuit Training fame) and David Munrow, former Directors of Physical Education at the Universities of Leeds and Birmingham respectively, re-assessed some of the female's ideas sympathetically,[102] while others became enthusiastic advocates of the females' ideals.[103]

Notwithstanding these overtures to conciliation, the balance of power throughout the 1960s shifted, and the shift was towards those values which underpinned the male perspective as it began to emerge in the gymnastics debate through the 1950s. This shift is clearly illustrated in the scramble to prove physical education's degree worthiness in the quest for an all-graduate profession that the Robbins Report[104] made possible with the creation of the BEd degree.[105] It was the males who took the lead in this quest,[106] and the new degree programmes drew heavily on the which emerging scientific sub-disciplines of exercise physiology, motor learning theory and biomechanics.[107] Another factor in this shift was the dissolution of the female colleges, which by the mid 1960s were in the process of being merged into other, larger institutions, and so their distinctive identities taken, or else closed completely. While this was not an abrupt affair,[108] the influence of the female physical educators as a group with a distinctively alternative perspective to the male view of physical education was by the end of the 1960s well and truly broken. In a field that until the late 1940s had been dominated by women for over fifty years, the rise of the male scientific functionalist discourse to power and influence during the decade and a half following the end of the second world war was little short of dramatic. In the final section of this chapter I want to offer an explanation of how and why this occurred.

Politics, Power and Patriarchy

The educational gymnasts initially thrived within an already existing female tradition in physical education. They had institutions to practice and develop their art, schools in which to apply it, and a progressive educational movement to legitimate it. Their ideas were also extremely influential in the state primary sector, and through this educational gymnastics developed a base of support and gained official government backing. However, these very conditions that fostered their version of physical education also limited its ability to move beyond a certain point. The insularity of their institutions, for one thing, restricted to those women who could afford to pay their fees, worked against them in the late 1940s when the government began to demand more teachers than they could possibly hope to supply.[109] They found they could not compete with the larger institutions being set up to meet this demand, and there resulted a series of takeovers, amalgamations and closures that had almost entirely undermined their professional infrastructure by the 1960s.[110] Perhaps this process could have been slowed but for two other forces which were also built in to the context in which educational gymnastics developed.

The first of these was their influence in the state sector primary schools and the fact that educational gymnastics very quickly came to be associated with primary school physical education. Because of the continuities between its non-competitive, aesthetic and creative features and the child-centred movement that was bringing about sweeping changes in primary classrooms, educational gymnastics was championed, as we have seen, by teachers of younger children, particularly teachers of Infants.[111] The way towards status and prestige, however, lay in the new secondary schools modelled on the subject-orientated grammar schools. While the arrival of mass secondary schooling had given the primary schools more scope to experiment, it was the secondary sector which was expanding rapidly, and it was there that the various Labour and Conservative governments in the late 1950s and the 1960s focused their attention, particularly on the transitional period from school to work and higher education. Progressivism in the primary school also worked against the achievement of an enhanced status and influence for the educational gymnasts' version of physical education by its very non-proprietariness, stressing instead the value of an integrated curriculum which attempted to dissolve subject boundaries.[112] This was little short of disastrous for a curriculum topic which could not present a coherent and unified public image of what physical education was and the knowledge it encompassed.

The second force at work lay in wider social and political trends. While the educational gymnasts were promoting humanitarian ideals focused around the notion of individual worth, the radicalism of postwar social reconstruction was, as we saw in Chapter 3, proving to be a sham.[113] Beneath the consensual politics of right and left, Britain was moving during the 1950s into a consumer-orientated materialism that sprung from the new technologically-produced affluence. Equality of opportunity came to mean something quite different in Labour educational policy from what it had meant to the child-centred progressives.[114]

The early radical intent of leftist policy for social change through the raising of a collective consciousness and personal enrichment through the acquisition of liberal culture, was drowned in the clamour of voices from the middle and right of the Labour party which in contrast adopted a purely quantitative conception of equality based in the fair distribution of educational goods. As one recent commentator put it, the doctrine of equality of opportunity within Labour educational policy in the late 1950s and early 1960s resembled a competition that produced winners and losers, and drew on the meritocratic ideology of just reward for hard work and talent.[115] This conception of equality of opportunity was quite at odds with the liberal humanism of the educational gymnasts where 'each girl in the class should work individually, trying to improve her own standard but not unduly conscious of or worried by the greater abilities of the girls around her'. The problem for the educational gymnasts was that the ideals of both liberal and radical progressivism were marginalized in the consensual educational policies of the day, and 'equality' became a slogan masking a profound materialism. Thus the discourse of progressivism in educational gymnastics, and the version of the subject it presented, had little support in the realities of broader educational policy and practice.

The male orientation, on the other hand, grew out of a different set of circumstances, and these created a contrasting set of possibilities to those of the educational gymnasts'. Their functional, scientific and competitive discourse from the start was in tune with a number of powerful trends. One of these was the widespread popular acceptance of competitive sport in schools and its role in the promotion of national prestige, a matter to be adressed in detail in the next chapter. The great demand for teachers to meet the needs of mass secondary schooling was also a particularly significant event for male physical educators. Because there were fewer of them compared to the women, greater attention was given to meeting this shortfall in the years immediately following the war.[116] The institutional settings in which scientific functionalism was fostered, in the universities, large teacher training colleges and secondary schools, were therefore relatively unhindered by tradition and the men were in a better position than the women to respond to contemporary challenges. These factors helped the males to maintain a higher profile in relation to developments in the wider educational arena and in society at large. Furthermore, universities with their increasing bias towards technology, and the secondary schools with their subject-specific organization provided a fruitful environment in which to pursue professional status.

All of this suggests that the conditions in which the male scientific functionalist discourse arose created a range of possibilities that were denied to the female physical educators. However, none of it entirely explains why such disparate discourses emerged in the first place or, more to the point, why they were so firmly identified with 'the sex of the individual'. This is not to deny that some women were appointed to the university departments,[117] nor to deny that some men did teach educational gymnastics. Perhaps the insularity and elitism of the female tradition was an important factor in allowing two distinctly different discourses to exist, but while this point explains how their conditions of emergence were dissimilar, it does not tell us why it was that the women as a group chose to move away from the functionalism of Swedish gymnastics towards a progressive, child-centred form of the subject, while the men reformulated the functionalism of the Swedish system within a scientific discourse. Perhaps, as

Fletcher has speculated, the quite disparate experiences of men and women during the second world war, and the male experience of armed combat was the crucial moment in drawing female and male physical educators so far apart.

Or perhaps more to the point is the nature of patriarchal norms and practices in which the events that have been discussed here were embedded. Scratton and Hargreaves[118] both suggest that while the female discourse formed a radical alternative to the male version of physical education in one sense, in another it did little to challenge women's roles as wives and mothers. Scratton claims that while, on the one hand, girls' physical education presented a radical challenge to Victorian notions of the frail, illness-prone and delicate constitution of the female, on the other girls' activities were still framed and limited by patriarchal views of correct conduct, biological capacity and emotional instability.[119] Hargreaves lends support to this line of argument in her claim that from the beginning of the female tradition in physical education, the gymnasts' support for female emancipation was based on 'a nationalistic sentiment, confirming the contemporary Social Darwinistic position about the vital importance of motherhood to evolution, and the encompassing belief that educational arrangements should be geared to the role of women as mothers'.[120] Thus, the familism of the Victorian era based on patriarchal authority and a strict hierarchy of command and definition of roles was, as Fletcher has shown in her study of Bedford Physical Training College, still present in the women's colleges in the 1950s. The fact that educational gymnastics came to be associated with the physical education of girls and small children in itself says much about the limits set by patriarchal structures on the extent to which any oppositional group may be permitted to form radical alternatives. In the next chapter, we turn to look at the rise of competitive team games in mass secondary school physical education during the 1950s, and the key role bourgeois patriarchal forces played in the male physical educators' rise to dominance.

Notes

1 Board of Education (1933) *Syllabus of Physical Training for Schools*, London: HMSO.

2 There has been a growing volume of feminist literature recently concerned with physical education and sport. See for example the collection of papers on the 'Gendering of sport, leisure and physical education' in the special issue of the *Women's Studies International Forum*, **19**(4), 1987 and Fletcher, S. (1984) *Women First: The Female Tradition in English Physical Education 1880–1980*, London: Althone; Hargreaves, J. (1985) 'Playing like gentlemen while behaving like ladies: Contradictory features of the formative years of women's sport. *The British Journal of Sports History*, **2**(1), 40–52; Scratton, S. (1986) 'Images of femininity and the teaching of girls' physical education', in Evans, J. (Ed.) *Physical Education, Sport and Schooling: Studies in the Sociology of Physical Education* Lewes: Falmer Press, pp. 71–94.

3 The college was permanently housed at Dartford ten years later from 1895.

4 Webster, C.M. (1958) 'The training of the woman teacher of physical education', *Physical Education*, **50**, 85–90.

5 See Saunders, W. (1951) 'Why exclude olympic gymnastic apparatus work?' *Journal of Physical Education*, **43**, 85–88.

6   For discussions of progressivism in British education see Hamilton, D. (1986) Some Observations on Progressivism and Curriculum Practice. Unpublished paper, University of Glasgow; Jones, K. (1983) *Beyond Progressive Education*, London: MacMillan; Finn, M.E. (1983) 'Social efficiency progressivism and secondary education in Scotland, 1885–1905', in Humes, W.M. and Paterson, H.M. (Eds) *Scottish Culture and Scottish Education 1800–1980*, Edinburgh: John Donald, pp. 175–196.

7   McIntosh, P.C. (1968) *PE in England Since 1800*, London: Bell, pp. 231–3.; see also Harris, J. (1961) 'The development of the Keep Fit Association of England and Wales', *Physical Education*, **53**, 38–41.

8   McIntosh, note 7, p. 242.

9   *The Leaflet*, **45**(9), 1946.

10 For example, between 1945 and 1955, Scandinavian gymnastics are mentioned in the *Times Educational Supplement* on only four occasions — 12 June 1948, 31 July 1948, 31 March 1950 and 22 April 1955 which contrasts starkly with the frequent comments on the promotion of games and sports, and the provision of playing fields.

11 See Fletcher, note 2.

12 Carlquist, M. (1955) *Rhythmical Gymnastics* London: Methuen.

13 Professor Olive Wheeler, in Wheeler, O. (1945) 'The changing conception of physical education', *Journal of Physical Education*, **37**, p. 3. Wheeler went on to argue that the physical educator 'should never regard the body as mechanically determined — 'a combination of carbon compounds, ammonia and soluable salts' — or as an intricate machine, tenantless and uncreative'.

14 Wardle, M. (1947) 'Free formation and individual work', *Journal of Physical Education*, **39**, p. 8.

15 Read, C.M. (1945) 'Gymnastics and physical education II', *Journal of Physical Education*, **37**, 130–132.

16 Squire, M.E. (1945) 'Gymnastics and physical education I', *Journal of Physical Education*, **37**, 101–104.

17 Cox, G.M. (1946) 'Gymnastics and physical education III', *Journal of Physical Education*, **38**, 57–60.

18 Squire, note 16, p. 104.

19 See Fletcher, note 2, p. 113 on the fate of Swedish gymnastics at Bedford Physical Training College.

20 Small, R.B. (1976) The Effects of Individuals On, and Developments Within, The Scottish School of Physical Education in the 20th Century. Unpublished paper, Jordanhill College of Education, Glasgow.

21 Randall, M. (1961) *Basic Movement. A New Approach to Gymnastics* London: Bell.

22 According to Jones, note 6, p. 38 this is an important feature of progressivism.

23 Carlquist, note 12, p. 2.

24 Laban, R. (1948) *Modern Educational Dance* London: MacDonald and Evans.

25 As we can see from this remark from an influential spokeswoman for the educational gymnasts, Ruth Morison. 'The limitations imposed by contemporary life tend to disrupt natural harmonious movement and produce stilted, restricted, isolated actions, and to develop bad habits of movement and carriage which in their turn cause tensions, cramps and the resultant ills'. Morison, R. (1969) *A Movement Approach to Educational Gymnastics* London: Dent, p. 6.

26 Rubinstein, D. and Simon, B. (1966) *The Evolution of the Comprehensive School, 1922–1966* London: RKP

27 See Hamilton and Jones, note 6.

28 Board of Education (1931) *The Primary School* London: HMSO, p. 139.

29 Jones, note 6, p. 2.

30   Fletcher, note 2, p. 132.
31   Thomson, I. (1978) 'The origins of physical education in state schools', *Scottish Educational Review*, **10**(2), 15–24.
32   *TES* 31 January 1948.
33   *TES* 27 July 1946.
34   Wardle, note 14, p. 10.
35   Ministry of Education (1952) *Moving and Growing: Physical Education in the Primary School, Part 1*, London: HMSO; Ministry of Education (1953) *Planning the Programme: Physical Education in the Primary School, Part 2*, London: HMSO.
36   McIntosh, note 7, p. 262.
37   For instance, *TES* 25 July 1952, p. 636; also *TES* Book Review 10 June 1955, p. 618.
38   *TES* 11 September 1953, p. 779.
39   Swain, M.O.B. (1954) 'Some impressions of PE in England'. *The Leaflet*, **55**(4), p. 5. Note also lack of written texts on these ideas; see Karn, E. (1952) 'The "old" and the "new" in Physical Education'. *Journal of Physical Education*, **44**, 64–65, which reveals something of the almost anti-intellectual dimension of the educational gymnasts, which was to become another source of problems later.
40   Report in *The Leaflet*, **55**(5), 1954, p. 6, on the first ever 'men-only' course at the Art of Movement Studio; and note the comments of DT Williams, a male teacher, in *The Leaflet*, **62**(5), 1961, p. 38. He first encountered educational gymnastics in 1956.
41   See Fletcher, note 2, pp. 134 & 136.
42   Swain, M.O.B. (1988) *Physical Education in England, America and NSW 1940–1960 and Allied Subjects* NSW: ACHPER.
43   Roberts, C. (1953) 'Movement training for girls', *Journal of Physical Education*, **45**, p. 93.
44   See Fletcher, note 2, p. 128.
45   Moyse, Y. (1949) 'A brief outline of some of the activities of the Ling physical education association'. *Journal of Physical Education* **41**, 31–53 and 77–89.
46   Jennifer Hargreaves, note 2, pp. 47–48.
47   Editorial, *The Leaflet*, **49**(7), p. 140.
48   Wardle, note 14, p. 8.
49   McIntosh, P.C. (1957) 'From treadmill to springboard', *The Leaflet*, **58**(5).
50   O'Dwyer, J. (1951) 'Open Letter — A plea for proportion', *Journal of Physical Education*, **43**, 46–47.
51   Karn, note 39, pp. 63–64.
52   *TES* 19 January 1951 and 26 January 1951; *The Leaflet*, **53**(5), 1952.
53   The Ling Association Easter Conference, 'Gymnastics for Secondary School Girls', reported in *The Leaflet*, **53**(5), 1952, p. 70.
54   Swain, note 39, p. 5.
55   Karn, note 39, p. 10.
56   Colson, P. (1952) President's Address to the AGM. *The Leaflet*, **53**(4), p. 50.
57   Even into the 1960s, certificate trained physical educators were not allowed to share a school staffroom with other (degree qualified) teachers.
58   Thomson, note 31.
59   See McIntosh, note 7 and Thomson, note 31 for more detailed discussion; see also the comment in *TES* 24 October 1523, reviewing McIntosh's book in its first edition, published in 1952.
60   Thomson, note 31.
61   Letter in *The Leaflet*, **45**(1), 1946, pp. 9–10.
62   Reported in *The Leaflet*, **44**(10), 1945, p. 194. One reason for the disproportionate numbers of male to female teachers in this case may have been due to the lack of availability of female teachers, who were in such demand that they could

virtually select which schools they wished to teach in, and certainly would not have had to work in the government sector unless they wanted to. Another possible factor could have been the larger number of boys staying on to Senior Secondary stage; in Scotland, only male teachers taught male pupils, and female teachers female pupils. A third factor, noted below (in note 63) would have been the view that women could not be promoted to positions of responsibility since they were liable to marry and leave teaching.

63 The next big push for more teachers came in the late 1950s and early 1960s with the creation of the Wing courses, see Thomson, I. (1986) 'Professional training in physical education and sport within a binary system of higher and further education in England 1944–1985,' pp. 61–74 in *Trends and Developments in Physical Education* (Proceedings of the VIII Commonwealth and International Conference) London: E & FNSpon. Determining actual numbers of teachers being produced by the specialist colleges between 1935–1960 is not easy due to complexity of training arrangements. However, one source (Foster, R. and Sagar, H. (1960) 'The future training of specialist teachers', *The Leaflet*, **61**(5)) provides some illustrative statistics. The total number of women in all training colleges 1949–50 was 746, and in 1959–60 1052. The total number of men produced by all sources in 1935 was 60 per year, 100–120 in 1939, 220 in 1949 and 350 in 1955. This difference in numbers is offset however, by the high attrition rate of women, evidenced in the repeated complaints of shortages of women teachers and pleas for married women to return to work throughout the postwar years and well in to the 1960s — see for example, *The Leaflet*, **49**(5), 1948; *TES* 9 October 1949, p. 574; *The Leaflet*, **57**(9), 1956; *The Leaflet*, **62**(1), 1961. It is important to note also the prevelant attitude of the time with regard to women and careers; for example, the *TES* 31 July 1948, p. 1 & p. 432 *Report on International PE Congress pre 1948 Olympics* — Miss M. Crabbe and Dr H. Schofield on the 'Training of Teachers' — 'Whereas women could specialize in this field alone, men had also to be trained as 'general practitioners', so that when they grow older they could undertake other class teaching. The Ministry did not, Dr Scholfield pointed out, consider this essential for women, since they were liable to marry and leave.'

64 Brown, H.C. (1958) 'The training of the man teacher of physical education', *Physical Education*, **50**, 91–94.

65 Brown, note 64, p. 92.

66 Brown, note 64, p. 93.

67 Brown, note 64, p. 93.

68 For example, see the report on a gymnastics Conference in *The Leaflet*, **57**(1), 1956.

69 *The Leaflet*, **45**(6), 1946, p. 120.

70 The conference topic was 'Physical Education Today and in the Future', and was organized by the Scottish Joint Consultative Committee on Physical Education which was made up of representatives of the separate male (Scottish Physical Education Association) and female (Scottish League of Physical Education) associations. There is a report on the conference in *The Leaflet*, **56**(1), 1955.

71 Munrow, A.D. (1955) *Pure and Applied Gymnastics* London: Arnold. Munrow was the first Director of the Department of Physical Education at Birmingham University.

72 In the second edition of *Pure and Applied Gymnastics*, published in 1963, Munrow commented on the debate around his definition of gymnastics presented in the first edition. 'Certainly the impact of the word 'artificial' in the definition has been unfortunate, especially on supporters of Modern Educational Gymnastics. Some of them might subscribe to the present definition of 'systematized exercises designed to produce particular effects on the body'...Thus a small

area of agreement could be found on which to stand together and discuss what are likely to be substantial areas of disagreement.', p. 22.

73 Munrow, A.D. (1956) 'Looking back and looking forward in gymnastics', *Journal of Physical Education*, **48**, 18–24.

74 See McIntosh, note 7. The shift to research is discussed in detail in Chapter 6.

75 See for instance Squadron-Leader Winterbottom, in Winterbottom, W. (1945) 'Physical training in the Royal Air Force', *Journal of Physical Education*, **37**, 9–11, and Brigadier T.H. Wand-Tetley, C.B.E., in Wand-Tetley, T.H. (1946) '"Purposeful" Physical training in the army"'. *Journal of Physical Education*, **38**, 140–143.

76 Marwick, A. (1982) *British Society Since 1945* Harmondsworth: Penguin.

77 Developed at Leeds University by Morgan and Adamson. See Morgan, R.E. and Adamson, G.T. (1957) *Circuit Training* London: Bell.

78 See Centre for Contemporary Cultural Studies (1981) *Unpopular Education* London: Hutchinson.

79 Munrow, A.D. (1955) *The Leaflet*, **56**(1), p. 6.

80 Conference on 'Gymnastics in the Secondary School', Munrow's comments reported in *The Leaflet*, **57**(1), 1956, p. 2.

81 Munrow, note 72, p. 276.

82 See *The Leaflet*, **48**(4), 1947, pp. 90–92.

83 Munrow, note 72.

84 Randall, M. (1956) 'The movement approach — A need for clarification'. *Physical Education*, **48**, 15–17.

85 Randall, note 21, p. 12.

86 Randall, note 21, pp. 25–6.

87 Indeed, educational gymnastics was sometimes called 'Basic Movement' or 'Movement Training'.

88 McIntosh, P.C. (1948) 'Skill and physical education. *Journal of Physical Education*, **40**, 130–137.; Munrow, A.D. (1952) 'Transference of training'. *Journal of Physical Education*, **44**, 49–54.

89 Roberts, note 43, p. 96; a similar point was made by Nahapiet, K. (1955) Transfer of training. *The Leaflet*, **56**(4); and in J Wright's response in *The Leaflet*, **57**(4), 1956, p. 21 to Randall, note 84.

90 Holding, D.H. (1965) *Principles of Training* Oxford: Pergamon

91 Knapp, B. (1963) *Skill in Sport* London: RKP, pp. 110 and 166.

92 Knapp, note 91, p. 110.

93 Knapp, note 91, pp. 112–113.

94 See Carr, D. (1981) 'On Mastering a Skill', *Journal of Philosophy of Education*, **15**(1), 87–96, for a devastating critique of this psychologistic approach.

95 Munrow, note 72, pp. 280–281.

96 Randall, note 21, pp. 20–22.

97 Munrow, note 72, p. 278.

98 See Stuart, N. (1964) *Competitive Gymnastics* London: Stanley Paul; and Allison, J. (1963) *Advanced Gymnastics for Women* London; Stanley Paul.

99 See Whitehead, N. (1970) 'The present and the future'. *SSPE/SAPE Conference Report* Jordanhill College, Glasgow, p. 24.

100 Miss J.D. Browne, Principal of City of Coventry Training College in 'The training of teachers' *The Leaflet*, **66**(1), 1965.

101 Webster, M. (1969–70) 'Physical education today and tomorrow', in the *Physical Education Yearbook 1969–70*, pp. 7–14.

102 Munrow, A.D. (1972) *Physical Education: A Discussion of Principles* London: Arnold; Morgan, R.E. (1974) *Concerns and Values in Physical Education* London: Bell.

103 Carlisle, R. (1969) 'The concept of physical education'. *Proceedings of the Philoso-*

phy of Education Society of Great Britain, Vol. 3; Curl, G. (1973) 'An attempt to justify human movement as a field of study', in Brooke, J.D. and Whiting, H.T.A. (Eds) *Human Movement as a Field of Study* London: Kingston pp. 7–17.

104   Robbins Report (1963) *Higher Education* London: HMSO.

105   See Thomson, note 63 and Fletcher, note 2 for detailed accounts.

106   See *The Leaflet,* **66**(9), 1965, p. 74 and the letter from Margaret Rosewarne Jenkins concerning the lack of female representation on BEd study group report; see also Fletcher, note 2, p. 148.

107   See for example Henry, F.M. (1964) 'Physical education — An academic discipline', *The Leaflet,* **66**(1), 6–7.; and Chapter 6 in this book.

108   But as Fletcher, note 2, p. 139 has commented 'their descent has been prolonged and uncertain, sometimes more like the movement of a kite, which, when almost grazing the ground, may lift off on a sudden upstream and soar again, or eventually tumble'.

109   McNair Report (1944) *Teachers and Youth Leaders* London: HMSO.

110   See Fletcher, note 2.

111   The key agents in the dissemination of educational gymnastics from the specialist physical education colleges to the generalist infant teachers were the Inspectorate and LEA Advisors, many of whom were women.

112   'Physical education is not a subject, it is an aspect of the curriculum.' *TES* 27 July 1946.

113   CCCS, note 78.

114   See Jones for a discussion of this point, note 6.

115   Bennett, D. (1982) 'Education: Back to the drawing board', in Smith, R. (1985) *The Inequalities Debate: An Interpretive Essay,* Geelong: Deakin University Press, p. 85.

116   Thomson, I., note 63.

117   Though as Fletcher, note 2, p. 135 observes, women were not admitted to the advanced diploma course at Leeds University until 1966, 11 years after it began.

118   See note 2.

119   Scratton, note 2, p. 73.

120   Hargreaves, note 2, pp. 47–48.

Chapter 5

The Games Ethic, Mass Secondary Schooling, and the Invention of Traditional Physical Education

Competitive team games and sports had been part of the cultural fabric of British life for almost a century by the end of the second world war, although the actual activities played had from the beginning been strongly flavoured by the gender and social class of the participants. Team games also occupied a central role in the education of wealthy males from the mid 1800s, though later this practice was taken up by upper class women and other less wealthy members of the bourgeois class. However, while participating in and spectating at competitive sports contests was a popular leisure-time pursuit across the social class spectrum in Britain, games and sports did not form a substantial or significant part of physical education programmes in the state sector until the introduction of mass secondary schooling in the late 1940s. In a very short space of time, competitive team sports had become the core of physical education and the largest part of the programme. In the process, the meaning of school physical education was itself reconstructed. Within a decade and a half, a version of physical education that had until the 1950s only been 'traditional' to the private schools in Britain became 'traditional physical education' for everyone, for the masses as well as the wealthy.

This spectacular rise to prominence of competitive games and sports in secondary school physical education was sponsored most enthusiastically by the newly arrived male physical educators, whose numbers relative to the female members of the profession increased dramatically after the war. Their appropriation of games playing and a version of the public school games ethic was an important means of enhancing their status, in relation both to their mainly middle class female colleagues and other teachers. In this, the male physical educators were given considerable ideological support by the educational press and other ruling class interests, who viewed games playing as a vehicle for the dissolution of a range of social ills. At the same time, the public school games ethic had to be sanitized and reconstructed for use in the mass secondary school system, and reconstructed in a form that could enlist the identification and support of working class pupils.

This was because the games ethic was strongly flavoured by the circumstances in which it first arose, in the education of ruling class males, and later took on a life of its own so that it achieved a mythical status long after the 'cult of athleticism' which had supported it in the public schools had lost much of its initial fervour. The myth about games playing and the educational qualities to-be gained from participation were taken up and propogated vigorously by the bourgeois class (males almost exclusively) and in the process came to embody and symbolize their cherished ideals — success, dynamism, vigor, competitiveness, individualism and fair play. Part of the success of competitive team games among the bourgeoisie was their symbolic value as a mark of social superiority, through which they could simultaneously emulate their social superiors and distance themselves from their inferiors. In addition, the mythology surrounding the educational value of games playing was used as a political tool as early as the first world war as a means of fostering national identity. By the 1940s and 1950s, the myth had persuaded politicians and other ruling class agents, themselves descendants of the original myth-makers, that games were a cure for such social ills as teenage crime and delinquency. By extending the logic of games as a means of fostering national identity, games playing also came to be seen in the 1950s as a 'common denominator' for children from different social class and later ethnic groups, as mass secondary schooling expanded and school physical education programmes expanded in turn. As we saw in Chapter 3, the 1950s marked the dawning of mass consumerism, and this also manifested itself in the expansion and increasing professionalization, commercialization, and commodification of competitive sport.

This chapter is an account of the reconstruction of the public school games ethic for use in the mass secondary school after the second world war, and the invention of 'traditional physical education' built on this reconstructed myth of the educational value of games playing. It briefly traces the roots of the public school games ethic and outlines the social and political conditions of its origin and development in the schools of the bourgeois class, before examining the extent to which competitive games and sports became part of mass secondary school physical education programmes through the 1950s. It then locates the invention of 'traditional physical education' in a nexus of social forces in postwar Britain, highlighting in particular the growth of state intervention in popular physical recreation after the war, attempts to use games to build national identity, and the discourse of games playing as a means of combatting delinquency among working class youth.

The Evolution of the Games Ethic and Bourgeois Class Identity

The 'cult of athleticism' and its accompanying 'games ethic' were born in the public schools of the male bourgeois classes in Victorian Britain, and formed a powerful educational ideology that was to become influential well beyond the boundaries of space, time and social class. The playing of the competitive team games and sports which constituted the cult — football, rowing, cricket, racquets and fives — rose to prominence between 1850 to reach a peak in the schools themselves around 1914.[1] As it was formulated and formalized during this period, the cult of athleticism was very much in tune with the needs of its creators at this time.[2] The civil and political unrest which had marked the first three decades of the nineteenth century gave way to a new prosperity and significant changes in the social structure in train with developments in industrial capita-lism.[3] It was at this time, towards the mid 1850s, that a new, many layered and diversely constituted class emerged, formed in part by an 'industrial aristocracy',[4] a new middle class of managers and other professionals, and a range of other occupational groups centered on manufacturing. Together, these groups formed the bourgeoisie. During this period, the English public school was resurrected from a less than illustrious past, and the cult of athleticism and games playing were at the centre of its reformation.[5]

The public schools served a number of apparently contradictory purposes for the bourgeois males, not the least of which was as a vehicle for social sponsorship and limited mobility on the one hand, and the preservation of exclusiveness and privilege on the other. The merchant classes had been continuously invading and replenishing the English aristocracy from the sixteenth century onwards.[6] However, the advent of industrial capitalism brought profound changes to the structure of society, including massive shifts in population from rural to urban areas, the development of the factory system, and the creation of wealth. The new, powerful upper levels of the bourgeoisie which emerged from this upheaval set about consolidating their places in the social hierarchy at levels which reflected members' material wealth. The reformed public school was one of the institu-tions invented to fulfill this project, and the cult of athleticism was central to its success. Besides satisfying a demand for leisure complementary to work, games provided a way of disciplining and 'normalizing' the male youth of the ruling group to take their place in the social order, and produced a sense of class identity and cohesion among the ruling class groups of which they were members. More than this, the ethos surrounding games playing came to constitute and symbolize the central values of these groups, and later, as we will see, came to be seen by them as a way of uniting an increasingly divided nation. The games ethic came to express 'the quintessential bourgeois English qualities that were felt to make the English superior to foreigners',[7] involving a 'subscription to the belief that important expressive and instrumental qualities can be promoted through team games (in particular loyalty, self-control, perseverance, fairness and courage, both moral and physical)'.[8] At its height, games playing was celebrated ardently as 'a magnificent preparation for life',[9] and spawned a clutch of cliches such as 'play the game' and 'it's not cricket' which were later to become by-words of the British way. Not everyone agreed with these sentiments, and games playing was also vilified for the excesses and anti-intellectualism it induced and 'the licence permitted public school boys under the cover of a wide-flung cloak of moral texture',[10] but these criticisms did little to halt the spread and influence of the cult of athleticism in the latter decades of the nineteenth century.

The games ethic infused the physical education of bourgeois girls' schools in much the same way as it had done for boys, although the activities played were different and the same excesses did not always apply. Games such as netball[11] and lacrosse were introduced into girls' schools by the 1880s and 1890s,[12] and these emphasized the cooperative and therapeutic aspects of play rather than the physi-cally vigorous and competitive character of the male games. While in the wider societal context sport was part of the emancipatory movement for upper class women, challenging notions of the delicate female constitution and other mores concerning clothing and display of the body, games playing in the girls' schools was still framed within patriarchal notions of womanhood and motherhood.[13]

Women were not expected to become leaders in politics, the military or business, and so the characteristics and values that marked the male ethos were seen to be unnecessary for females.[14] And while women's participation in sport lead to greater freedoms for some, old ideas nevertheless died hard. McIntosh tells us of a letter, from one Miss Conroy a high school headmistress, published in *The Lancet* in 1922 which stated that

> eighty per cent of gymnastics teachers had breakdowns, that playing strenuous games developed a flat figure with underdeveloped breasts, that athletic women suffered from nerves, heart trouble, rheumatism, suppressed menstruation and displacements, that they decried marriage, that their confinements were always difficult, that their children were often inferior, and that most athletic women seemed to have stifled what is finest in women — love, sympathy, tact and intuitive understanding.[15]

This sort of pernicious nonsense was enough to make games playing, at least, less popular among girls than boys. In addition, there were as we saw in the previous chapter, other factors unique to female physical education which forged the particular form that characterized physical education programmes in the elite schools for girls. Notably, it was not the ethos which surrounded female games playing that had the most significant influence outside the public schools, but the male ethos, though the female version did survive to make an impact on the games playing of lower middle and working class girls in the 1950s.

Before long, the cult of athleticism began to be imitated by other social groups at the lower end of the bourgeois class. Excellence in games had become by the 1870s both a mark of the distinctiveness of public school education and a measure of the school's quality. Since these schools were the training grounds of the upper classes for leadership in all of the major political, economic, military and legislative institutions in society, and games were considered by many of their advocates to be the ultimate testing ground of the qualities a member of the ruling classes had to possess, they became a prominent feature in the curricula of the schools in those sections of the bourgeois class that existed outside the 'industrial aristocracy' and had aspirations to improve their social status. Indeed, Mangan has argued that the grammar schools of the Victorian and Edwardian eras evolved with concerns for social status and prestige uppermost, and they therefore modelled themselves on their social superiors, the public schools. More than this, they also sought to simultaneously distance themselves from their social inferiors, and games played a key role in this process.

> The evolution of the grammar schools involved in large measure, imitation of its upper class superiors and segregation from its working class inferiors. In an accurate reflection of public school priorities, games and games fields were the expensive symbols of emulation, distancing, ambition and success. The reason is not hard to find. Technological competance in an industrial era was less valued than an image of gentility in a strongly hierarchical social system. The deferential absorption of the athletic mores of the public schools reveals a significant cultural hegemonic process at work.[16]

Mangan develops this case through detailed reference to various grammar schools and their respective fortunes. His message is clear: where schools rose in status and were successful according to such criteria as admission of its Head to the Headmasters' Conference, they invariably included organized games, interhouse sports competitions, sports days and the awarding of school colours as central features of their curricula. Where schools were less successful, Mangan claims that lack of organized games almost always played a key role in their demise. So pervasive was the games ethic throughout the private schools system that by the early twentieth century games 'were no longer attractive, valuable adjuncts of the system; they were sine qua non of institutional existence'.[17]

Mangan proposed three reasons for the widespread acceptance of games and the games ethic in both public and grammar schools. One reason, he claims, was that protagonists believed games actually worked as an instrument of social control within the schools; they saw games as effective and practical instruments for creating enthusiasm, fostering team spirit and letting off steam. A second reason he suggests was that games provided these schools with a visible and highly dynamic medium for the development of 'Englishness', of 'fair play' and 'the British way' which was unmatched by other curriculum activities. And a third, that games playing, or at least the paraphenalia required to play games such as playing fields and other facilities, were prominent symbols of superiority.

> Playing fields were part of the social and cultural capital to be acquired in the struggle to maintain social position. In this process they served as a means of demonstrating image. They were at one and the same time emblems of similarity and separateness. But above all they were symbols of superiority — not merely social but moral. Schools without them were suspect. They were either inferior institutions of narrow vocationalism or anachronistic institutions of dangerous intellectualism.[18]

This use of playing fields as highly visible symbols of social superiority, and the use of games playing in a process of emulation and distancing provides a clear indication of the hierarchical nature of British society during the Victorian and Edwardian eras. It also reveals something of the transitory nature of this hierarchy, however, since games playing and the schools themselves were a necessary means of obtaining the moral and other cultural credentials for entry into the upper echelons of society. The spilling of the games ethic and games playing over into the schools at the lower levels of the bourgeois classes can be seen as merely an extension of the original function of the games ethic in the public schools themselves. The consolidation of this ethic in the grammar schools, many of which achieved the status of 'public school' during the Victorian and Edwardian period, did much to cherish and perpetuate its key values in a living form within the upper strata of the bourgeoisie. Furthermore, by the 1870s, the games ethic began to be viewed by elements of the ruling groups as an expression not just of class, but of national identity;

> with the advance in rivalry between the great powers and the extension of the franchise, dominant groups and the political parties found it convenient to tap the widespread suspicion of foreigners and outsiders and to identify their own interests with the 'national interest'; and so

appeals in terms of the national good, often mixed with chauvinism, became an increasingly important element in the emergent pattern of hegemony; and sporting imagery and symbolism played a certain part in this kind of appeal.[19]

How are we to understand the emergence of this games playing tradition and the ethos that surrounded it, and its subsequent adoption by consecutive waves of aspiring bourgeois males? Mangan has suggested that the acceptance of the games ethic by the grammar schools is evidence of a 'significant cultural hegemonic process at work'. Implicit in the notion of cultural hegemony, as we saw in Chapter 2, is the idea of control by negotiation, consent and permissible opposition. As Gramsci had conceived it, hegemony attempted to explain how domination was possible without coercive force being used. He recognized that this control was achieved through a willing acceptance by factions of the domin- ated classes of the naturalness of their domination, a willingness that was tem- pered by the apparent permissibleness and legitimacy of alternative, oppositional and dissenting values. By emphasizing the cultural dimensions of this process, Gramsci sought to draw attention to the taken-for-grantedness of hierarchies of power and their saturation of everyday life to the extent that the operation of social control is co-extensive with culture. Indeed, the crux of the notion of hegemony is that the nature of control and domination is hidden or masked by its very acceptance by the dominated group as everyday and ordinary and so unquestioned and unquestionable.[20]

To what extent can it be argued that the diffusion of the games ethic from the upper levels of the social hierarchy down through the bourgeoisie is a process of domination by negotiation and consent? On the one hand, as Mangan has argued, the bourgeois males were involved in a process of deferential absorption of the values of the upper sections of their class. But it would seem that in this process, the upper classes had more to lose than their middle level counterparts, since the wherewithal of games playing supplied them with the symbols of social and cultural legitimacy necessary for their entry into a higher strata of society. Indeed, we know on the basis of Mangan's evidence that games were a crucial aspect of the curriculum of any grammar school that wished to elevate its status to public school, and were therefore a prime instrument in allowing the upper classes to be invaded from below and so their exclusiveness placed at risk. On the other hand, this invasion was also a replenishment, not (at least to begin with) a process of dramatic transformation. In order to gain entry to the exclusive upper levels of the bourgeois class, only particular social and cultural values were acceptable, and these were defined by the upper class males themselves. In this sense, the process is indeed one of domination by consent, since it is the values of the upper classes that define the rules of entry to their level in the social hierarchy. At the same time, this continual infiltration of the ruling groups could not avoid affecting these values, and throughout the cycles of invasion and replenishment, traditional values would have been continually recast and remade in order to meet the challenges of new situations and circumstances and to fulfill the projects of the invaders.

The circumstances in which the public schools arose are the key to under- standing the ways in which the games ethic worked to the advantage of upper level bourgeois males, and any subsequent transformations of the values embodied in games playing within other social and temporal contexts. I suggested at the beginning of this section that the creators of the ethos surrounding games playing in the public schools considered that games met particular needs, as they perceived them, at this time. The 1830s and 1840s represented a period of consolidation of collective self-consciousness in Britain after more than fifty years of social unrest. The working classes emerged for the first time as a more or less unified group whose cohesion was not so much due to shared material circumstances or spiritual characteristics as a recognition that their interests were defined against those of the bourgeois classes, the owners of industry and others closely associated with the management and control of the manufacturing process. The emergence of this force in British politics lead in turn to an alliance of landed and industrial wealth and to an awareness of the need to create a highly visible identity befitting members the ruling groups.[21] The public schools came to be seen by sections of the upper classes as a vehicle for creating this identity and projecting it in dramatic fashion through the cult of athleticism.

There are direct analogies between this perception of the uses of games playing among factions of the bourgeoisie and what Foucault has called the encitement to discourse on sexuality and the body among these same, evolving bourgeois groups. Foucault argues that, contrary to the received opinion that the Victorian bourgeois classes repressed sexuality, their near obsession with the body and sexuality was a central aspect of the formation of their class identity and the insulation and preservation of this identity from other social groups. He has suggested that we should not

> picture the bourgeoisie symbolically castrating itself the better to refuse others the right to have a sex and make use of it as they please. This class must be seen rather as being occupied, from the mid–eighteenth century on, with creating its own sexuality and forming a specific body based on it, a 'class' body with its health, hygiene, descent, and race.[22]

Just as the aristocracy had marked off its exclusiveness on the basis of blood, so the bourgeoisie built the boundaries of its exclusiveness on the basis of 'its progeny and the health of its organism'. Games playing was part of this discourse on sexuality since it too invoked an intensification of attention to the body, and in particular the moral virtues surrounding athletic displays.[23] In this context, the games ethic was not so much an instrument of domination, but a means of self-affirmation among ruling class groups, a highly visible, dramatic and dynamic medium for the display of their exclusiveness. Indeed, it might be argued that games playing, as an aspect of the bourgeois discourse on sexuality, was one of the (few) media in which public display of the male body and physical prowess could be gazed upon, adulated and celebrated. Consequently, the symbolic significance of the body among the bourgeoisie should not, as Foucault goes on to suggest, be underestimated.

> It seems in fact that what was involved was not an asceticism, in any case not a renunciation of pleasure or a disqualification of the flesh, but on the contrary an intensification of the body, a problematization of health and its operational terms: it was a question of techniques for maximising life. The primary concern was not repression of the sex of

the classes to be exploited, but rather the body, vigor, longevity, pro-geniture, and descent of the classes that 'ruled'. This was the purpose for which the deployment of sexuality was first established, as a new distribution of pleasures, discourses, truths, and powers; it has to be seen as the self-affirmation of one class rather than the enslavement of another: a defence, a protection, a strengthening, and an exaltation that were eventually extended to others — at the cost of different transformations — as a means of social control and political subjugation.[24]

As an element in the development and sustenance of class consciousness and a dramatic medium of self-affirmation, games playing was the literal embodiment of the sacred values of the bourgeois class. Foucault's comment concerning the different transformations of this discourse is a matter of particular interest, given the class-specific benefits its creators considered it provided for them, when we consider its relocation within the lives of lower middle and working class people whose material and social needs and circumstances demanded different responses. Indeed, if games playing formed a crucial part of the bourgeois school curriculum because it served the functions of fostering class indentity and simultaneously distancing the bourgeoisie from their perceived social inferiors, what role did it play in the schools of the lower middle and working classes?

Mangan has suggested that until 1900 games were denied by State officials to the elementary schools and thereafter not greatly encouraged by them.[25] There had been advocacies for children who attended the state-run elementary schools to play games from before the turn of the century, and a view of physical education incorporating games was introduced into official discourse by 1906 in a set of regulations issued by the Board of Education.[26] These regulations suggested that provision be made for state school pupils to play sports and field games as part of their physical education. This idea rested uneasily within the frame of the therapeutic view of physical education which contained it, even though it is given greater and greater prominence in the 1919 and 1933 syllabuses. But other factors helped this emergent view along. The Fisher Education Act of 1918 had instructed local education authorities to provide playing fields for sport, and there was also the influence of the playground movement in the USA and the setting up in 1925 of the National Playing Fields Association. The extension of compulsory schooling to age fourteen in the 1920s lead to the realization that the young adolescent required a different form of physical education than that outlined in the 1919 Syllabus, and the 1933 Syllabus represented a marked expansion in the kind of programme that could, potentially, be offered to the state school pupil. The 1933 Syllabus devoted an entire chapter to 'The Organization and Coaching of Games' and recognised 'the value of Organized Games, as an adjunct to physical training in promoting health, moulding the character and developing team spirit in general'.[27] Nevertheless, the 1920s and 1930s were the years of the Depression, and few of these ideas would have become reality for most state school pupils until after the second world war and the beginning of mass secondary education.[28]

The practical difficulties in providing the facilities for games playing in the elementary and post-elementary schools were not merely administrative or economic problems alone. Given the function of competitive games and sports in consolidating bourgeois class identity, there had been resistance to the lower middle and working classes gaining entry to particular sports, and substantial barriers were erected by many sports associations and clubs in the late 1800s to exclude the lower orders.[29] Running somewhat contrary to this exclusionary policy, there was a widespread belief among the bourgeois classes during the last decades of the Victorian era that competitive games and sports could transcend class divisions and conflicts. However, as Hargreaves[30] has noted, the pressures for the consolidation of class identity were the stronger in this period, and it is not until the 1920s and in the aftermath of the first world war that this elaboration and extension of the games ethic became more prominent in the public sphere. An example of this is McIntosh's description of a scheme aimed at overcoming class antagonism during the Depression.

> Games were encouraged not only for their physical and moral value but as instruments of social policy in the hope that they would break down class barriers and mitigate the bitterness of industrial strife...The most notable attempt to achieve this was the Duke of York's camp started in 1921 and held annually; 400 boys were invited, 200 boys from public schools and 200 working in industry. The common denominator was found in games.[31]

This example reveals the widespread manifestation in public discourse, by the early 1920s, of the completion of the process of transformation of the games ethic from an element of bourgeois class indentity to an element of national culture, as an aspect of life common to all classes. Even when the hierarchical structure of games and sports are themselves taken into account, organized around the pivotal amateur/professional distinction, this notion represents a clear departure from the use of games as a medium for demonstrating class superiority. At the same time, we need to be aware of the political function of this transformation. Clearly, the rhetoric of a national culture is consciously and deliberately conciliatory and unitary, an essential and desirable ideology during any period of class conflict and political unrest. In contrast to this rhetoric, though, is the practical reality of what lower middle and working class children actually did in school physical education at this time. The evidence suggests that they were unlikely in large numbers to have been playing games like football, cricket, racquets and so on for the simple reason that the facilities were not available for them to do so. This gap between the rhetoric of games as a 'common denominator' and the reality of lack of provision for the masses was to remain an enduring problem up to and beyond the 1950s.

After the first world war, the cult of athleticism began a long and gradual decline in influence within the male public schools. It was assailed on many sides, by those critics from within who felt the value placed on games to be excessive, and by pressures that affected the public school system as a whole; 'new political principles, creeping embourgeoisment, declining national prosperity and a reformulation of educational ideals'.[32] Nevertheless, such was the strength of the idealism it had generated, the ethos of games playing continued to exert a powerful influence within the schools over the next fifty years leading up to the mid-twentieth century. For instance, describing the attitudes of Birmingham University students to physical activity at a conference in the 1950s, David Munrow remarked

Not only did the public schoolboys bring with them the games of their schooldays, but they brought also the climate of opinion and the traditions of behaviour in which these games were played. Briefly these were a tacit acceptance that some sort of exercise was good for you, but that it did not much matter what it was, that the moral effects of playing were more important than the physical, and that winning was pleasant but by no means essential. There was also a sturdy tradition of complete independence and self-government in the administration of the games by the students and undergraduates themselves. As a corollary there was relatively little interest in rules — provided somebody was in charge — even less in technique and, although physical virtuosity was admired (sometimes excessively), it was still a 'good thing' to play games, even for rabbits...For many (students) it provided some opportunity for strenuous activity and a habit of mind which accepted games playing as a natural feature of youth and manhood.[33]

Between the beginning of the decline of the cult of athleticism in the public schools and the advent of mass secondary schooling, a period of approximately thirty years, the mythology and symbolism associated with the games ethic as an educational ideology continued to infiltrate the rhetoric of social reform and the education of the working classes. This is in some respects entirely unsurprising, since many of the policy makers were beneficiaries of a public school education, and whether they themselves were athletes or 'rabbits', they could not have avoided being touched by what by the 1950s was a one hundred year old tradition of athleticism.

Mass Secondary Schooling and the Expansion of Physical Education

The rise and subsequent decline of the cult of athleticism in the male public schools occurred without the influence of a professional body of physical education teachers. Games had formed a part of the curriculum of the female Swedish gymnasts from the first appearance of their training courses in the 1880s, and indeed the Ling Association adapted the rules of basketball to create netball in the late 1890s and administered the game, publishing rule books and instructional booklets, until the formation of the All England Netball Association in 1926.[34] But, as we saw in the previous chapter, gymnastics formed the core of the professional physical educator's art until the end of the second world war. It was at this time, and as a result of two inter-related factors, that gymnastics forfeited this pre-eminent role and by the end of the 1950s, competitive games and sports became firmly established in its place. These two factors were the introduction of secondary schooling for all through the Butler Education Act in 1944 which among other things involved raising the school leaving age to fifteen in 1947, and the influx of males into the physical education profession in the postwar period.

It had been conceded as early as the 1919 Syllabus that it was desirable for older elementary and post-elementary pupils to participate in an expanded range of activities beyond gymnastics and drill. Pupils who attended the selective

government run or aided secondaries and grammar schools had played competitive sports and games in the private school tradition since the turn of the
century. But these schools catered for only a small number of pupils and even
then facilities were in short supply.[35] So the introduction of secondary education
for all and the raising of the school leaving age presented the Ministry of
Education with a considerable challenge in terms of supplying the school buildings, specialized facilities within the schools like science labs and playing fields,
and the staff that were required to fulfill the terms of the legislation. For physical
educators, the challenge was how to adapt the existing forms of physical education within the limitations set by lack of facilities and teachers to the needs of
large numbers of older pupils who, unlike their grammar school peers, encompassed a wide range of academic and physical abilities. A survey of physical
education in girls' secondary schools reported in 1946 showed that gymnastics
and games dominated the curriculum, with little time provided for dancing,
swimming or athletics.[36] In the boys' secondary programmes apparatus and some
free standing (Swedish) gymnastics vied for time with major games like cricket
and football and other activities like boxing.[37] In the elementary schools, physical
training in the form of Swedish gymnastics and drill were, as we saw in Chapter
4, giving way to less formal methods and modified exercises. This was the
situation that faced the physical education profession at the end of the war, and
their discussions in the years immediately following the implementation of the
Butler Act were taken up with the problem of how to cater for the older pupils.[38]
The unanimous response was to provide older pupils with more freedom
of choice of activities, and while this notion was proposed with much
qualification,[39] it was to have far reaching consequences for physical education,
since choice was predicated on the existence of a range of activities from which to
choose. In this response to the challenge of mass secondary schooling, the
influence of the progressive movement within the physical education profession
and some other sections of the secondary school community can be seen,[40] in
addition to the coming force of the popular recreation movement which was in
its beginning stages in the immediate postwar period but, as we will see shortly,
was to have a substantial influence on physical education by the late 1950s.

While competitive sports and games had formed a part of the female tradition since its establishment, it was the males who were largely responsible for
their rise to dominance in schools after the war. The Ling Association had
followed a consistent policy of opposition to over-competitiveness from the late
1800s up to the 1940s, displaying on the one hand open anatagonism towards the
excesses of the male public school tradition and on the other appreciation and
support for a distinctive upper class feminine approach to games and sports. At
their annual conference in 1925 'professionalism in women's games and participation for children in Junior County Teams was deprecated', the latter point being
restated forcefully at the 1932 gathering. The 1928 conference focused on the
introduction of 'Competitive Athletics for Schoolgirls', and while this innovation
received a generally favourable response, the discussion centred entirely on concerns over whether lavatory and dressing room facilities would be suitable for the
schoolgirl athletes.[41] As late as 1948, the Editorial in *The Leaflet* took a dim view
of competitive gymnastics at the London Olympics held in that year, and
antagonism towards competition continued among the educational gymnasts
throughout the 1950s and 1960s.

The men, on the other hand, were from the beginning of their specialist courses strong advocates of competitive games and sports. While in the 1930s and 1940s Swedish gymnastics complemented games in their college curricula, this sharing of time did not last for long. At the 1949 Lingiad held in Stockholm, the bastion of Scandinavian gymnastics, the male physical education students from Loughborough and Carnegie colleges performed work that 'splendidly contrasted in type and presentation' with the activities of the host nation, and left the Scandinavians 'not knowing what next to expect from the British'.

> The Carnegie programme opened with quickening and strengthening activities all conducted competitively. It then gave four series of games skill practices and competitions. The games taken were cricket, basketball, soccer and rugger. Each series showed the separate skills of the game being practised and then applied the skills in a competitive phase. Twenty-five activities were packed into fifteen minutes and the work was a good test of stamina as well as a fine demonstration of speed and skill. Cricket greatly intrigued the audience and Rugby Touch brought them to their feet.[42]

During the late 1940s and early 1950s competitive sports and games quickly became the staple of the male specialist college curriculum.[43] At the Scottish School of Physical Education based at Jordanhill College in Glasgow, this enthusiasm for games extended beyond the curriculum, and the college had first claim on all students in their chosen sport, exemptions being granted to professional footballers only. Students were also required to attend a Friday afternoon pre-match briefing whether they were in college on that day or in schools on teaching practice, non-attendance incurring disciplinary action.[44] This system was established under Hugh Brown, Director of the SSPE between 1958 to 1974, who was an ardent advocate of games.

> The curriculum in the Colleges of PE is ever-widening. This is something that I rejoice to be able to report, and my only comment is 'high time, too!'. We are British people — for which I can find no cause for apology — and we are a games-playing nation. It has always puzzled me, for instance, that gymnastics should be regarded as being synonymous with Physical Education. Gymnastics is a part — a very valuable part — of a vast subject, and in some countries it may have been looked on as being the main fraction of the whole. No longer is that so here. However good a system may be, the folly of adopting it in its entirety and foisting it upon people, unadapted to peculiar needs, is at last recognized. What may delight the Germans or the Danes, and what suits their national characteristics, does not necessarily make a similar appeal here. Now we are recognizing this![45]

Brown's statement is strongly flavoured by the notion that games playing is part of the national culture of the British, and in this he was expressing a point of view that had gained considerable and widespread legitimacy by the 1950s. This enthusiasm for games playing among the male physical educators and the nationalistic justification for expanding physical education programmes to accomodate this enthusiasm can be explained in two ways. The first is to see this appropriation of games as an extension of the male domination of competitive sport and games in general.[46] The second is to view the promotion of this new expanded version of physical education as a means of enhancing the status of male physical educators. We saw in the previous chapter that while the female physical educators were with few exceptions from the bourgeois classes, male physical educators tended to be drawn from the lower end of the social class spectrum and their social and professional status in the 1940s and 1950s was certainly inferior to that of women. By adopting and championing competitive team sports in contrast to non-competitive gymnastics, the males were, consciously or not, emulating the public school tradition of athleticism, a move which conceivably could be seen to offer enormous benefits to the male physical educators by virtue of association with this bourgeois tradition alone. The other side of the males' push for status was the application of the new scientific knowledge derived from the fields of exercise physiology, biomechanics and skill acquisition to their teaching, and competitive games and sports provided a more appropriate medium than Swedish and educational gymnastics for the use of this new knowledge.[47] Not only did the association with team games provide the newly arrived male physical educators with a ready-made 'tradition' that was at least a century old and had been an intrinsic part of the education of the upper classes, it also supplied them with a medium for the application of the new knowledge that was rapidly being incorporated into their specialist courses.

By the end of the 1950s, team games formed the core of an expanded physical education curriculum that included a wide range of indoor games and other activities like swimming and in some places, outdoor activities like hill-walking and canoeing.[48] The role of games in the existing grammar and other selective secondary schools was consolidated through the late 1940s and early 1950s,[49] and was very quickly becoming established in the new secondary modern and comprehensive schools.[50] In an article which appeared in *The Leaflet*[51] in July 1961, Vivien Jacobs outlined the planning and organization of physical education in Holland Park School, a London comprehensive opened in September 1958 with an initial intake of 1700 pupils. The school had extensive facilities for swimming, gymnastics and indoor games, outdoor court games such as basketball, netball, tennis, and space for jumping and throwing. While these facilities allowed the school to offer a wide range of activities on-site, games and games-related activities formed the major part of the programme, and pupils were bused to London County Council playing fields twenty minutes from the school to play major team games such as soccer, rugby, hockey, netball, and cricket, and minor activities like tennis, rounders and athletics, to Wimbledon Common for cross-country, and to Putney Reach for rowing. Given the large numbers of pupils involved in any one games session (up to five hundred), Jacobs not surprisingly expressed concern in her article over matters of control, order, discipline and organization. Despite these problems though, the viability of this option of bussing pupils to various venues for their physical education lessons was not questioned. One of the reasons for this was a practical one; the on-site facilities at the school could not accomodate the large numbers of pupils allocated to the physical education department at any one time. But the large amounts of time spent on games[52] were justified on a different basis than practicality.

> We are a Comprehensive School, and naturally we believe in the comprehensive system. In the Physical Education Department we felt that games was one subject, at least, in which we could carry out the system completely and beneficially...We were convinced that there would be an all-round improvement, and that lower intelligence groups would not debase the standards, the view held, unfortunately, by so many people.[53]

Here, in the new comprehensive schools that were supposed to exemplify the egalitarian spirit of social reconstruction in postwar Britain, pupils were allocated to Grammar, Secondary Modern and Remedial streams during their first three years, and for those who stayed on past the compulsory leaving age, to Academic, Technical, Commercial and General streams.[54] If the egalitarian principle could not be applied in practice to what Jacobs describes as the academic work of the school, then perhaps games could provide the common denominator that would allow expression of this ideal. Clearly, though, as we can see from Jacobs' comment, this was not an uncontested idea. And while games were now available to all pupils, even the allegedly 'less intelligent', the issue of segregation begs the question of the function these games were to serve for the different streams of pupils. Jacobs' suggested that third and fourth year pupils in the Secondary Modern and Remedial streams were 'extremely difficult to manage' and that they were consequently gaining little from playing games. She noted, however, that these 'problem pupils' participated more readily when streams were mixed, implying that this mixing had a civilizing effect on them. The disaffection of the pupils in the lower streams and their hostility to the school in general, the effects of streaming itself, and the imposition of cultural values that were foreign to the pupils who were assumed to need exposure to them, were not raised by Jacobs. The notion emerges, however, that these more probable sources of 'the problem', which were implicit in the school's broader structure and function, could be ameliorated by the benign influence of games playing since it possessed properties that were somehow common to all students, regardless of their social class or intelligence. Significantly, at Holland Park School, it was the physical educators who supported this common denominator view of games and claimed for themselves the role of integrating the various social class groupings among the pupils.

A survey of secondary modern schools conducted by the CCPR in the Eastern Counties of England in the summer of 1960 reveals that the Holland Park curriculum was not uncommon. On the basis of responses from just under five thousand pupils surveyed, tennis (male and female), soccer (male), swimming (male and female), cricket (male), netball (female), athletics (male and female) and hockey (female) emerged in that order as the pupils' most popular activities and played most regularly at school. Gymnastics rated a mention, but was popular only among a very small number of pupils. However, while the opportunity to play games seemed to be available to pupils in these parts of the country by the end of the 1950s, and were accepted as the major part of school physical education, few of these secondary modern pupils wished to continue with their favourite sports after leaving school.[55] This apparent lack of willingness on the part of the secondary modern and comprehensive school pupils to take advantage of the range of activities now available to them was a cause for considerable and continuing concern in some quarters as we will see later in this chapter, but it did not arrest the rate of growth of competitive games and sports in physical education programmes, and the 1960s saw the consolidation of games at the centre of the curriculum. Whitehead's[56] end of decade surveys of boys' and girls' physical education in a range of types of secondary schools mainly in the North of England shows the dominance of the national games of soccer, rugby and cricket for boys, and hockey and netball for girls and athletics for both. He also made a number of interesting observations. The first was that the so-called major, traditional, national games were clearly the main priorities of physical education teachers, particularly males, and that there was little attention being paid to the popular physical activity leisure time pursuits of adults.[57] This observation is interesting for the reason that it contradicts the accepted opinion of the previous three decades that team games could fulfill this leisure-time function, an issue that we will explore in greater detail below. His second observation was that while games had rapidly become the mainstay of school physical education in the postwar period, they were more often taught by non-specialist teachers. Paradoxically, only specialists were permitted by local authority inspectors to teach indoor lessons, particularly those involving gymnastic equipment. So while the gymnasium had continued to remain the specialists' preserve, the core of the physical education programme was often taught by non-specialists. This suggests that in terms of propriety, the development of games skills in the gym were seen to be the physical educator's main responsibility, while games playing, significantly, was not under their sole ownership and control but was the property of a wider section of the school community. As for Whitehead's view, he applauded the efforts and enthusiasm of the non-specialists, and while he was prepared to concede that 'the *coaching* could be good' among non-specialist teachers, he suggested that 'educational principles are not applied to the extent that they might be'.[58] This paradox raises the question again of the function of games in the expanded secondary system and the use that the schools, and the physical education teachers within them, made of competitive team games. In order to understand this, we need to look outside the schools at what was happening in sport and recreation in the postwar period, and through this to consider the legacy of the games ethic of the public schools and its transformations in the era of social reconstruction and mass secondary schooling.

Sport, Recreation and the Consolidation of Traditional Physical Education

An Editorial in one of the January 1951 issues of the *Times Educational Supplement*[59] discussed what the editor called the 'two traditions' in English education, with the 'haves' on one side and the 'have nots' on the other. In the next issue, a response appeared in the form of a letter from Peter McIntosh, then a lecturer in the Department of Physical Education at Birmingham University, in which he suggested that the 'two traditions' were most sharply defined in physical education, the 'haves' being represented by team games and the 'have nots' by drill and gymnastics. He argued that:

> There was almost no mingling of the two traditions before the twentieth century. Indeed, there has often been antagonism between them: the

public schools have looked down on physical training as mere pedantry, while the protagonists of physical training have decried games because they are neither systematic nor primarily designed to promote health. In spite of considerable intermingling of recent years the fusion is still far from complete. There will only be a single national tradition of physical education when the State's schools can provide adequate playing fields and facilities for all children and when the public schools realize and appreciate the value of scientific and systematic physical training. Apparently a deficiency of insight is as difficult to make good as are deficiencies of space and money.[60]

From McIntosh's perspective in 1951, the key obstacles to creating a national system of physical education that was not differentiated on the basis of wealth and class were a wilfulness on the part of the public schools to concede that physical exercise properly conducted had a role to play in maintaining physical fitness and health, and a lack of money and space to provide the playing fields on which the 'have nots' could play the major team games. With the benefit of hindsight, we can now see that in the immediate pre- and postwar years it was this latter obstacle which received most attention in discourse on physical education and mass participation in sport, while McIntosh's challenge to the public schools fell on deaf ears. The feeling of the time was not that the public schools should change, but on the contrary that their version of physical education should be emulated.

Hargreaves,[61] also with the benefit of hindsight in the mid 1980s, identified a number of forces at work in the immediate postwar period in relation to sport and recreation in the community which I suggest were instrumental in bringing about the rise to prominence of games in the State secondary schools. The first of these was increasing State intervention in sport and physical recreation outside the school system, which Hargreaves claims was an important part of increasing government intervention in civil society generally.[62] While this intervention was at first relatively uncoordinated, it began after the second world war to draw school and community physical education and recreation into the State's sphere of influence and the service of 'the national interest'. A second and closely related factor which has already been discussed had been in place since the end of the 1800s, and this was the view that competitive games and sports were a unifying force and a means of promoting national identity. By the end of the 1930s, Hargreaves argues sport had become

> more firmly perceived in commonsense terms as a unifying activity to which all sections of society could relate, and as nothing to do with power and conflict...Sport more than any other aspect of popular culture, and possibly even of national culture, had come to serve as a common reference point for different social classes and other social categories, which on other grounds were opposed.[63]

This view of sport a common denominator and a unifying medium in society was entirely consistent with the consensual politics of the day, and indeed had much to do with creating the notion that sport was above and beyond politics. On the basis of this view, the new secondary schools began during the 1950s to be given the role of bolstering Britain's sagging international prestige by providing what politicians argued was a huge pool of untapped talent, including sporting talent. Moreover, as a result of the work of sports lobbyists, the idea that international success in sport was predicated on government funding gained ground in ruling circles through the 1950s and early 1960s, as did the realization that success in international sport could compensate for declining influence in the world economic, political and military spheres. And a third factor which boosted the fortunes of competitive sports and games in schools was the apparently widespread public concern for social order, fuelled by the intensification of consumer culture, affluence and materialism and the emergence in train with these of youth subcultures, particularly in relation to working class youth and their use of leisure time. The 'leisure problem' was to be solved through participation in wholesome, harmless and morally beneficial activities like games. Echoing the sentiments of the Victorian public school Headmasters, games not only provided an outlet for youthful energy, but kept potential troublemakers in public view for at least some of the time. These three forces combined to form a powerful undercurrent that swept through the late 1940s and with growing momentum through the 1950s and on into the 1960s, to install competitive sports and games at the heart of school physical education. They operated at different levels of society and so together played an important role in forming popular opinion and commonsense attitudes to games and sports and their 'educative' potential. These forces did not work in isolation, but were instead different sides of a self-conscious movement in British society towards postwar social reconstruction in an era of declining influence as an international power. Given the significance of these three inter-related forces, each merits a little more detailed attention.

Popular Recreation and State Intervention

We need to dispel the idea from the beginning that the British ruling class and more specifically the government, intentionally and cynically intruded in community recreation and sport for the purposes of promoting their own interests or controlling the masses. What happened instead was a much more complex and gradual process of intervention, intensifying from the mid 1920s onwards. Along the way, successive British governments actually resisted becoming directly involved in funding and organizing sport, much to the frustration of some sports lobbyists.[64] Despite this initial reticence though, their involvement steadily increased after the second world war and by the 1960s had lead to an explicit harnessing of competitive games and sports in schools and the community to the power structure and to the projects of ruling class interests. None of this was straightforward and obvious, especially to the people actually involved at the time. On the other hand, as Hargreaves[65] rightly stresses, none of this involvement was uncontested either but, as we will see, was the outcome of a range of diverse pressures, interests and forces. The two major avenues for State involvement besides government funded schooling were the provision of playing fields and the work of the National Playing Fields Association (NPFA), and the promotion of mass participation in recreational physical activity and the work of the Central Council for Physical Recreation (CCPR).

The NPFA was formed during the Depression years of the 1920s as a direct response to philanthropic concern for the plight of the unemployed and the civilizing effect of games and sports.[66] A voluntary organization, the Association from the beginning was under the patronage of Royalty and was financed by public subscriptions and charitable donations. By 1935, it had funded 908 projects at a cost of just under three million pounds.[67] Nevertheless, the provision of playing fields and other sports facilities continued to be in short supply in the postwar period. In an address to the NPFA in 1951, the Honorary Secretary of the Amateur Athletic Association reported that of the sixty-six cinder tracks that existed in England and Wales, thirty-seven were privately owned and another twenty-one were owned by the London County Council, the latter figure highlighting the disproportionate distribution of facilities around the country. Scotland had seven tracks and there were none Northern Ireland.[68] The availability of facilities varied between sports and regions, but the situation in athletics was reflective of the general state of affairs. The 1949 annual report of the NPFA, delivered by its President the Duke of Edinburgh, bemoaned the acute shortage of playing fields, and this was to be a consistent message in subsequent annual reports throughout the 1950s.[69] Funding had been and remained the key problem. Despite a highly successful £250,000 fund raising campaign in 1951 as part of the Association's silver jubilee, including £115,000 from a 'cinema appeal' and £15,000 raised at Butlin's Holiday Camps,[70] the government came under increasing pressure during the late 1940s and 1950s to provide funds for playing fields.[71] The 1944 Education Act created the precedent for this pressure by allocating the functions of the defunct National Fitness Council's Grants Committee, which operated under the terms of the 1937 Physical Training and Recreation Act to the Ministry of Education, 'thus involving the government more intimately than ever with the leisure pursuits of the community at large'.[72]

A decade after the establishment of the NPFA, the National Association of Organizers and Lecturers in Physical Education cooperated with the Ling Association to form the Central Council for Recreative Physical Training in 1935. Community recreative physical training had reached the proportions of a 'movement' by the mid 1930s and the function of the CCRPT was to coordinate the various and diverse community physical recreation groups which had been growing steadily in number from the 1920s. Like the NPFA, the CCRPT was under Royal patronage from the beginning; indeed, as Hargreaves has noted 'the membership of the Council read like a roll-call of the Establishment'.[73] The use of physical training in the title of the Council was testimony to its origins in the Keep Fit movement and other forms of physical exercise, but in 1944 it changed its name to the Central Council for Physical Recreation to reflect a change of focus away from physical exercise to incorporate a wider range of physical pastimes including outdoor activities and competitive sports and games.[74] The CCPR's responsibilities included coordinating the activities of its affiliated associations, clubs and groups, but its immediate concern in the postwar period was the provision of courses for recreation leaders and participants. In order to do this, the Council employed a number of officers and regionally-based 'technical representatives', and set up facilities to house their activities. Its first national test for leaders of physical recreation was in place by 1940, with over one thousand men and women qualifying,[75] and its first national recreation centre opened in 1946 at Bisham Abbey.

In his Presidential Address to the CCPR AGM in September 1949, Lord Hampden claimed that as the Local Education Authorities began to meet their responsibilites to provide facilities for physical recreation under the terms of the 1944 Education Act, the CCPR's role would shift from local to national level, and this pattern began to emerge as predicted over the following decade. At the same meeting, a National Sports Development Fund[76] was approved that was to help extend the influence of the CCPR and to set up recreation centres around the country.[77] Bisham Abbey offered 'training holidays' in its first year to males and females in the sixteen to twenty-five age range.[78] Two new national centres quickly followed, Glenmore Lodge, an outdoor activities centre in 1949 and Lillieshall Hall in 1951, the latter funded by a £120,000 gift from the South African government, and opened by Princess Elizabeth in the presence of sports star Roger Bannister and administrator Stanley Rous.[79] These additional facilities allowed the CCPR to extend its services, and by the end of the 1947–48 financial year, it had run 750 training courses, 1450 lectures and demonstration classes, enrolled 19,000 students, and organized summer-time rallies at sea-side resorts.[80] Over the next few years, it created a network of personnel and facilities that laid the ground for its continuing expansion through the 1950s and into the 1960s.[81]

Both the NPFA and the CCPR operated outwith the direct control of the government, and according to McIntosh 'were in the mid-20th century pursuing an ideal of sport for all which broke down or took no notice of social and educational distinctions which had been such a feature of physical education and recreation fifty years earlier'.[82] In one sense, McIntosh was correct. There can be no question that in the immediate postwar period, the opportunities available to lower middle and working class people to participate in recreational physical activity improved greatly, and sports and games which had previously been restricted to the wealthy and privileged were opened up to a wider cross-section of the population.[83] But there was a cost to pay for increased opportunity, and this was a higher level of formalization and regulation of the recreational and leisure time pursuits of this section of the population.[84] Even though at this stage the State's entry into this sphere of life is relatively uncoordinated, the patronage of the aristocracy and the provision of indirect funding and other material assistance drew popular physical recreation into the State's sphere of influence and drafted it into the service of 'the national interest'.[85] The association with prominent sports performers such as Bannister and administrators like Rous was not insignificant either. From the early 1950s onwards, the case for extending the provision of playing fields and other sports facilities to promote the national interest began to be more frequently heard in the public sphere, proponents arguing typically that 'improved facilities should result in improved standards of performance. Good facilities provided for secondary school, together with expert and enthusiastic teaching will provide the means of improving standards of performance in our national games and athletics'.[86]

National Identity, the National Interest and the Invention of Tradition

The games ethic of the public schools may have been in decline from the end of the first world war, but its power as an educational ideology outside the public schools had become stronger by the end of the second. The resilience of this ideology and its continuing influence within educational discourse was in no small part due to the dynamic, physical and competitive features of games themselves and the symbolic values attached to these features, displaying the 'basic themes of social life — success and failure, good and bad behaviour, ambition and achievement, discipline and effort'.[87] Since sport encapsulated these key themes, it was an easy step to view competitive matches against rival schools and other groups as symbolic struggles, comparing not just the skills of the opposing players but also the worth of the institutions they represented. This use of competitive games and sports was a feature of life at all social levels, and from local to international arenas, with community pride and self-worth linked closely to the outcome of a match. And while a view of competitive sport as a means of fostering community, class and national identity had from the mid 1800s been an intrinsic part of games playing, it was only with the provision of playing fields and other sports facilities on a mass scale that the possibility of achieving a consolidation of national identity through sport emerged. Besides the need to promote mass participation in sport to meet this end, however, the male public school version of games playing had to be simultaneously recast as the 'tradition-al' form of physical education and the birthright not merely of the bourgeois class, but of everyone. It was in the new secondary schools in the 1950s that this recasting of the games ethic began to take place, and it was at this point that this 'games playing tradition' was invented.[88]

The games ethic of the male public schools was almost a century old by the mid 1950s, but this does not mean that it occupied an inert role; on the contrary, this tradition fulfilled an active role in creating the possibility of using games and sports as an element of national culture. As we saw earlier, games were con-sidered by factions of male bourgeoisie to be a key medium for the purposes of promoting and maintaining class identity. In order for the ethic to be generalized to become the property of all classes and extended beyond class affiliations to foster a popular national identity, certain features of this public school version of games playing had to be omitted and others retained and emphasized. In this respect, the games ethic in its extended form in the 1950s was a selective version of its former self. Raymond Williams has highlighted the key features of this invention of tradition more generally as:

> an intentionally selective version of a shaping past and a pre-shaped present, which is then powerfully operative in the process of cultural definition and identification...from a whole possible area of past and present, in a particular culture, certain meanings and practices are selected for emphasis and certain other meanings and practices are neg-lected or excluded. Yet, within a particular hegemony, and as one of its decisive processes, this selection is presented and usually successfully passed off as 'the tradition', '*the* significant past'.[89]

In this process of reconstructing *a* traditional form of physical education as *the* tradition, the interests of the ruling group were selectively chosen and established as the interests of the nation. None of this denies that games and sports had been played by people at all levels of the social system for well over one hundred years. The point is that it was a sanitized version of the bourgeois males' games ethic that formed the value structure on which competitive sports and games in the mass secondary schools in the 1950s were based and justified, not the many other alternative approaches to games playing, some of which were organic to the working classes, their material circumstances and cultural values. And it was through this selective device of 'tradition' that success in international sports competitions could come to represent the state of the nation, its corporate health, and its future wellbeing.

In the process of recasting the public schools' games playing ethic as 'traditional physical education', a number of commentaries relating to the development of national culture and national identity were prominent in physical education and sport discourse in the postwar period. There was a widespread idea that Britain was a nation of sports spectators and not active participants. An early expression of this notion came from Sir Ernest Baker who was quoted as saying in an Address to a NPFA Conference in 1947 that 'the NPFA existed as an expression of a universally felt want for open spaces. Team games were one of Britain's chief contributions to the world, and active participation in them needed encouragement at a time when we were fast becoming a nation of game watchers, football-pool fillers, and radio listeners'.[90] There was also frequent expression of disgust at the use of sport as 'a political tool', particularly by 'totalitarian' regimes.[91] Eminent figures like Harold Abrahams openly deplored the 'West-East war in sports' represented by the Olympic Games medal tallies,[92] while others vilified the 'Iron Curtain teams (who) have shut themselves up in ideological seclusion'.[93] Many comments of this kind appeared during the cold-war era, and were used as much as a means of promoting a favoured 'British' perspective on competitive sport as they were a renunciation of the alleged misuse of sport by countries governed according to alternative political ideologies. One example of this was the *TES*'s reporting of incidents of player violence in Yugoslavian football matches, followed by scarcely concealed sarcasm in the comment that 'the bourgeois rules of conduct favoured in our own schools and universities perhaps deserve another trial this year, even at the risk of appearing a bit reactionary'.[94]

Indeed, the *Times Educational Supplement* was an important force in the reconstruction of the public schools' games ethic at this time and was an unashamed proponent of the ruling class position.[95] Photographs and commentaries on sport, particularly male public school and elite sport, appeared frequently in the pages of the *TES* throughout the entire postwar period, while virtually no space was given to the version of physical education favoured by the female physical educators. A photograph on the front page of a March 1950 issue showed children on a cross-country run leaping a ditch accompanied by a caption which claimed the photograph showed 'modern physical education in striking contrast to earlier methods'.[96] In another issue that year, the *TES* reported on an MCC inquiry into youth coaching, and printed on the same page a photograph of Field-Marshall Sir Claude Auchenleck, President of the London Federation of Boys' Clubs, opening new playing fields at New Eltham in London.[97] In a 1951 issue, it reported on the AAA Schools Consultative Committee's recomendations on equipment regulations for school competition[98] and on the MCC's youth cricket coaching scheme again in a 1952 edition.[99] The *TES* also reported regularly on CCPR and NPFA conferences, courses and other events, on the Olympic Games, and many aspects of school sport throughout the 1950s. Not all sports were treated with equanimity however, as a report from a 1950 edition of the *TES* illustrates. A brief comment appeared on the front page on an incident that had come to the attention of the Birmingham Education Committee concerning the alleged 'victimization' of a grammar school boy who wanted to play soccer (not rugby) and to become a professional player. The boy's peers had apparently been giving him 'a thin time', and the school Headmaster was reportedly 'appalled' that the boy should complete a grammar school education only to become a professional footballer.[100] The mere fact that this incident and all of the other sports related activity reported regularly in the *TES* were considered newsworthy is in itself an indication of the positioning of this educational newspaper within the power structure.[101]

Not only did the *TES* report and highlight a selection of episodes and events relating to physical activity and sport, but it consistently under-represented what physical education actually consisted of for most teachers and pupils of the subject at that time.[102] Many of the key themes in the discourse of this era, reflecting the selection of particular aspects of sport and physical activity as worthy of serious concern, are graphically illustrated in this editorial comment that appeared in the *TES* in June 1951.

> Sport in England remains under a cloud. The South Africans beat us at cricket; a United States golfer is Amateur Champion; an Australian tennis player is supreme at Wimbledon. The tide may be about to turn in athletics, but it does not seem to have done so yet. In spite of a tradition and a comparatively large population to choose from, the record remains one of failure and defeat. Nor is this low standard of skill and prowess the only criticism. It is said that the British have become a nation of spectators, not sportsmen. Gambling is needed to stir enthusiasm. Bodily exercise and vigorous physical activities have long been succeeded by the sedentary enjoyment of expert entertainment. Professionalism has ousted the sportsman and made nonsense of the Englishman's love of games. 'Bodily exercise profiteth for a little time,' said St. Paul, possibly having in mind some of the muscle-bound athletes with enlarged hearts and fibrositis who do most to extol the animal aspect of games...But the need today is not so much physical fitness as the development of sound character and healthy interest — the war has shown that severe military training can turn the flabbiest civilian into a commando, if necessary. And if, incidentally, a certain sporting patriotism enters in, what of it?...In England, every instinct would be against State intervention in sport, but private bodies have done and are doing much...with such bodies as the National Playing Fields Association, the CCPR is doing practical work to combat the evil of the passive circusgoer. And in the course of encouraging more young people to play sport instead of watching it, it may well, one day, enable England to win some international events.[103]

This statement embodies all of the key elements of the ruling class perspective on 'traditional physical education' and reveals that the selective process had already reached an advanced stage by the early 1950s. Its dramatic listing of the evidence of 'failure and defeat' conveys the impression that the natural order of things has somehow been upset, and hints, with the passing references to spectatorship and gambling, that the malaise in sport is indicative of deeper problems in society. The loss of a glorious past (that never in fact existed) is nostalgically mourned ('bodily exercises and vigorous physical activities have long since been succeeded'), while the baser features of modern sport are vilified and scorned ('muscle-bound athletes with enlarged hearts and fibrositis who do most to extol the animal aspect of games'). Only six years after the war, there is still some symbolic mileage to be gained in recalling military success, contrasting 'severe' military training with 'flabby' civilians, and patriotism is mentioned in the same breath. There is also an inescapable moral tone in the support given to groups such as the NPFA and the CCPR for their work in 'combatting the evil of the passive circus-goer'. The final statement that as a result of their efforts 'England ...may win some international events' is deliberately understated, suggesting that it is not winning alone but winning with apparent effortlessness that reveals the superiority of the English. The entire editorial is also blatantly chauvinist, with no suggestion that women's sport may be worthy of consideration, an omission that was not missed by one female reader who wrote to the Editor the following week that England's female hockey team 'is still regarded as the greatest exponent of the game'.[104]

While the *TES* was an important producer, legitimator and communicator of 'traditional physical education', it was not the only active agent in promoting the patriotic and socially cohesive functions of competitive games and sports. Even the Ling Association's *Leaflet* considered the educational value of games and athletics in 1946, with the Editor arguing that games could be useful as a medium for physical, mental, moral and social training, but then characteristically qualifying this by suggesting 'over-keen' competition had no place in physical education.[105] Other commentators took a more positive if idealistic view. Lord Aberdare, a member of the International Olympic Committee Executive and Organizing Committee for the 1948 London Olympics, eulogized that 'the gathering together of young amateurs (i)s one of the best ways to enable the different classes in a country, as well as the units of different civilizations, to become well acquainted with each other and thus to promote a better understanding between nations',[106] while Phillip Noel-Baker suggested that the Olympics were not, as the Cambridge University Union had once moved, a 'faked antique' but corresponded 'to something eternal in the human heart'.[107] At a more practical level, this common denominator view of games and sport was displayed in another form in a report on the resumption of the Duke of York's camp following its abandonment during the war, claiming that the camp for seventy-seven boys from industry and their thirty-three fee-paying school guests and incorporating games as a key element, had been an 'undoubted success'.[108]

The issue of the State's role in promoting participation in games and sports in schools and the community was beginning to be much more closely linked to notions of national identity and culture by the mid 1950s. In August 1954, the House of Commons debated the issue of government funding for sport after a Labour MP Mr Ellis Smith claimed 'the country had had some severe shocks in the international football games at Wembley, Berne and Balse'. He argued that the Ministry of Education was 'responsible for British football' since 'our boys' were being coached at the Ministry's expense (through school physical education programmes), and that with greater financial outlay, Britain could turn out more Bannisters, Chataways and Matthews. Mr Pickthorn, the Minister of Education, refused to accept responsibility for the defeat of British football teams, and was quoted as saying that

'the Ministry's first responsibility was to the schools, and what could be done by central direction to see that games were properly organized would be done. Commenting on the quotation that the Battle of Waterloo was won on the playing fields of Eton, he observed that the games then were wholly unorganized, and that the boys did the whole thing and made their own rules, so it was not a good argument to use either way'.[109]

Good argument or not, the symbolism of the playing fields of Eton and the Battle of Waterloo remained a powerful force among sections of the sports lobby, who argued that Britain's approach to organizing competitive games and sports, from schools through to elite international levels, were drastically out of date. In 1956, UNESCO published a report on 'The Place of Sport in Education', which the British government did not contribute to because, according to McIntosh, they considered that the exercise was not 'practical or worthwhile enough'. McIntosh quoted Mr Lloyd the Minister of Education as saying

I have read the report and while it is interesting, I must point out that the English idea of sport is such that the English do not like professional professorial discourses on sport. At the same time, I can see that there is some rather interesting information, perhaps, for some countries which are backward in education matters.[110]

Notwithstanding the condescension and ambivalence his comment reveals, events began to overtake the Conservative government in the latter half of the 1950s. The staff of the Physical Education Department at Birmingham University, of which Peter McIntosh was a member, produced a survey and analysis of British sport in a booklet 'Britain in the World of Sport', which attracted widespread interest[111] and which was an important factor in the establishment of the Wolfenden Committee in 1957. McIntosh also published an open letter to the Minister of Education in *The Leaflet* early in 1958, deploring the British government's recalcitrance on the issue of its role in organizing and funding sport, and requesting a change of policy.

As an Old Harrovian you will be familiar with the great tradition of sport in our public schools. You will know too that games and sports which were first refined and organized by the boys and old boys of those schools have now spread to the far corners of the world. They provide common ground upon which men and women of different languages, races, religions and political creeds can meet and they reflect credit upon us. However, the world has changed since our export of games began and what could once be achieved by individual enterprise now needs government support. For lack of such support even in our own Commonwealth the influence of Britain upon sport is waning, while that of other great powers is waxing. We still have a unique and valuable contribution to make to sport in the world and to sport in the education of the world's citizens.[112]

At the heart of McIntosh's argument was the trinity of the public school tradition, the common denominator thesis, and the pride of the nation, and this letter suggests that these three themes were in the process of being closely linked towards the late 1950s in relation to competitive games and sports. Whether or not this particular letter was written in this way to have the biggest possible impact on its intended target, the Minister of Education, McIntosh and his Birmingham colleague David Munrow were two of the most articulate and prolific speakers and writers among the sports lobbyists during the 1950s and early 1960s. Both had championed the cause of internationalism within physical education, with Munrow particularly involved in various international study groups and conferences on physical education and sport.[113] Munrow and McIntosh held similar views on the importance of competitive games and sports as an element of popular national culture. It was Munrow's deep conviction that 'the part played by sport in our own culture pattern is under rated by many sociologists, politicians and educationists,'[114] while McIntosh argued that 'sport is now a prominent and important feature of culture' and that moreover 'the world's most popular sports came from Britain'.[115] In addition, both believed that something was amiss in the world of sport, and that urgent action was required to tackle the problem. McIntosh suggested that while the world's most popular sports came from Britain 'it has proved easier to export the sports than the spirit of the sport. Today this spirit is in danger of being lost both abroad and at home and teachers are concerned as never before to see that sport is harnessed to education and not education to sport'. Despite these dangers however, 'sport offers tremendous opportunities for self-discipline as for self-expression, it provides a common ground on which humble members of every race and nation may meet, it could even provide a link between grammar, technical and modern schools in Britain, and perhaps even between different streams in a comprehensive school!'.[116]

Beneath the nationalistic rhetoric, this notion of competitive games and sports being harnessed to educational ends and employed as a means of bringing a divided society together, not of celebrating the divisions as the bourgeois version of games playing had done, was a prime motivating factor for those members of the sports lobby like McIntosh and Munrow who saw themselves first and foremost as physical educationists. In this, the physical educationists within the sports lobby played an important role in inventing 'traditional physical education'. But their's was not the only voice among the calls for a more organized approach to competitive games and sports, and not everyone shared this concern for the educational values of sport. By the mid 1950s, some members of the sports lobby saw a more organized and centralized approach to British sport as a major factor in determining success in international competition, and some argued strongly that a combination of the new scientific knowledge derived from studies of skill acquisition and work physiology applied to physical education in the new secondary schools was the key to providing world class performers. The phenomenal success of the Australian swimmers at the 1956 Melbourne Olympics raised the question of whether Britain should copy the Australian's 'whole-sale preparation'.[117] Some commentators were in no doubt about the answer to this question. In an article that appeared originally in the *Sunday Times* and later in *The Leaflet*, Alexander Nicol claimed the 'we have ceased to be world beaters at football' and blamed the lack of 'high pressure training' of players which could be traced back to schools.

> If our footballers are to hold their own, our men will have to train harder and faster, and start doing it when younger. Their insufficiencies go back to schooldays. Our boys are said by critical observers to be less strong, especially in the arm, than the boys of many continental countries. They are not taught to develop their strength.[118]

Nicol went on to damn Swedish gymnastics as mere 'physical jerks' which 'do nothing to make the boys stronger', and to report on experiments in strength training at Leeds University using scientific methods and built on the principle of progressive overload. A response from I J MacQueen, an Anatomist at the University of Sheffield, strongly endorsed Nicol's remarks, suggesting it was 'British apathy' that lead to such a 'poor showing at the Olympic games and other international sporting events'. He agreed that schools were a major source of blame.

> A study of any school timetable shows that out of a working week of about thirty-five hours, only one or perhaps two hours are designated to 'gym'. Again 'gym' at most schools means the uninspiring armwaggings that do next to nothing to make the boys stronger...Who wants powerful muscles anyway? is the cry. The answer is — any athlete who hopes to stand any chance at all in modern international competition.[119]

These views of Nicol and MacQueen shared the concern for Britain's national prestige in sport with other sports lobbyists within the Establishment, the CCPR, and the Birmingham group, but their blatant exhortation to athletes to train harder and their view of the prime purpose of school physical education to supply the international sports arena with star performers would clearly have been repugnant to some of these other lobbyists. This does not mean that others would not have been sympathetic to the views of Nicol and MacQueen, but we need to note that there were tensions and contradictions within the discourses of the various parties who were proponents of competitive games and sports at this time.[120]

Another issue which reveals similar tensions and contradictions, and which has continued to greatly vex sports organizations and governments since, was the relationship between sport and politics. Some of the sports lobbiests like Phillip Noel-Baker argued that sport, as 'something eternal in the human heart', was above politics, while others saw the politicization of sport as something done by less than respectable 'totalitarian' regimes. And some, like Peter McIntosh, more realistically argued that sport and politics were inseparable and always had been. He suggested however that sport *could* transcend class, race and national barriers to become a 'cohesive agent', but recognized the potential of too much politics to destroy what he called the unreality of sport. He described himself as a supporter of the view of sport as an end in itself and an outlet for personal and international competitiveness in a 'non-harmful' way, a view which was to become something of an orthodoxy in physical education circles in the following two decades. 'The final conclusion' he suggested 'is a paradox; sport, if performed as an end in itself, may bring benefits to man (sic) which will elude his grasp if he treats it as little more than a clinical, a social or a political instrument to fashion those very beliefs'.[121] On the grander social stage, the relationship between sport and politics may have been easier to discern (though no less difficult to resolve), but the use of competitive games and sports for less obvious social and political purposes, such as maintaining social class identity, ruling class hegemony, and social control, were less yielding to critique by those involved in the action at the time. It was the use of competitive games and sports for this latter purpose that by the end of the 1950s had become consolidated within the collective wisdom of educationists, politicians and some social commentators to represent a third force at work in the promotion of games and sports in physical education.

Delinquency, Social Control and Games

Concerns over a perceived increase in juvenile crime during the first world war lead to the setting up of Juvenile Delinquency Committees (JDCs) and the publication of a Juvenile Delinquency Report by a Standing Committee of the Home Secretary, which suggested that boys and girls who became members of youth organizations on leaving school were less likely to be involved in crime. The work of the JDCs was transferred in 1937 to the short-lived National Fitness Council (1937–1939), establishing a direct and formal association between physical activity and the control of delinquency. The National Youth Committee (1939–1942) and the Youth Advisory Council continued this work through the war years, the term 'juvenile' being dropped because it had by this time come to be associated with delinquency, the courts and crime. By the end of 1941, all 16–18 year olds were required to register with a youth organization, the main purpose being 'to reach those who had left school and were no longer under educational supervision and discipline',[122] and within the organizational framework of the youth services, the Board of Education issued a series of circulars on youth organizations during the war, with physical recreation awarded a key role within them.[123] In all of this activity in relation to youth organizations, which was sustained through the war years and the 1950s to receive fresh impetus and direction from the Albemarle Committee whose report was published in 1960, there was a concern to maintain supervision and control over working class youth[124] during the period of leaving school and becoming established in 'regular' employment.

While the raising of the school leaving age to fifteen in 1947 relocated the 'problem' of working class youth in the new secondary modern schools, much was made of the effects of the new affluence of the postwar period on young adults who, it was claimed, had greater spending power and more leisure time to fill than ever before.[125] Cinema going,[126] gambling, and other elements of popular leisure culture such as the emerging rock 'n' roll music, were seen to be symbolic of a more egalitarian and materialist spirit among subordinate groups,[127] in some cases, as we saw in Chapter 3, as definitely antisocial. One philanthropic upper class commentator claimed that working class youth 'are getting completely the wrong idea of the purpose of life; making as much money as they do, they have got it into their heads that the things in life which are worth having can be bought'.[128] Schools, it was claimed, could do much to counteract this philosophy of 'I want: I see: I take',[129] and the idea that physical activity could be used as a means of regulating and supervising the activity of working class youth had become well established in ruling class circles by the end of the 1940s.

The *TES* was once again to the fore in reporting examples of the socially therapeutic power of games, citing an instance in Harmondsworth, London where 'hooliganism, which reared its ugly head last summer, was eliminated by employing two games supervisors after play centre hours to organize cricket, in which local boys' clubs have also taken part...particular attention was paid to Saturday morning activities by which it is hoped to break the cinema habit'.[130] From the point of view of members of the Establishment, delinquency was a relatively straightforward question of keeping working class youth occupied. The Duke of Wellington, reporting in his capacity as President to the AGM of the London and Greater London Playing Fields Association, suggested that there was an urgent need for playing fields to combat juvenile delinquency and that 'many juveniles became delinquent because of sheer idleness'.[131] In a House of Commons debate on juvenile delinquency in 1950, a similar comment was made by a Miss E Burton, who was reported to have said that

> unless something vigorous and attractive was done for our young people we had no right to complain if they went into activities of which we did not approve. While more playing fields were not the whole answer to juvenile delinquency they were part. Young people had nothing to do at night or on Sundays.[132]

While much of this discourse was concerned either explicitly or implicitly with social control, part of it, as John Hargreaves[133] has rightly pointed out, was an extension of the logic of the welfare state in which the masses were to be provided for by a benign and caring government. Saturating this discourse was a commonsense, patriarchal conservatism which scoffed at trendy progressive ideas,[134] and drew on certain knowledge of human nature to assert with confidence what was good for working class youth. In containing working class delinquency, the countervailing qualities to be gained from 'team games well played...loyalty, dependability, unselfishness, and above all, courtesy'[135] were the values of the reconstructed bourgeois games ethic.

The Wolfenden Report[136] embodied all of this patriarchal conservative concern along with a proportion of worldly knowledge, level-headed commonsense, and the occasional sliver of acute insight thrown in for good measure. This report articulated in an elaborate and sophisticated form the key features of the postwar rise to prominence of competitive games and sports, and formed the basis for the reorganization of the administration and funding of British sport over the next two decades.[137] It was commissioned in October 1957 by the CCPR to examine factors affecting the organization of British sport, and the Committee, which included David Munrow, interpreted its remit widely, reviewing the situation at that time across all sports and forms of physical recreation including major and minor games, outdoor recreational activities, amateur and professional sports, and other matters such as facilities, coaching, and the influence of the media. The Committee endorsed the emphasis placed by the Albemarle Report[138] on physical recreation in the Youth Service, and paid particular attention to 'the needs of young people'. In a now well known and often quoted statement, it expressed the quintessentially bourgeois view of the role of games and sport in meeting these needs.

> It is widely held that a considerable proportion of delinquency among young people springs from the lack of opportunity or the lack of desire for suitable physical activity. The causes of criminal behaviour are complex, and we are not suggesting that it would disappear if there were more tennis courts or running tracks: nor are we concerned to press for wider provision of opportunities for playing games just on the ground that it would reduce the incidence of those various forms of anti-social activity which are lumped together as 'juvenile delinquency'. At the same time, it is a reasonable assumption that if more young people had opportunities for playing games fewer of them would develop criminal habits. [139]

Such an assumption is only 'reasonable', of course, within a particular view of games playing; at the same time, the Wolfenden Committee were, in stating this view, merely confirming a widespread conviction that had been growing in strength since the end of the war that games did have these therapeutic powers. [140] The way in which this bourgeois view was treated in the Report in itself reveals the extent to which this version of games playing had been successfully reconstructed as *the* traditional form of physical education. In the early pages of the Report, the Wolfenden Committee went to some lengths to caricature what was intended to be understood as an obsolete and slightly ridiculous version of the bourgeois games ethic, in order to legitimate those elements of the ethic that have been selectively retained. For instance:

> 'Character-building' is a description commonly applied to games, especially team games...it is easy to exaggerate (and to react from) this kind of claim. It is not in actual fact obvious that those who have been brought up on competitive team games are more un-selfish, co-operative and self-sacrificing than those who have not; and we should not wish to press this particular argument too far. But within limits we believe that the playing of games or the sailing of a boat does at least provide the opportunity for learning this kind of lesson.

> Certainly it can be said that in Britain there is an ingrained respect for certain attitudes which have their roots in sport. The word 'sportsmanship' means something important and valuable; and the notion which underlies it is perhaps still one of the traits on which we customarily pride ourselves most. It is easy to ridicule the 'That's not cricket, old boy' attitude. But in its deeper (and usually inarticulate) significance it still provides something like the foundations of an ethical standard, which may not be highly intellectual but which does have a considerable influence on the day-to-day behaviour of millions of people. [141]

The sentiments expressed in these statements are not nostalgic hankerings for good times past; on the contrary, they express a reconstructed version of the bourgeois games ethic that is intended to have relevance and authority in the here and now. The very idea that the values embodied in games playing form an ethical standard that is the measure of the everyday behaviour of millions of people reveals the extent of the saturation of bourgeois hegemony. It also shows how far these values had penetrated physical education discourse, and the level of sophistication the process of reconstructing the bourgeois games ethic had reached by the end of the 1950s. This reconstructed tradition formed the legitimating framework of the Wolfenden Committee's analysis of the problems facing British sport, and lead directly to the identification of 'The Gap' as one of the key difficulties requiring urgent resolution.

The notion of 'The Gap' was borrowed from the Albemarle Report, and in the Wolfenden Report signified 'the manifest break between, on the one hand, the participation in recreative physical activities which is normal for boys and girls at school, and, on the other hand, their participation in similar (though not necessarily identical) activities some years later when they are more adult'.[142] Identifying this issue as one of the leading concerns of their Report, the Wolfenden Committee strongly endorsed the recommendations of the Albemarle Report concerning the role of organized physical activity in the Youth Service, and greater linking between youth groups, statutory bodies, sports clubs and schools.[143] In addition to a more cohesive approach to organization, the Committee also expressed an optimistic view that the infrastructure of coaching, facilities and other services that would facilitate participation were on the way to being put in place. However, the Committee members scarcely conceal their puzzlement over the apparent reluctance of youth to take advantage of the opportunities being offered to them. The CCPR survey of secondary modern school leavers in the summer of 1960, showing that few of these working class adolescents had any desire to continue their involvement in organized sport and games,[144] confirm that the Committee's concerns were not groundless. After giving some lengthy consideration to what was clearly to them a surprising and unexpected obstacle to mass participation, they speculated that the resistance of school leavers might be rooted in resentment to continuing regulation and organization of their lives and an intrusion into their new found freedom. Rather than seeing this for what it was — a clash of class ideologies — and as a problem that afflicted the whole Welfare State, of which the State system of schooling was a part, the Committee saw the problem as one of immaturity on the part of working class youth. Given this perspective, intervention was for their own good, and the tone of the Committee's recommendations was couched entirely in terms of providing opportunities for youth who might otherwise be deprived; 'we find it discouraging that so many fall away; and for their sakes we hope that something may be done urgently'.[145]

While this philanthropic tone is the dominant one, other interests were also expressed in the Report which clearly demonstrate its bourgeois affiliations. Not only were the young missing out on the opportunity for 'healthy enjoyment', but there was a 'waste. . .of the national investment in the provision of facilities for school games'.[146] This statement could doubtless have been read in a number of ways. Within the political and sports communities, 'The Gap' was less a problem of missed opportunity for wholesome personal development and more an issue of lack of supply of sports men and women who could excel in international competition.[147] For the physical education profession, and especially for the males, 'The Gap' represented an opportunity to confirm their indispensibility to the development of British sport. But beneath all of these interests, 'The Gap' can be seen as an expression of concern over social control. When this concern is placed in its temporal context of ruling class attempts to control the allegedly delinquent behaviour of working class teenagers, what the Wolfenden Committee were advocating was a very extensive network of supervision and surveillance during the post-school 'problem' years. This is not to accuse any of the members of this Committee of engaging in a conspiracy to dominate the masses; indeed, to judge from the Report, their belief in the wholesome and therapeutic power of organized physical activity is sincere and profound. Rather than damning members of the Committee, their sincerity in itself reveals the pervasiveness and power of the reconstructed games ethic among some members of the physical education profession and many members of the Establishment and, more generally, the bourgeoisie.

The Wolfenden Report was generally well received and many of its recommendations finally acted upon.[148] Its solutions to the problems afflicting British sport focused on more and better organization, facilities and coaching,[149] and these were predicated on the provision of funding from the British government.[150] The setting up of the Sports Council in 1965 was the outcome of this and other pressure from the sports lobbyists, an event that continued the trend toward State intervention which began with indirect funding of sport through the Ministry of Education after the war. The inevitability of this outcome of greater State intervention was prefigured by the almost simultaneous publication of policy statements on physical recreation and sport by the Labour opposition and the ruling Conservatives in 1959, just before the release of the Wolfenden Report.[151] While each party's policy statement differed in approach, with Labour in particular making much of teenage delinquency and the lack of provision of sports facilities, their recommendations were virtually identical, both supporting the idea of a Sports Council of Great Britain. This outcome was entirely consistent with the consensual politics of the 1950s, and it is not insignificant that this sudden interest in sport emerged at the same time that education became an election issue. Discourses on both education and sport were mired in the egalitarian rhetoric of the day, and the Sports Council's Sport for All slogan had close affiliations with the ideology of comprehensive schooling and the notion of equality of opportunity which, as we saw in Chapter 3, had become by the early 1960s a debased materialist concern for the equitable distribution of educational resources. Both sport and education were dominated by the same meritocratic myth that 'IQ (or in the case of sport, Talent) + Effort = Merit', and physical education straddled both institutions, being located within schools and drawing its substance from competitive games and sports. In this respect, the reconstructed games ethic appeared as the ideal form of physical education for the new mass secondary schools, at one and the same time supplying the common denominator to unite divided groups, a means of combatting recalcitrance and delinquency among working class adolescents, and a cohesive force forging group solidarity, and more broadly, national identity.

Traditional Physical Education as Myth

The playing of team games and the educational values to be derived from this had achieved mythical proportions among sections of the British bourgeoisie long before the cult of athleticism reached its peak in their schools around 1914. We saw earlier in this chapter that this myth performed a number of class-specific functions for the bourgeois males in relation to class identity and the identification of their own interests with the nation's. In this latter regard, ideas about patriotism and right conduct generated from games playing may have made some impression on popular consciousness, but it was not until much later that a reconstructed and sanitized version of the myth began to have anything like a widespread impact or appeal. One of the things that had to happen to the myth was the eradication of the idea that games playing demonstrated social superiority, in order to accommodate the alternative notion that games were a common demoninator that could transcend barriers of class and wealth. Other important modifications included an elaboration of the notion of character building as a counter-vailing influence on delinquency, and the establishment of the idea that access to facilities for participating in games and other sports was a right of everyone, not just the privileged minority.

The myth was being continually reconstructed to suit different purposes and circumstances between the end of the first world war and the beginning of the second, but it was in the late 1940s and through the 1950s and its use in the mass secondary school system that this process of reconstruction accelerated and the myth began to take on its contemporary form. It was at this point that what had been a form of physical education traditional to the schools of a specific social class group was installed as *the* traditional form of physical education common to all social classes, for females as well as males, and that bourgeois hegemony was extended through organized physical activity and sport. The Wolfenden Report represented something of a peak in this process in as much as it brought together the various strands of the debate on physical education, recreation and sport from the end of the second world war, and expressed a sophisticated version of 'traditional physical education' that was to form the basis for work in schools over the following two decades, embodying each of the key elements of the selective tradition, in particular the promotion of national culture and the supervision and therapy of potentially delinquent working class youth. In this respect, the Wolfenden Report effectively consolidated what was to become the official discourse in physical education and played a key role in further legitimating and extending bourgeois hegemony. At the same time, as John Hargreaves[152] has pointed out, we cannot read-off the effects of this official discourse from the discourse alone, and deduce that participating in competitive games and sports actually developed national culture or controlled delinquent youth. Though participation may have had this influence in some specific instances, it was not the actual impact, for example on working class youth literally being cured of delinquency through the therapeutic powers of games, that was the decisive factor in extending bourgeois hegemony. Rather, the effectiveness of 'traditional physical education' for this purpose was in its continuing function as a myth.

The CCPR survey of 1960 showed that working class youth were by and large not particularly interested in participating in so-called national games outside compulsory schooling, and this pattern of non-conformity continued to be a feature of the response of sections of the working classes to participation in organized physical recreation beyond the 1960s.[153] Hargreaves has argued that such non-compliance on the part of the working classes demonstrates the tensions and contradictions inherent in the often contradictory functions competitive games and sport are required to perform in contemporary society. He suggests, as an example, the situation where sport is on the one hand sold as family entertainment and yet on the other often involves displays of violence and dissension that are counterproductive to this use; or where in consumer culture the prime targets for the control function of games and sports, such as the unemployed and certain ethnic minorities, may be inaccessible to media influence and so remain untouched.[154] These contradictions suggest that the effects of the bourgeois games ideology are certainly neither literal nor straightforward.

> We can dismiss the idea that sports nowadays embourgeoisify the work-
> ing class...involvement in sport, whatever section of the class we
> consider, does not induce an identification with, or facilitate mixing
> with bourgeois elements, or lead to the adoption of a bourgeois lifestyle
> ...we know the middle and upper classes effectively place obstacles in
> the way of the lower classes mixing with them in sporting activity; and
> we also know that working class people on the whole do not aspire to
> join them.[155]

What this example points to is the fact that in terms if its practical effects, a hegemonic ideology is rarely absolute or universal. Indeed, it is precisely because of such disjunctions in practice that hegemony needs to be constantly recon-structed. The more profound effects of the ideology surrounding competitive games and sports derive from its function as a myth. It does not require literal belief or adoption to be effective, since it operates mainly as a metaphor, not for games and sports, but for other aspects of social life, such as the allegedly natural order of society, proper social conduct, and the underpinning principles of the political system sloganized in terms like equality of opportunity. Hargreaves shows how the ideology of bourgeois sport and games performs this mytholo-gical function, in this case in relation to social mobility.

> Social mobility through sport can exert an effect and make an input
> to hegemony by functioning as a myth about, and as a symbol of, the
> openness of society...sport as a social institution therefore gives convinc-
> ing substance to the ideology that the ambitious, hard working, talented
> individual, no matter what his (sic) social origin, may achieve high
> status and rewards, and so reproduces the belief among subordinate
> groups — some individuals from which are actually successful in
> sports — that the social formation is more open and amenable to change
> that it really is.[156]

It was this mythical quality of competitive games and sports that the members of the Wolfenden Committee were alluding to when they caricatured the quaint and faintly ridiculous relics of the public school tradition, but then suggested that the 'That's not cricket, old boy' attitude actually stood for something above and beyond cricket. As proponents of the 'games playing as a common denominator' ideal and affiliates to the ruling class, though, their view of the operation of this myth was that it provided inspiration and an ethical standard for the right conduct of everyday life for all. A less partial view of the myth suggests a less benign set of outcomes. As Hargreaves' example shows, the myth serves the interests of the ruling class by masking the actual state of affairs in society and constructing a reality that is patently false. His example of social mobility through sport is a good case in point, since on closer examination it is clear that only a small fraction of working class people become wealthier or achieve a higher social status through their sporting ability. As we saw in Chapter 3, the same can be said for education. Indeed, it is obvious that despite the increase in the numbers of working class people now participating in organized physical recreation either in school or their own time, sport itself remains an inegalitarian institution, and certain sports such as golf, yachting, rugby union, and equestrian to name a few remain the preserves of the wealthy.

The reconstructed bourgeois games ethic which emerged from this postwar period as 'traditional physical education' was mythical in two interrelated senses, then. The first is that the entire notion of 'traditional physical education' was in itself a myth, since it purported to be *the* tradition rather than simply *a* tradition in physical education. Clearly, since competitive games and sports were never a substantial part of the physical education programmes of working class schools until after the second world war, this claim was unfounded. So the myth of 'traditional physical education' effectively concealed or at least obscured its class-specific origins. This was an important function since it facilitated appeals to a common heritage and a shared interest in the well-being of the nation. And it was mythical in a second sense in so far as it obscured not merely its origins, but the fact that the values of its originators (or at least their heirs) continued to be represented through the educational ideology surrounding competitive team games. In this second sense, the myth of 'traditional physical education' is consistent with reconstructed bourgeois sport in its widest sense, and indeed occupies a key role in the overall process of the production of bourgeois values.

The power of the mythical and symbolic properties of games and sports to influence the practices of individuals and groups cannot be underestimated, even when the educational values awarded to games playing are treated with scepticism. Physical educators were key proponents of 'traditional physical education', but there was dissent among sections of the profession regarding the educational values of games in the public arena by the mid 1960s. We know that the females had resisted the excesses of the male bourgeois games ethic from the beginning, and many educational gymnasts continued to do so through the 1950s and 1960s. However, there was dissent among the males too. Teachers at a 1968 Conference in Scotland on 'The Place of Organized Games in the Curriculum' discussed the issue of the 'carry-over' between what is learned in games and other aspects of life, and reported that 'when considering competition in adult life in commerce, industry, the professions or anywhere else, (the group) was completely agreed that the experience of children in 'game situations' would be of no value whatever'.[157] In a paper presented at another professional gathering two years earlier, KB Start poured scorn on many of the educational benefits alleged to derive from participation in games, arguing through a sustained critique that any literal interpretation of the games ethic was in contemporary consumer society naive, and the values it purported to embody redundant for many working class pupils.[158] While such explicit dissent was rare in the late 1950s, there were few physical educators a decade later who would have been able to take the ideas of the Wolfenden Committee on the educational value of games seriously, since they had the evidence of their own experience that team games did not have the practical effects the rhetoric claimed for them. Nevertheless, as surveys in the late 1960s and early 1970s by Whitehead and Kane[159] showed, the role of competitive team sport, as the mainstay of physical education programmes, was by this time unquestioned. In this respect, the myth of 'traditional physical education' suited the purposes of the male physical educators, even though they were themselves privately sceptical of its educational value. This myth provided them with a legitimate and respectable rationale for games teaching while they were drawn more and more through the 1960s into developing the base in the pyramidial structure of British sport. The function of servicing elite sport became the dominant but unstated purpose of physical education programmes in many schools, and in this physical education teachers were aided and abetted by the new scientific knowledge of skill acquisition, exercise physiology and biomechanics. In the next chapter, we turn to examine the emergence of this scientific functionalism in male physical education discourse in the 1950s, and its 'hard core' of fitness training centering on the development of strength and endurance.

Notes

1 Mangan, J.A. (1981) *Athleticism in the Victorian and Edwardian Public School*, Cambridge University Press.
2 As Mangan, note 1 and Hargreaves, J. (1986) *Sport, Power and Culture*, Cambridge: Polity Press, both point out.
3 Thompson, E.P. (1962) *The Making of the English Working Class*, Harmondsworth: Penguin.
4 Mangan, note 1, p. 14.
5 See Mangan, note 1, for a detailed account of this process.
6 Thompson, note 3.
7 Hargreaves, note 2, p. 75.
8 Mangan, J.A. (1983) 'Grammar schools and the games ethic in Victorian and Edwardian eras', *Albion*, **15**(4), 313–335.
9 Mangan, note 1, p. 7.
10 Mangan, note 1, p. 207.
11 Netball was the result of the Ling Association's modifications to basketball.
12 See McCrone, K.E. (1988) *Sport and the Physical Emancipation of English Women* London: Routledge, pp. 60–85, and her discussion of games at the North London Collegiate School, St Leonards and Roedean, where games did not become firmly established until this time.
13 Hargreaves, J. (1985) 'Playing like gentlemen while behaving like ladies: Contradictory features of the formative years of women's sport', *The British Journal of Sports History*, **2**(1), 40–52.
14 See McCrone, note 12, p. 88.
15 McIntosh, P.C. (1952) *PE in England Since 1800* London: Bell (First Edition), p. 189. This comment needs to be seen in the context of the development of scientific medicine in the nineteenth century as a powerful body of professional knowledge centred on the control and surveillence of populations, and as a major propogator of what some feminist theorists have described as the uterine tradition, through which a woman's purpose in life was identified with her biological capacities for childbirth and mothering; see Turner, B. (1984) *The Body in Society: Explorations in Social Theory* Oxford: Blackwell, and Matthews, J.J. (1987) 'Building the body beautiful: The femininity of Modernity', *Australian Feminist Studies*, **5**, 18–34.
16 Mangan, note 8, p. 313.

17 Mangan, note 8, p. 336.
18 Mangan, note 8, p. 330.
19 Hargreaves, note 2, p. 55.
20 Gramsci, A. (1971) *Selections from Prison Notebooks* London: Lawrence and Wishart. See Chapter 2 for a more detailed discussion of hegemony and its place in the theoretical framework of this study.
21 Thompson, note 3, p. 21.
22 Foucault, M. (1981) *The History of Sexuality: An Introduction*, Harmondsworth, Penguin, p. 124.
23 See Mangan, note 1, on the religious connection in the public schools, p. 27; and problems of discipline, pp. 31–34; and McIntosh, P.C. (1968) *PE in England Since 1800*, London: Bell (Second Edition), p. 58 for the view of games as an antidote to (homo)sexual misbehaviour. See also the comment in note 15.
24 Foucault, note 22, p. 123.
25 Mangan, note 8, p. 330.
26 McIntosh, P.C. (1976) 'The curriculum in physical education — An historical perspective', in Kane, J.E. (Ed.) *Curriculum Development in Physical Education*, London: Crosby, Lockwood and Staples, pp. 11–45.
27 Board of Education (1933) *Syllabus of Physical Training for Schools* London: HMSO, p. 37.
28 The writers of the Syllabus suggested that 'in most schools games now form part of the general curriculum'. These were more likely to be games like Fox and Geese, Blind Man's Bluff, etc. viz. 'It is too commonly assumed that the games to be played should be football and cricket for boys, netball and tennis for girls, regardless of the fact that these games require a high degree of physical co-ordination as well as specially prepared pitches, the cost of which would be altogether prohibitive for the thousands of schoolchildren for whom provision must be made'. They also make one of the earliest official statements about the role of sports and games in post-school leisure. 'Unless children are taught to play and enjoy organized games while at school it is unlikely that later they will occupy their leisure hours in healthy open air exercise of this nature'. Board of Education, note 27, p. 37.
29 The key to exclusion was the amateur/professional distinction; see Hargreaves, note 2, pp 46–47.
30 Hargreaves, note 2, p. 46.
31 McIntosh, note 15, pp. 199–200.
32 Mangan, note 1, p. 207.
33 Munrow, A.D. (1958) Physical Education in the Universities. Proceedings of the Second British Empire and Commonwealth Games Conference, Barry, Glamorgan, p. 2.
34 Moyse, Y. (1949) 'A brief outline of some activities of the Ling Physical Education Association', *Journal of Physical Education*, 41, p. 83.
35 *The Leaflet*, **45**(6), 1946, pp. 123–124.
36 *The Leaflet*, note 35.
37 *The Leaflet*, **49**(7), 1948.
38 Conference Report, 'Physical education of girls and boys in their last year at the secondary grammar and secondary modern school', *The Leaflet*, **49**(1), 10–11, 1948.
39 For example 'the possibility of allowing the Grammar School boy some free-dom of choice'; 'it might be wise to allow them (the VI Form girls) some latitude of choice in physical education, in consultation with the teacher'; *The Leaflet*, note 38, p. 10.
40 For example, in Rubenstein, D. and Simon, B. (1966) *The Evolution of the Comprehensive School, 1922–1966* London: Routledge and Kegan Paul.

41 Moyse, note 34.
42 Report, *Journal of Physical Education* 1949, p. 123.
43 See Whitehead, N. and Hendry, L. (1976) *Teaching Physical Education in England — Description and Analysis* London: Lepus, pp. 43–71.
44 Small, R.B. (1976) The effects of individuals on, and developments within, the Scottish School of Physical Education in the 20th Century. Mimeo, Jordanhill College of Education, Glasgow.
45 Brown, H.C. (1958) 'The training of the man teacher of physical education'. *Physical Education*, **50**, p. 92.
46 Hargreaves, note 2.
47 See Chapter 4; and McIntosh's comments — 'Posture training has been overdone, the present need is for knowledge on 'skill learning'. Are we teaching skills the best way? How can we experiment and compare different methods?' in McIntosh, P.C. (1953) *The Leaflet*, **54**(10), p. 10.
48 McIntosh, P.C. (1963) 'Practical aspects of physical education', *The Leaflet*, **64**(8), 62–64.
49 For example, *TES* 5 February 1949, p. 86, picture of senior pupils at Tiffin's Boys' School, Kingston-on-Thames, having their weekly golf lesson with the professional at Home Park Golf Club; *TES* 24 February 1950, front page picture of 'Lacrosse at Kensington Gardens'; *TES* 31 March 1950, picture of four boys with a football headed 'Talking Over The Rules'; *TES* 28 April 1950, picture of seven schoolboy athletes at the steeplechase waterjump, caption reads 'The London Athletic Club's Annual Schools' Challenge Cup meeting was held at the White City Stadium last weekend, when the trophy was won by Latymer Upper.'; *TES* 6 October 1950, front page picture of ancient building in background, game of rugby in foreground, caption reads 'The school scrum half throwing out a long pass in the match between Taunton School and their Old Boys. Taunton has had one of the strongest school sides in the West Country in the last few years. In 1948 they won the public schools' seven-a-side tournament'.
50 *TES* 18 May 1951, picture of fencers headed 'School Fencing Team', caption reads 'Members of the Stoke-under-Ham Secondary Modern School practising fencing, which is proving to be a popular sport with both boys and girls.'; *The Leaflet*, **58**(5) 1957, article 'Physical Education in Cornwall' shows games to be well established for boys and girls.
51 Jacobs, V. (1961) 'The planning and organization of physical education in a new comprehensive school'. *The Leaflet*, **62**(6), 45–48.
52 Basically on a ratio of three periods of games to one of all other activities, and some of these 'other activities' involved skill practices for games like cricket and for athletics; see Jacobs, note 51, p. 46.
53 Jacobs, note 51, p. 47.
54 Jacobs, note 51, p. 48.
55 CCPR (1961) 'A survey in the eastern counties of England on the sports interests of secondary modern school leavers'. *The Leaflet*, **62**(3), 23–24.
56 In Whitehead and Hendry, note 43, pp. 22–42.
57 Whitehead and Hendry, note 43, p. 38.
58 Whitehead and Hendry, note 43, p. 31.
59 Editorial, *TES*, 19 January 1951.
60 McIntosh, P.C., Letter to the *TES*, 26 January 1951.
61 Hargreaves, note 2.
62 An example being the Welfare State; State intervention in the education sector was evidenced in the introduction of mass secondary schooling, see Lawson, J. and Silver, H. (1973) *A Social History of Education in England* London: Methuen, p. 431, for a comment.

63 Hargreaves, note 2, p. 92.
64 See for example the Birmingham University, Physical Education Department Report, 'Britain in the World of Sport' (1956); and Report in *The Leaflet*, **59**(3), 1958 of the Minister of Education's response to the UNESCO Report, 'The Place of Sport in Education'.
65 Hargreaves, note 2, pp. 135–137.
66 McIntosh, note 23, pp. 223–224.
67 McIntosh, note 23, p. 238.
68 *TES* 9 March 1951, p. 192; there would have been many more grass tracks, but these would have been of variable standard.
69 *TES* 6 May 1949; and NPFA Annual Reports, 1950–1960.
70 *TES* May 1951.
71 There was a question in House of Commons to Chancellor of Exchequer Sir Stafford Cripps concerning a grant to the NPFA; Cripps responded that funding was made available through the Ministry of Education and the 1937 Physical Training Act, *TES* 30 April 1949. Michael Astor, chairman of NPFA grants committee, addressing a conference of local authorities, was told by a representative of the Minister of Education that there could be no hope of money from the government due to financial stringency, *TES* 30 October 1953, p. 920. The *TES* 30 October 1953 reported on a debate in House of Lords on playing fields for new towns.
72 McIntosh, note 23, p. 251. By 1947, part of the salaries of the AAA's four National Coaches was being paid by the Ministry of Education, McIntosh, note 23, p. 264.
73 Hargreaves, note 2, p. 89.
74 *The Leaflet*, **44**(5), 1945.
75 Seventy-five per cent of women and only twenty-five per cent of men were already qualified teachers, *TES* 24 April 1946.
76 One of the CCPR's fund-raising activities for the National Sports Development Fund was an exhibition at the Wembley Festival of Youth and Sport. Princess Elizabeth and Prince Phillip attended the Festival, and the *TES* description of the finale provides some idea of the complicitness of the CCPR with the power structure, and also demonstrates the intermeshing of nationalism, patriotism, and militarism. 'The finale was apt and impressive. The RAF marched into the arena as markers, each man bearing a flag; at a blast from the whistle the boys of the army and the navy scampered from the sides with incredible speed to shape themselves into a living E and P. A moment's pause, and the Empire Pool Orchestra struck up the National Anthem to conclude an absorbing and interesting exhibition which, it is hoped, will have materially benefitted the fund it was designed to aid'. *TES* 12 June 1948, p. 1 & p. 334.
77 *TES* 24 October 1946.
78 *TES* 21 September 1946, p. 450.
79 *TES* 15 June 1951, p. 484.
80 *TES* 9 October 1948, p. 574.
81 See for example the *TES* October 1949, 13 February 1953, 21 August 1953, 11 September 1953, 8 October 1954.
82 McIntosh, note 23, p. 280.
83 This is not to say that they played together though, see Hargreaves, note 2, p. 111.
84 Sir Ernest Baker claimed that 'Leisure has to be nationalized if there is to be a common provision of facilities', *TES* 18 October 1947, p. 558.
85 Hargreaves, note 2, pp. 89–90.
86 Report on an Address given by RE Presswood, Director of Education for Cardiff, to the NAOLPE Conference, in *The Leaflet*, **55**(8), 1954, p. 5.

87   Hargreaves, note 2, p. 12.
88   Hargreaves, note 2, p. 67.
89   Williams, R. (1977) *Marxism and Literature* Oxford University Press, pp. 115–116.
90   *TES* 18 October 1947, p. 558.
91   Munrow, A.D. (1956) 'Looking back and looking forward in gymnastics', *Journal of Physical Education*, **48**(1), 18–24.
92   Abrahams, H. (1957) 'The Olympic Games, 1956'. *Journal of Physical Education*, **49**, 1–8/20.
93   *TES* 18 July 1952, front page.
94   Editorial, *TES* 8 September 1950.
95   Its elitism and upper class point of view was at times quite blatant. An example is provided by an Editorial comment about 'racy talk', which presented a generally dismissive view of what the Editor saw as the American influence in British sports journalism. The Editorial went on to say 'The sporting pages of the papers form the only reading matter of millions; perhaps if local government debates were reported like this more than 40 per cent of the eligible voters might be constrained to vote', *TES* 11 April 1952, p. 308. See also Joan Simon's analysis of the role of *The Times* and the *TES* in projecting a ruling class view of 'social reconstruction' during the war years, Simon, J. (1989) 'Promoting educational reform on the home front', 'The *TES* and *The Times* 1940–1944. *History of Education*, **18**(3), 195–211.
96   *TES* 17 March 1950.
97   *TES* 14 July 1950, p. 562.
98   *TES* 26 October 1951, p. 831.
99   *TES* 24 April 1952, front page.
100 *TES* 6 October 1950, front page.
101 The examples cited are merely a brief selection to illustrate the point. In addition to the reporting described, the newspaper ran a regular column from the late 1950s and through the 1960s called 'In Corpore Sano', which reported on interschool sports matches and other elite competition, outdoor pursuits, and other sports news. See, for example, *TES* 22 January 1960, p. 120, an article on Lacrosse as a 'Moral Substitute for War'; *TES* 2 September 1960, p. 262 'Youth at the Helm', report on a sailing regatta; *TES* 2 February 1962, p. 187 report on a rugby union match between two secondary modern schools; *TES* 23 March 1962, p. 557 report on a school Head of the River race at Putney Reach; *TES* 4 May 1962, p. 881 report on public schools' foil and sabre championships; *TES* 30 October 1964, p. 761 'Sport the Real Theatre' report on pre-Olympic Conference on Sport held in Tokyo.
102 See Chapter 4.
103 Editorial, *TES* 15 June 1951.
104 *TES* 22 June 1951, p. 507.
105 Editorial, *The Leaflet*, **45**(5), 1946.
106 Lord Aberdare (1948) 'Olympics I', *Journal of Physical Education*, **40**, p. 115.
107 Phillip Noel-Baker, reported in the *TES* 9 October 1948.
108 *TES* 5 October 1952, p. 735.
109 *TES* 6 August 1954, p. 760.
110 In McIntosh, note 23, 281.
111 See Anthony, D. (1980) *A Strategy for British Sport* London: Hurst.
112 McIntosh, P.C., Letter to the *The Leaflet*, **59**(1), 1958, p. 5.
113 For instance, see *The Leaflet*, **58**(10), 1957.
114 Munrow, note 113, p. 71.
115 *The Leaflet*, **58**(5), 1957, p.
116 McIntosh, note 115, p.

117 *The Leaflet*, **58**(3), 1957.

118 Nicol, A. (1954) Training for Strength. *The Leaflet*, **55**(2), p. 1.

119 MacQueen, I.J., Letter to *The Leaflet*, **55**(2), 1954, p. 10.

120 On this issue of international competition, the Wolfenden Committee's rational pleading in 1960 provides us with some idea of the pervasiveness of at least the sentiments if not the substance of Nicol *et al's* views. 'Naturally the public is pleased by national success; the public has normally expected it, since so many sports and games originated in this country and were later adopted abroad. Correspondingly, there is a natural tendency to regard defeat as a disaster...It is not the end of the world if British teams are defeated, still less is it a symptom or proof of national decadence. To talk, as some do, as if sport could properly be used as an instrument of international diplomacy, or as if a nation's authority in world affairs at large are to be measured by its successes or failures at the Olympic Games, seems to us to reveal a serious lack of sense of proportion.' Wolfenden Report (1960) *Sport and the Community* London: CCPR, p. 73.

121 McIntosh, P.C. (1963) *Sport in Society* London: Bell, p. 203.

122 Graves, J. (1942) *Policy and Progress in Secondary Education* London: Thomas Nelson, pp. 169–171; See also Lawson and Silver, note 62, p. 416 who explain that this need was brought about by the need for evacuations in the early years of the war which resulted, among other things, in large scale inattendance at school.

123 Board of Education (1940) 'The Service of Youth' Circular 1486; Board of Education (1940) 'The Challenge of Youth' Circular 1516; Board of Education (1940) 'Youth, Physical Recreation and Service' Circular 1529; Board of Education (1941) 'Youth Service Corps' Circular 1543; Board of Education (1941) 'Registration of Youth' Circular 1577.

124 The *TES* report 24 May 1947, p. 247 suggests that youth clubs were not seen as appropriate or necessary for grammar school boys and girls.

125 Marwick, A. (1982) *British Society Since 1945* Harmondsworth: Penguin, pp. 148–149.

126 See the *TES* 24 May 1947, p. 247; *TES* 13 May 1949; *TES* 31 March 1950, p. 240.

127 Hargreaves, note 2, p. 184.

128 Henriques, J. (1955) 'Physical activity and the young delinquent', *Journal of Physical Education*, **47**, p. 2.

129 As one speaker at a NAOLPE Conference in 1952 put it, *TES* 25 July 1952, p. 636.

130 *TES* 13 May 1949.

131 *TES* 12 July 1947, p. 359.

132 *TES* 22 December 1950, p. 980; see also the *TES* 31 March 1950, p. 240 and the comments of Lt-Col. Edmundson.

133 Hargreaves, note 2, pp. 182–183.

134 For instance, Henriques, note 128, p. 3; 'There are schools — they are called progressive schools — which are definitely based on the principles of no rewards, no punishments, no competitions, and no repressions. Well, it sounds awfully nice, but it is no preparation for life. Life is not like that. There is competition and surely competition is not a bad thing. The desire to compete is almost innate in human nature.'

135 Henriques, note 128, p. 5.

136 Wolfenden Report, note 120.

137 See Anthony, note 111 on this issue.

138 Albemarle Report, in note 120 for a commentary.

139 Wolfenden Report, note 120, p. 4.

140 For example, 'Today, games are part of the life of every school. It has to be

remembered that young people who learn games now have not been brought up in homes in which the sporting spirit has been unconsciously embued. If we want to help them fit into a community, the recognition that certain rules must be obeyed, as in games, should help them to accept the basic principles of society. Loyalty to the team or to the gang, so strong in the adolescent, should be extended until the gang includes an ever-larger group, and loyalty to truth might also be reached'. Webster, C.M. (1958) 'The training of the woman Physical Education teacher', *Physical Education*, **50**, p. 88. The bourgeois values associated with games playing were also extended to cover outdoor leisure and adventure activities — 'Have you ever watched a Teddy gang at work? I have. I have seen them beat up a single enemy, leaving him bleeding and unconscious on the pavement. And the terrible thing about it all was the cold, passionless, miserable atmosphere in which they did it. Are we being unduly sentimental when we believe that the beauty of mountains, rivers or lakes can be some kind of antidote to this tawdry misery? My own experience of taking many hundreds of young people to the mountains for their first visit convinces me that most respond with eager happiness to peacefulness and beauty.' Bell, W.O. (1962) Changing Objectives in Physical Education. *Physical Education*, **54**, p. 9.

141 Wolfenden Report, note 120, pp. 5 and 6.
142 Wolfenden Report, note 120, p. 25.
143 Wolfenden Report, note 120, p. 29.
144 See note 55.
145 Wolfenden Report, note 120, p. 28.
146 Wolfenden Report, note 120, p. 28.
147 Anthony, note 111.
148 Anthony, note 111, Chapter 5.
149 A point supported with qualification by the *TES* 30 September 1960, front and p. 400.
150 'It seems inevitable that if sport were left to be self-financing without support from the central government, local authorities, the great charitable trusts or benevolent industrial firms, those which require buildings or land and all within the great conurbations would decline almost to the point of extinction. Is this the prospect which any modern society or any government of whatever party could, should or would be ready to accept?' McIntosh, note 121, p. 142.
151 See Anthony, note 111, pp. 52–54.
152 Hargreaves, note 2, pp. 135–137.
153 Hargreaves, note 2, pp. 101–102.
154 Hargreaves, note 2, pp. 135–137.
155 Hargreaves, note 2, p. 111.
156 Hargreaves, note 2, p. 111.
157 SSPE/SAPE Conference Report 1968, p. 23 (Jordanhill College Library).
158 Start, K.B. (1966) Sport and Education. Aspects of Sport and PE, SSPE Symposium, Jordanhill College of Education, Glasgow.
159 Whitehead, note 43; Kane, J.E. (1974) *Physical Education in Secondary Schools*. London: Macmillan.

Chapter 6

Health, Fitness and the Rise of Scientific Functionalism

The calculated use of physical education as a means of contributing to the health of school children was restricted mainly to the state elementary school system, despite the long association between physical activity and health in physical education discourse stretching back to at least the mid 1800s. The female Swedish gymnasts did champion the role of their system of gymnastics in promoting health. But, with the exception of the work of a few of their number through Inspectorate and Advisory positions, their influence was limited to the girls' private schools. Their conception of the relationship between physical activity and health was embedded in a medico–health rationale, which built on the same logic as the view of the purpose of physical education in elementary schools. However, their objectives diverged dramatically from those of the elementary school teachers. In the bourgeois girls' schools, physical education was relevant to health in so far as it developed elegance, poise and posture, and the sound physical functioning that was a prerequisite to child-bearing. In the elementary schools, the concerns were rather different, focusing instead on the role of physical activity in compensating for and possibly remedying inherited and acquired physical defects. The result was that up until the middle of the 1950s, the use of organized physical activity to promote health was associated with the masses, and indeed, was with few exceptions[1] never taken seriously by the male public schools.

The demise of the influence of the Swedish gymnasts in physical education coupled with the influx of large numbers of male physical educators into the state secondary schools after the war, severely undermined the traditional, medico–health conception of the link between physical activity and health. In its place, a new view of this relationship began to emerge during the 1950s, crystallized in the notion of physical fitness. In contrast to the traditional therapeutic view of physical education's role in promoting health, this new view was embedded in 'scientific physical education', which was itself framed by the canons and procedures of experimental methods and statistical analyses. New insights into the process of skill acquisition and the mechanics of body movement deriving from experimental work began appearing in physical education discourse by the early 1950s. But it was the new knowledge of the physiological responses of the body to exercise that led the way in reconceptualizing the physical activity/health relationship, and this experimental work was pioneered mainly by male physical educators through the 1950s. In the process, it was their definitions of fitness that dominated this new view of the relationship between exercise and health, with the hard core of fitness being formed by strength and endurance. While their functionalist view of this relationship owed much to the preoccupations of the Swedish gymnasts, the male physical educators' application of experimental methods to investigate physical activity marked a distinctive break with their predecessors. The outcome was the development of scientific functionalism which, as a way of understanding physical education, was to play a key role in defining physical education after the 1950s, first in college and university programmes and later in schools.

This chapter locates the emergence of scientific functionalism within the demise of the traditional, medico-health conception of the physical activity/health relationship. The positioning of school physical education in medico-health discourse at the turn of the twentieth century is discussed, as a means of previewing the subsequent fall from grace of the Swedish gymnasts and the expansion of health education in schools after the second world war beyond purely medical and structural-postural concerns. The rise of scientific functionalism is then examined in relation to 'scientific physical education' and the development of the new knowledge centring on fitness, strength and endurance. The chapter concludes with a synthesis of the new view of fitness and health which emerged from the 1950s and which was linked to the solution of problems such as coronary heart disease that were claimed to have their source in sedentariness and the other ills of affluence.

The Positioning of School Physical Education in Medico-Health Discourse

Concerns over the health and physical well being of working class children in the state elementary school system arose out of a number of interconnected events from the middle to the end of the nineteenth century. As the factory system became more widespread by the 1850s and the urban centres began to grow at an accelerating rate,[2] there was considerable philanthropic attention directed at the living conditions of the masses and the effects of these conditions on their health. A number of surveys of slum dwellers, revealing the extent of deprivation and squalor at the heart of Britain's great manufacturing cities, made a considerable impact on the consciousness of the bourgeoisie, and the notion that the physical condition of the race was deteriorating became an accepted fact in ruling class circles by the late 1800s.[3] The mid nineteenth century also marked a new phase of imperial expansion in order to protect Britain's trading interests. Such expansion required a regular supply of fit manpower to fill the ranks of the army and navy, and so the matter of physical deterioration was a cause for grave concern to the merchant classes. And by 1880, the effects of schooling itself, with its compulsory internment in a classroom for up to eight hours a day, brought to light the fact that some working class children were not fit enough to benefit from the State's benevolence. The interests expressed through each of these events were focused in the late 1800s in the notion of national efficiency and, as part of this concern, in the question of whether physical training should be made compulsory in the state elementary schools.

William Jolly, appointed an HMI in 1868, was a vociferous supporter of physical education, and his various speeches and reports reflected the range of arguments for the inclusion of physical education in the elementary school curriculum that had their source in these events. In a paper read to the British Association in Glasgow in 1876, he strongly advocated a national system of 'rational physical education' as the basis for improving the health of school children.

> Systematic Physical Education should, beyond doubt, be carried on in all our schools, and, if any national improvement in health and physique among the masses of our people is to be effected, it can be achieved only by systematic physical culture in our *Common* schools.[4]

Jolly had been much impressed by the 'scientific physical education' of Archibald McLaren at Oxford, the writings of Dr Mathias Roth and the expanding literature on physical education and health from the United States, and he used this information to identify four pressing problems that rational physical education could overcome: 'deteriorated physique', 'organic defects', diseases of the eyes, nose, throat, chest and spine, and 'misery and death' due to 'ignorance of the commonest laws of health'. 'These formidable evils' he alleged 'are largely produced by our present defects and errors in school buildings, furniture, and practice, and by the neglect of physical training in our schools'. Jolly made three recommendations to remedy this neglect; that grants be offered for physical training (under the system of payment-by-results), that hygiene or 'the principles of health' be included as a specific subject and made compulsory, and that physical education be made a compulsory part of teacher training. In putting his case, he was clearly aware that a broad range of parties had an interest in physical education.

> With such evils to be cured and such advantages to national health and education to be gained by its means, surely it becomes not only our profit but our duty to do all we can to secure (physical education). Ambition itself prompt us to efforts to prevent our being ignobly beaten by other nations in a matter of national advantage. Self-interest of the most utilitarian kind should urge its adoption, for any improvement in the health and strength of our people will raise the working power and skill of the artisan, and increase the value of his labour. Our Government should foster it, if only on the grounds of national defence, for it would furnish better recruits, and improve the national courage and endurance by its Spartan training. Our teachers and School Managers should encourage it, for if it did nothing more, it would improve discipline by its vigour-giving, cloud-dispelling effects, raise the mental work done, and increase even monetary results.[5]

Jolly himself may have been a pragmatist in attempting to sell physical education by citing as many advantages as possible, but his comments reveal the battle ground physical education was already becoming as a range of interest groups — the government and the army, the merchants, industrialists and factory owners, and the school administrators and teachers — pursued their own advantage through the establishment of a form of physical education in the state elementary schools. It is also significant to note that, apart from staving-off 'misery and death', there was little suggestion in Jolly's arguments that health might be something of value to the working classes for *their* own well-being, rather than some-one else's.

By 1880 and on until 1895, however, the effects of compulsory schooling on children's health had become an important topic of debate in itself.[6] The concern was that 'over-pressure', brought on by the rigours of school work, was a major cause of physical deterioration among poorer children. The fact that some children's health was badly affected by schooling, or more precisely, that some children were not fit enough to cope with schooling in the first place, was readily conceded by all sides in the debate. The two main points at issue were, rather, how many children were actually affected and how the problem could be remedied. Some saw the introduction of school meals as the key to improving attendance and performance at school, while others, like Jolly, argued for exercise as a means of improving health. This latter claim was countered by the suggestion that, if children were in poor health in the first place, physical exercise would simply be another form of over-pressure. Thomson[7] has suggested that the argument was partially resolved in 1895 when the School Codes in England and Scotland were altered to recognize some form of physical training as eligible for a grant,[8] though he contended that the deciding factor in choosing to implement physical education was at this stage a concern to combat the poor discipline that was prevalent in the schools at the time rather than promote health.

A number of shock defeats for the British Army in South Africa during the Boer War brought to a head the question of what form of physical training should be adopted in elementary schools,[9] and presented the militarist lobby with an opportunity to drive home their preference for military drill. However, while Anne Williams[10] in her recent historiography of health and fitness in physical education is correct to suggest that the addition of physical training to the School Codes in 1895 'aimed for discipline rather than for health',[11] she perpetuates a particularly damaging misconception in her claim that physical education's 'initial acceptance into elementary education was for military more than medical reasons'. There had been, as is clear from Jolly's speech, some agitation for military drill before 1876, but this connection between militarism and physical education has been clearly shown by Thomson[12] to have been inflated. Attempts to introduce military drill into state elementary schools came to a head in Britain in a five year period between 1898 and 1903. Thomson singles out Sir Henry Craik, Secretary of the Scottish Education Department, as one of the major protagonists for military drill, and claims that Craik used the full range of the powers of his office to establish military drill in Scottish schools.[13] It was in large part on the basis of his and his coalition's agitation that the *Royal Commission on Physical Training*[14] was appointed in 1902, ostensibly 'to inquire into the opportunities for physical training now available in state-aided schools and other educational institutions', and Craik intended to use it as a means of furthering his ambitions for military training. In the event, his plans came unstuck. The Commissioners were much impressed by the determination of teachers and headmasters to resist military drill, and the larger School Boards in Scotland simply ignored the important Circular 279, issued in 1900, that threatened to reduce school grants if they did not meet approved standards in teaching military drill. The Commissioners also accepted, after much consideration and a survey of the health of school children conducted by Dr MacKenzie and Professor Hay, the contentious idea that exercise could not cure disease, but properly conducted could have a beneficial effect on minor defects and deformities. The notion of 'nutrition' lay at the core of the Commission's views on health; it was 'the unifying concept which brought together the four component parts of a sound approach to improving health, namely food, clothing, fresh air and exercise'.[15] It was also accepted by the Commissioners that the wrong kind of exercise, or exercise for under-nourished children, could have a deleterious effect. The main impact of the Commission's recommendations was to encourage the government of the day to empower the School Boards to introduce regular and systematic medical inspections and school meals. The case for military drill, on the other hand, had been thoroughly routed. In response to a debate in the House of Lords in February 1905, Balfour, the Secretary of State for Scotland and previously a supporter of Craik and his ambitions for military drill, commented 'I am prepared to advocate ordinary physical drill as part of the general curriculum of education; I am not prepared to advocate to the same extent anything which seems to train the military side of human nature'.[16]

It was thus in the context of a medical, and not a militarist, rationale that physical education was positioned in the curriculum of state elementary school in the early 1900s. Exercise was defined *by* medical practitioners *in* medical terms; it was one of four factors in securing the health of working class school children, and above all it was a therapy that could be applied under medical supervision to improve minor physical defects and deformities. This doesn't deny that, in practice, physical training may have been used or viewed by school headmasters and teachers as a means of controlling and disciplining large numbers of children. Nor does it deny that governments might have believed there was still some military advantage to be gained from physical training. Notwithstanding these views, the way in which physical education was conceived within the official discourse of the time was in medical terms. As we saw in the previous chapter, though, the disciplining or social control function of physical activity did not disappear from this discourse, but at this time it was not the main framing or defining rationale.[17]

This medical definition of physical education and the positioning of physical education within a functional, medico-health rationale was institutionalized in 1908 through the establishment of the School Medical Service within the Board of Education, with Dr George Newman (later Sir George) as its Chief Medical Officer. While Newman was a strong advocate of physical education, overseeing the publication of three syllabuses between 1909 and 1933, the real work in maintaining the health of school children was from the beginning to be done through medicine. At first, the School Medical Service merely inspected children, but by 1912 grants were made available for treatment as well as inspection, and by the end of the first world war, inspections had been extended from elementary to all state-aided schools.[18] Consonant with these developments, student teachers in training were required to become familiar with 'the main principles of healthy living' and the maintenance of 'hygienic conditions in every part of school work'.

The role of physical education as an arm of the School Medical Service altered little between the two wars. While consecutive syllabuses issued by the Board of Education did reflect a broadening view of physical education subject matter, the practical circumstances of the state schools, lacking specialist teachers, facilities, equipment and playing fields, meant that there was little challenge to this role. The 1933 Syllabus, the last to be published under Newman's direction, revealed the extent to which the logic of the late 1800s had been carried forward with only minor and relatively superficial alteration into the 1930s, and how the medico–health rationale continued to frame physical education's part in the working class child's school experience. According to the author/s of the Syllabus 'the ultimate test by which every system of physical training should be judged, (is) to be found in the *posture and general carriage of the children*'.[19] Newman confirmed that medical matters were the leading concerns in the use of physical education in his Prefatory Memorandum to the Syllabus. While he acknowledged that 'suitable nourishment, effective medical inspection and treatment, and hygienic surroundings' were essential to good health, 'a comprehensive system of physical training...is indispensible as much for the normal healthy development of the body as for the correction of inherent or acquired defects'.[20] Newman also carried forward in his preface the nineteenth century preoccupation with physical deterioration among the lower orders, remarking that 'the Board wish to record their conviction that the development of good physique is a matter of national importance, vital to the welfare and even the survival of the race'.[21] Adjusted to the conditions of the Depression years of the 1930s, Newman merely extended the late nineteenth century view of physical education in arguing that it had a part to play in ameliorating the straitened circumstances of the masses.

> In exceptional conditions of unemployment, poverty, or economic distress it is particularly necessary to safeguard mental and physical health by means of wisely directed physical education of the body, which will lay the foundations of wholesome out-of-door recreation as well as protect normal growth, health and strength.
>
> The conditions of modern civilization with its crowded locations, confined spaces, and sedentary occupations; the increasing need for study and mental application; and the many social circumstances and difficulties which restrict opportunities for natural physical growth, all require that children and young people should receive physical training by well-considered methods devised in a broad catholic spirit to promote and encourage the health and development of the mind and the body.[22]

Neither of these statements would have been out of place thirty or even fifty years earlier, and their presence suggests that the ruling class view of the needs of the working classes had changed little in this time. It may be possible, following Williams,[23] to interpret as 'far-sighted' Newman's comment concerning 'habits of recreation that will be of value in the future', and references in a similar vein to 'the daily period of exercise', 'good habits of hygiene', and the problems caused by 'sedentary occupations'. However, even though the 1933 Syllabus did include an expanded view of physical education, these changes were merely a hat-doffing exercise to current trends, and did nothing to disturb the medico-health definition in which working class physical education was firmly set. In this respect, the 1933 Syllabus was not a blueprint for the future of physical education, but a backward looking confirmation of the past, with its roots deeply embedded in the attitudes of the late 1800s. Four years after the publication of the 1933

Syllabus, in 1937, the debate surrounding the *Physical Training and Recreation* Bill confirmed that formal, mass physical exercises had come to be closely associated 'with the playgrounds of the Board Schools, elementary schools and the military training of "other ranks"'.[24] This positioning of physical education within a functional, medico-health framework thereby marked it as the curriculum for the working classes. As we will see in the next section, it also set limits on the development of this view of physical education after the second world war.

The Undermining of the Medico–Health Framework and the Expansion of Health Education

The changes to the education system and physical education after the second world war broke the medical stranglehold on physical education in the state school curriculum, and at the same time undermined physical education's *de facto* status as health education. The previous two chapters have outlined some of the reasons for this. The female physical educators had up until the late 1930s worked within the medico–health framework, though not under the supervision of the School Medical Officers to any great extent since the gymnasts were concentrated in the private grammar schools and the School Health Service (as it was now known) extended only to those schools that received government funding. Of course, not all of the grammar schools were entirely self-funding, and those that received government assistance certainly would have been eligible for visits from a School Medical Officer. However, a survey of girls' secondary schools in 1946 revealed that 'there seems little co-operation between the medical officer and the physical education teacher',[25] suggesting that, where medical inspections did take place, the extent of the medical profession's direct influence on physical education may have been slight in these schools. In any case, by the end of the war the female gymnasts had begun to defect in large numbers from Swedish gymnastics and to reject the entire medico–health rationale for their work, turning instead o an aggressively anti-functionalist form of child-centred progressivism in their adoption of educational gymnastics. The second blow to the medical influence in physical education in the state schools came in the form of the male physical educators who began to populate the government-run secondary schools in large numbers after the war and to champion competitive games and sports. They, like the female gymnasts, located themselves in the secondary sector which, for a number of reasons,[26] had never been an entirely satisfactory site of operation for the School Medical Officers, and so were unhindered in their invention of 'traditional physical education' in the form of team games.

In the years immediately following the war, during which changes to the educational system, to teacher training in physical education and to the staffing of the new schools began to get under way in earnest, the relationship between the new and fast growing physical education profession's view of physical education's role in the curriculum and that of the School Health Service soon revealed itself as problematic. Part of the problem lay in the fact that the medical profession's view, as we saw with the 1933 Syllabus, had essentially changed little since the late 1800s. For instance, in an article on 'Public Health and Disease' that appeared in the *Journal of Physical Education* in 1946 by Dr Robert Sutherland, a great deal was said about bacteriology and the micro-level behaviour of disease bearing organisms, but only two paragraphs were included at the end on the relevance of this discussion for physical educators; 'in our attack on disease we must, therefore, consider what we can do to strengthen people's resistance as well as to reduce attack by infection'.[27] Sutherland considered the serious threats to health to be disease which could only be combatted through medical care. The work of the physical educator was merely an adjunct. The assumption in this and other medical discourse at the time was that 'health' was first and foremost a medical issue. So, if the physical education profession was to have a part to play in relation to the health of school children, then this part should rightly be defined by medical practitioners.[28]

This, in any case, was clearly the attitude of Dr J.L. Dunlop in an address to the Ling Association in 1949. Dunlop argued that:

> physical educationists try to inspire the children with an appreciation of physical fitness for its own sake, and to give these children a ground-work of knowledge in the various types of physical activity which will enable them to find and take a creditable part in suitable forms of healthy recreation when they leave school. In fact, physical education is a specialized aspect of the wider field of the School Health Services; but, like parallel lines, the two refuse to meet.[29]

Dunlop confessed to a degree of puzzlement over the separateness of the physical education and medical professions, though the reasons are not difficult to see. One of the most powerful of these is the fact that the School Medical Service was invented to cater for people who could not afford the cost of private medical treatment, while the female gymnasts were drawn exclusively from the bourgeois class and worked almost entirely within bourgeois schools. So a closer relationship between the physical educators and the School Medical Officers would have involved an undesirable association with a socially inferior form of physical education. Another forceful reason for the stand-off would have been the tradition of independence of the Ling Association and its mainly female constituents. This independence would have been reason enough to resist the medical profession's attempts to define the gymnast's function in schools. Dunlop nevertheless attempted to do just this in his Ling Association address, suggesting that in a closer association between the two professions, the physical educator could 'be identified as a kind of resident representative of the School Health Services'.[30] The physical educator's main task would then be to assist the work of the School Medical Officer; 'it would be a tremendous help to him (sic: the doctor) if there was someone on the teaching staff to whom he could talk about the child. He could tell them in general terms what he suspected might be wrong with the child, and give an indication of what might develop and what action might be taken'.[31] Dunlop considered that the physical educator could be more than simply a liaison, but her (in this case) activities should not encroach on the doctor's, suggesting that in training 'there might be less emphasis on the treatment of advanced orthopaedic conditions which are properly the province of the hospital service, and more on the early detection of diseases'. Not that teachers should be taught to diagnose diseases in any case, but they should 'know enough Anatomy and Physiology and medical terminology to study these subjects from sound textbooks, to answer questions intelligently, and to co-operate effectively with the school doctors'.[32] Besides being of assistance to the school doctor, the physical educator was in Dunlop's opinion the 'pre-eminent person' to teach hygiene, health education and sex hygiene.[33]

Despite this rather limited and unflattering role for physical educators mapped out in Dunlop's remarks, the medico–health framework nevertheless exerted a strong influence on the female physical educators' work within their own social class sphere, and persisted well into the 1950s, mainly among the Swedish gymnasts of the old school. They and others supported the view that the physical educator's role in relation to health lay in the traditional areas of hygiene and remedial work. One commentator claimed optimistically in 1947 that the link between the School Medical Officers and the physical education teachers was actually getting stronger.

> One often hears nowadays of a school doctor watching the gymnastic lesson and taking an interest in the pupils beyond the medical inspection. As a result, remedial gymnastic lessons achieve better and quicker results. One sees postural defects such as round shoulders, poking heads and flat foot cured in quick time through sympathetic teaching.[34]

There was support from politicians for physical education's contribution to 'the health side',[35] and also from some sections of the medical profession for physical educators to take an active role in closing the gap between themselves and doctors through remedial and rehabilitation work.[36] At a National Panel Committee meeting of the Ling Association in November 1948, participants claimed that some 'excellent co-operation' had been taking place between individual teachers, the Ling Association and School Medical Officers, but complained that there was too little contact with general practitioners. The meeting recommended to the Ling Association that personal contacts with the British Medical Association needed to be extended at local levels, that the Ling Association should offer lectures to medical practitioners, and that copies of the Association's Annual Report should be sent to selected members of the medical profession. In addition, as an outcome of the Committee's recommendations, the Ling Association itself proposed to write in protest to the Ministry of Health at an alleged tendency of LEAs to discontinue medical inspections of all school children except for entrants and leavers.[37] Later that year, the Ling Association's New Year Conference was devoted to 'Health Education in Schools', and concern was expressed over the evident neglect of health education in schools and teachers' apparent indifference to teaching about health matters.[38] One Lecturer in Health Education stressed the importance of the teacher's role in promoting hygiene among pupils, suggesting that 'the child needs to be stimulated and made conscious of the discomfort of dirt'. Meanwhile, at a conference on 'Health Education in Schools' in April 1949, the Scottish Council for Health Education concurred with the Ling Association's views on the importance of 'health teaching' in schools, considering that it should be aimed 'at the inculcation of right habits with the main emphasis on cleanliness and tidiness'. They also confirmed the key part physical educators should play, arguing that 'health teaching should be directly connected with physical education, both indoors and on the playing field...teaching of practical health principles should be in the hands of the physical instructors mainly'.[39]

Inevitably, with the expansion of the State secondary school system and the changes within the physical education profession, the Swedish gymnasts' view of the physical educator's role in health gradually began to fall apart as the 1950s progressed. While the physical educator's role in relation to hygiene was fairly widely accepted at this time, it was the treatment of postural and other physical defects that was becoming increasingly problematic. A conference on 'School Remedial Work' in 1951 revealed that some physical educators still considered this to be a legitimate part of their work, although many of the papers presented at the conference were delivered by medical practitioners.[40] Issues such as foot health continued to appear in the professional literature, but apparently remained important to fewer and fewer physical educators.[41] In 1957, a letter published in *The Leaflet* revealed the extent to which the traditional remedial gymnastics work of the female physical educator had been eclipsed, not only through change in the profession, but by the monopolizing activities of the medical profession. The letter was signed by a 'Gymnast of the Old School' who claimed to have been a member of the Ling Association for over thirty years, and following a career in teaching and as an LEA Adviser, was working as an exercise therapist in a general hospital. She complained that she was required to treat children with a range of preventable postural and foot problems and was thereby deflected from attending to patients who had suffered injuries and who were forced on to a waiting list. From her point of view, the problem lay in inadequate training of physical educators and neglect of remedial work in schools.

> What has happened to the training in School Remedials that used to be included in the syllabus in all recognized PE colleges? Is the present-day teacher unable to treat the type of condition I have described or even to prevent these cases of poor posture and inability to walk well developing in the children under their care? When a school uses the 'Posture Recorder', what happens to children shown by this appliance to have poor posture? Whose business is it to see that every child develops that habit of standing, sitting and walking well with easy deep breathing and strong, healthy feet? We in the Health Service are ready to do everything possible to rehabilitate the injured and sick patients who are sent to us for treatment, but we do grudge the time taken up doing work that used to be considered the primary aim of gymnastics in a school curriculum.[42]

A response to this letter appeared in the next issue of *The Leaflet* from a male teacher at St. John's School in Surrey, who pointed out that the fault may not lie with the profession at all.

> Too many PE teachers have 'burnt their fingers' by giving children with postural faults certain elementary exercises and then found themselves reprimanded by the SMO or head teacher for exceeding their duties. I do not think the fault in the whole question of the shortcomings of the school remedial work lies with the teachers or the training colleges, rather it may lie with the SMO and the Health Service. Had 'Gymnast of the Old School' looked into the pre-case history stage of the cases she

quoted, she might have found that the PE teachers had been told to keep their hands off medical and possible surgical cases and 'What did they think the Health Service was for?'[43]

This interchange reveals two important developments in the physical educator's relationship to the health of the school child by the mid 1950s. The first was that the traditional para-medical, remedial role of the Swedish gymnasts had finally been undermined, by a combination of educational gymnastics and new training methods from within, and by the influx of games-orientated men and the monopolizing activities of the medical profession from the outside. The second, while not stated explicitly as an issue in the exchange between Gymnast of the Old School and the St. John's School teacher, formed an undercurrent to their communication and was as far reaching as the the first development. This was a broadening view of health education in the immediate postwar period that went far beyond the physical dimensions of health. At the Ling Association Health Education Conference in December 1948, Dr Robert Sutherland modified some of the views expressed in his 1946 paper to present a concept of health education that encompassed physical, intellectual and emotional aspects, and appealed to physical educators to take 'a synthetic approach by considering what effect these exercises will have upon the intelligence, the emotions, and upon the social side of life'.[44] While his intent in this paper was to provide a rationale for the continuation of physical education as the *de facto* health education in schools, as a form of 'all-round development of the individual as well as the development of agility, physical strength and organic reserves', he showed by dint of his own argument that health was a multi-dimensional concept that drew on fields of study as diverse as anthropology, psychology, and sociology, as well as anatomy, physiology, nutrition and the like. The prospect of physical education encompassing this expansive terrain of ideas unhelpfully stretched the notion of 'physical education' beyond credibility and practicability, but it showed that health education could no longer be contained within concerns for disease prevention and treatment and the use of therapeutic exercise to remedy postural defects. In another paper published in the same volume of the *Journal of Physical Education*,[45] the Head of Accrington Girls' Grammar school described in detail the rationale and practice of health education in her school. In this case, health education was seen to be synonymous with the entire school curriculum, and health to permeate all other aspects of education. 'Health means wholeness' she claimed. 'There can be no separate section for mind and body. To attain wholeness and perfection, growth is necessary.' The influence of progressivist thinking is unmistakable in this account of health education, as it is in the attempt to use the concept of health as a means of integrating subject matter. While physical education had a part to play, its *de facto* status as health education was indefensible given the school's emphasis on such issues as slums and urban living, dietetics, hygiene, public health, smoke abatement, and mother craft; visits to places of relevance and interest like hospitals, nursery schools, and dairies; and collective project work on the part of the pupils. Both these examples of a broadening view of health education placed the Gymnasts of the Old School in an untenable position, since there was nothing in their training to prepare them to teach beyond the physical and functional aspects of health. They were caught between these two developments, robbed of their right to treat postural and other physical defects by the medical profession on the one hand, and outflanked by a more eclectic view of health education on the other.[46]

It needs to be stressed, however, that the erosion of the ideas associated with the Swedish gymnasts' role in health matters, and with the medical definition of physical education embedded in the state elementary schools of the pre-war era, was gradual and uneven throughout the postwar period. While, by the late 1950s, an older teacher may have been thought old-fashioned by her younger colleagues for her use of the Posture Recorder, echoes of the medico-health rationale and the idea of remedial work in physical education remained more pervasively in the form of beliefs, if not as actual practices. Hugh Brown for example, the Director of the Scottish School of Physical Education, proclaimed in characteristically Calvinistic fashion that:

> For a teacher to condemn tobacco and alcohol, and to have nicotine-stained fingers and an insatiable thirst is, obviously, nonsense. In fact, it is my belief that any man in our branch of teaching who smokes is a saboteur! If his school yard is littered with the discarded cigarette ends of his pupils he cannot wonder.[47]

Antagonism towards 'body pollutants' like tobacco and alcohol remained part of the physical education profession's popular view of its responsibility towards health practices in schools, even though the logical relationship between physical activity and the use or abuse of these substances was of no greater relevance to its work than it was to the teaching of the biology, chemistry or home economics staff. Similar beliefs about hygiene and other matters such as sexual behaviour also continued to be viewed by physical educators as part of their remit. This was particularly true of the role female physical educators adopted in relation to working class, adolescent girls who were close to school leaving age, and in this we can see the persistent presence of bourgeois protectionism and paternalism of the working classes, incorporating remnants of the patriarchal Victorian notions of the emotional and frail disposition of women. Dr Sutherland, in his 1948 paper, pronounced that physical education should engender 'grace, poise and expression' in girls, and provide an 'emotional and social outlet',[48] while at a 1960 Conference on Health, 'girls' movement training was acknowledged to be admirably suited to their needs and an outlet for the emotions'.[49] Moreover, it was through physical education lessons that working class girls were to be prepared for marriage and motherhood. At a 1952 Ling Association Conference on 'Gymnastics for Secondary Schoolgirls', the comment was made in a discussion group that:

> with regard to the task of keeping home and looking after children, it was pointed out that a mother was frequently called upon to make quick decisions, and it was believed that modern (educational gymnastics) work helped to train her to be self-reliant, to have self-respect and to set her own standards and to work to them — all essential qualities if she was to be successful in the home.[50]

More than a decade later and in response to another proposed raising of the school leaving age to sixteen following the Newsom Report, similar ideas were being expressed. One of the lecturers, a Miss Dawson:

> explained that one-third of the present population of women are married at nineteen and the 'Newsom' girls tend to marry earlier than those planning Further Education. Many girls in their last year may well have a steady boyfriend and physical education could help them prepare for marriage and motherhood...For those less interested in educational gymnastics, classes for poise, good grooming, developing clothes sense, and making good use of their figure might have more purpose. Instruction in the economy of effort in household chores: lifting of weights, training in family camping, could be given in curriculum time...It is characteristic of less able girls that they are fond of young children and like to 'mother' them. Perhaps girls who find no interest in playing field games could be happy to teach small games to young children in nearby primary schools.[51]

The relevance of these views of issues that had patently little to do with physical education in an epistemological sense becomes clear only when they are situated within the residual influence of the pre-war medio-health rationale, and more particularly in terms of the legacy of bourgeois opinions on the needs of the working classes. Health-related issues such as hygiene and grooming, tobacco and alcohol use, sex education and preparation for marriage and motherhood remained the property of the physical education profession who worked in working class settings long after the social and political circumstances that lead to the establishment of physical education within medico-health discourse in the early 1900s had been forgotten. During the late 1940s and early 1950s, and as the remedial role of the Swedish gymnast was being finally and irrevocably undermined, a new view of the relationship between physical education and health was emerging that owed much to the functionalism of the gymnasts, but which reformulated their notions of 'scientific physical education' within a powerful contemporary framework that promised to combat the twin evils of declining influence in the international market-place and failure in international sport through the development and promotion of physical fitness.

Fitness, Measurement and the Rise of Scientific Functionalism

The term physical fitness came to prominence in physical education discourse between the wars, exemplified most explicitly in the Keep Fit movement, though the question 'Fit for What?' exercised advocates until the second world war gave fitness an 'obvious' purpose and focus.[52] After the war, mass physical exercise and uniformed youth movements became less popular through their associations with Nazism, but the notion of fitness as the capacity to perform specific physical tasks[53] was, by virtue of their war experience, familiar to many returning soldiers and thereby formed one point of entry into popular consciousness. The success of the armed forces in preparing the British male civilian population for the rigours of armed combat consequently had a profound influence on the steadily increasing numbers of postwar male physical educators and, by the early 1950s, physical fitness was on the way to becoming established as the key linking concept between physical education and health. More than this, it was the development and measurement of strength through the application of the scientific principle of progressive overload that quickly formed the core of this new view of physical fitness, and in this we can see the projection of a conception of fitness that was explicitly gendered. It was fed by popular commonsense ideas of the time that suggested men's needs in physical education were quite different from women's, and most of this discourse was couched in psuedo–psychological expressions of 'human nature'.[54] In addition, this new view of fitness marked a departure from the way in which the Swedish gymnasts had conceptualized the effects of exercise on the body. As we saw in Chapter 4, strength was part of an internal dynamic that was focused in their terms by balance, proportion and harmony rather than the capacity to lift, throw, run, kick, or strike. The fundamental difference between the two views lay in the fact that the Swedish gymnasts had no wish to *do* anything in particular with their 'fitness'; if it had any utilitarian value, physical education developed a neuro-muscular framework on which more specific capacities might be developed. The male view was in direct contradiction of this principle, seeing fitness *as* a specific capacity to achieve some particular outcome, and it was the disparateness of the two views that underwrote the whole debate over gymnastics, discussed in detail in Chapter 4.

As I suggested in the previous section, elements of the medico-health legacy exerted a lingering but residual influence in physical education discourse through the 1950s and into the 1960s. But it was this new view of fitness that formed the dominant and favoured link between physical education and health, feeding at the same time into two specific concerns contemporary to the 1950s. The first was the demise of Britain's international sporting prowess, and the second, the country's diminishing influence as a world power, reflected in particular in the alleged self-satisfaction and moral and physical laxity of the workers which, it was claimed, was in large measure responsible for Britain's dismal performance in the international market-place. As we saw in Chapter 5, the conviction was being strongly expressed by the sports lobby in the late 1950s that lack of serious concern for physical fitness based on scientific principles was at the root of Britain's poor showing in international sport. And by the end of the 1950s, the proponents of the new view of physical fitness had begun to establish a more direct link between fitness and health, by claiming a key role in combatting the physical manifestation of the evils of affluence; sedentariness, the problem of the coronary heart disease and other related ills. The basis for these developments and associations between fitness and health lay in the establishment of 'scientific physical education' immediately following the second world war, and the growth of scientific research on the development and measurement of fitness and, in particular, strength.

Scientific Physical Education

The notion of 'scientific physical education' had been around since at least the mid 1800s, in Britain most prominent in the writing of physical educators like Archibald McLaren.[55] The Swedish gymnasts also employed the term in the title of their journal, *The Journal of Scientific Physical Training*.[56] In the sense in which it was used by both McLaren and the Swedish gymnasts, physical education was 'scientific' in so far as it was based on knowledge of human anatomy and physiology and applied by use of precise tables of physical exercises that worked through the entire range of possible movements of the joints and actions of the muscles in a systematic fashion. 'Scientific physical education' applied specifically to one or other of the systems of gymnastics, and not to the games and sports version of physical education practised in the male public schools. The use of the term within physical education circles after the second world war was not, therefore, unprecedented. However, with the demise of the influence of the female Swedish gymnasts, the meaning of 'scientific' that began to achieve widespread use in physical education discourse by the late 1940s was quite different from its predecessor. Clearly, this nineteenth century notion of science did not conform to the established twentieth century protocols and procedures of experimental, natural science, since it did not involve the collection of data, its manipulation by statistics, nor did it possess predictive power. In the 1940s and early 1950s in Britain, it was this view of science that found growing acceptance among male physical educators. Indeed, it was a rather uncritical acceptance of the natural science paradigm that led to ambivalence in some of the writing on the subject of 'scientific physical education' in the 1940s, since compared with the rigorous procedures and protocols of experimentation, physical education could only be seen to be deficient.

In one of the earliest discussions of physical education in relation to the natural science paradigm in British physical education discourse, David Munrow was not prepared to argue for a view of physical education as scientific in the same way that the gymnasts had done. Addressing a combined Ling Association and NAOLPE conference on 'Physical Education in Postwar Reconstruction' in 1942, he remarked with reference to physical education at Birmingham University that:

> In the university, there are to hand physiologists, psychologists and professors of education, all of whom can make a contribution to the advancement of our subject. Research work could be devised with the help of those having a full knowledge of experimental method, with its proper standardization of conditions, use of control groups and accurate analysis of statistical data. In the university, not only could further research be done but our present knowledge and beliefs, say in regard to the value of posture training, could be investigated. But it is the more indefinable, though not less valuable, effect of making physical education part of education, instead of apart from education, which I prefer to stress. Scientific enquiry is naturally to be welcomed though many of the factors with which physical education is concerned are not yet capable of exact measurement and I prefer to regard the subject as an art rather than a science.[57]

Munrow stuck by this view of physical education as an art consistently in the years that followed.[58] He did not deny, however, that there was a body of scientific knowledge which was of relevance to physical educators, but this was a different notion from the idea that physical education was itself scientific. Indeed, support grew rapidly after the war for the application of the natural science paradigm, with its experimental, predictive and quantitative procedures, to problems of apparent relevance and interest to physical educators, and Munrow and some of his colleagues at Birmingham were important and influential protagonists for scientific research in physical education.

The second world war had played an enormous role in generating new technologies, and one of the proclaimed successes of the armed forces was the creation of a technology of fitness development. In 1946, Brigadier Wand-Tetley described in the *Journal of Physical Education* how 'purposeful physical training' had been used by the British Army. He claimed that 'the science of body mechanics' had been applied to the development of 'dexterity and strength in the rifleman, to give him better neuro–muscular control and consequently to develop those qualities essential to good shooting'.[59] Troops were trained to lift and carry, and to vault from moving vehicles in full gear without injury. Although he did not use the term progressive overload in his paper, his description of endurance training, specifically tailored to the infantryman's needs, described this process precisely, explaining how troops were gradually trained to accomplish 'great feats of endurance without undue strain' by beginning with walking, then walking with a pack, gradually covering greater distances, then progressing from flat to hilly ground. Wand-Tetley suggested that in peacetime, 'skill and consequent enjoyment at games could be increased and the burden of industrial labour lightened considerably by the imaginative adaptation of purposeful training to sport and work'.[60] The Armed Services continued to contribute to physical education discourse into the mid 1950s,[61] and their work resonated strongly with the new view of fitness that had become established within the male division of the physical education profession. At the same time, there was little conscious celebration of the Armed forces' views on fitness among physical educators, despite this congruence. Perhaps the status conscious males were keen to distance themselves from the social inferiority they inherited from their predecessors, the army drill sergeants, and reluctant to foster associations with militarist forms of physical education in their raw state.

The influence of war-time developments in training were, nevertheless, far-reaching in physical education. In addition to creating a technology of fitness, the armed forces generated knowledge about the learning of specific tasks like shooting a rifle and operating complex machinery and instruments like radar. This work tapped an already existing and extensive body of experimental research on skill learning which was eagerly appropriated by physical educators after the war. One of the first syntheses of this literature and its application to physical education was carried out by Peter McIntosh in a paper on 'Skill and Physical Education' published in the *Journal of Physical Education* in 1948.[62] This was followed four years later by a paper on 'Transference of Training' authored by David Munrow,[63] in which he argued that the question of transference of training, particularly in relation to the Swedish and educational gymnasts' claims to be able to develop generalized co-ordination, and the extent to which skill practices contributed to the development of the whole skill, formed a highly appropriate field for investigation by experimental science. Closely linked to this interest in skill learning was 'human kinetics' or kinesiology, which focused on the mechanics of muscle actions, the movement of limbs, and the forces acting on the body in motion. During the 1940s and early 1950s, at least half-a-dozen books appeared on kinesiology, most of them from the United States, and in 1952, the first British book on this subject appeared. *Human Kinetics and Analysing Body Movements* was written by T. McLurg Anderson, Principal of the Scottish Physiotherapy School and Director of the Institute of Human Kinetics.[64] Anderson claimed that human kinetics was a scientific approach to research on the body that had been in the process of development from the late 1920s at the Scottish Physiotherapy Hospital.[65] In his book, he added to an extensive knowledge of anatomy and well-established physiological material a mechanical analysis, creating his own terminology to analyze movement and effort. He also used slow-motion filming of sports performers to produce line drawings as illustrations of his analyses, and while his professional experience was substantially in remedial medical work, his analyses of a number of athletic events demonstrated the direct relevance of this kind of work to the coaching of advanced and elite sports performers.[66]

These developments in applying the natural science paradigm to researching skill learning and body mechanics made important contributions to the notion of a scientific basis to physical education. However, it was mainly through physiology and its applications to exercise that the natural science method was introduced most powerfully to physical educators. By the late 1940s, the term scientific was still being applied to non-experimental research and teaching in physical education,[67] but this use contrasted markedly with new research that was emerging on the development of endurance and strength.[68] This experimental research in the physiology of exercise had an immediate and direct impact on the content of professional preparation courses. At a Ling Association National Panel Committee Meeting in 1949, concern was expressed over whether a 'scientific background' might soon be required of students in order for them to understand the physiology being taught in the colleges.[69] It also had a rapid and profound effect on the leadership of Ling Association. In 1950, an Editorial in *The Leaflet* on 'Research and Professional Status' commented that physical education was a 'young profession reaching maturity', and noted the growing volume of research being carried out at Birmingham, Manchester and Durham Universities where 'physical educationists are collecting facts, sifting evidence, and material is being prepared for publication'. In a prophetic statement, the editor concluded that the status of the profession depended on this research.[70] Two years later, *The Leaflet* published a notice from the 'Men's Advisory Sub-Committee' which proposed to run a course in 1954 that 'might be arranged in conjunction with the women members which would make a widespread appeal to men. Such a course might focus attention on a subject of fundamental interest to all, such as the physiology of exercise'.[71] This 'fundamental' interest in physiology of exercise was further promoted through the encouragement of some sections of the medical profession. In 1953 the Editor of *The Leaflet* celebrated the attention of the British Association to the 'Physiology of Athletic Training', which was the title of a lecture delivered by Professor Hemmingway, who was interested almost exclusively in the use of physiology to service the needs of elite athletes. This point was overlooked in the Editor's enthusiasm, however, in the comment that 'physical education surely is a science designed to promote physical health by judicious exercise of the body and let us not be afraid to add also the mind, in conformity with physiological factors. To this extent, therefore, medical science enters into the picture as well'.[72] In the same issue of

The Leaflet, Dr Roger Bannister published the results of a physiological study of 'The Control of Breathing During Exercise'.

The 1950s were an important period of gestation for this base of scientific knowledge for physical education. The ready and direct applications of some of this knowledge to work with elite sports performers and in schools also gave this new knowledge legitimacy, though at this stage this was confined mainly to male physical educators, sports coaches and some other interested parties. With the expansion of the curriculum in school physical education to include competitive games and sports, the pre-war notion of 'scientific physical education' was no longer a viable one by the 1950s, but there was considerable and growing support for a not entirely dissimilar idea among college and university based researchers. As early as 1955, David Munrow was arguing that researchers in physical education needed to take responsibility themselves for scientific and other research directly relevant to their interests since 'the study of the body's mechanical and psycho-physiological behaviour in acquiring and performing physical skills, is an area not being fully tackled by any other branch of learning'.[73] This notion was echoed a decade later by Franklin Henry, Professor of Physical Education at the University of California at Berkeley, who argued that the time was ripe for the development of physical education as an academic discipline at tertiary level.[74] Henry outlined what was to become, through the 1960s and 1970s, the accepted model for the development of degree courses in physical education based on a collection of sub-disciplines. He suggested that physical education 'considered as an academic discipline, does not consist of the application of the disciplines of anthropology, physiology, psychology and the like to the study of physical education. On the contrary, it has to do with the study, as a discipline, of certain aspects of anatomy, anthropology, physiology, psychology, and other appropriate fields'.[75] He accepted that there was no clearcut line between subject matter properly belonging to the sub-disciplines or to physical education, and suggested tentatively that 'the study of the heart as an organ is physiology, whereas determining the quantitative role of the heart action as a limiting factor in physical performance is perhaps more physical education than physiology'.[76] Despite this ambiguity, the idea underpinning both Henry's and Munrow's advocacy of physical education as an academic discipline was that there was sufficient coherence within the knowledge base of physical education to enable its consolidation as a distinctive field in its own right. And while neither wished to exclude non-experimental research from this scheme, the momentum behind such an idea was coming with few exceptions from the scientific functionalists, those researchers whose interests lay in the application of the natural science paradigm to the investigation of physical, functional phenomena.[77]

The few dissonant voices with regard to this view were to be found among the educational gymnasts when they could be stirred to commit themselves to a written critique, and even then their concerns tended to be expressed, as we saw in Chapter 4, mainly in terms of defending their practice from male attacks on their version of physical education. Within physical education discourse, no-one directly challenged the legitimacy of the natural science paradigm and the value of its procedures, and few questioned the notion of scientifically-based physical education. K.A. Schrecker's 1952 critique of the idea of 'scientific physical education' stood alone in the physical education literature as a dissenting view which attacked on its own terrain the basic premises upon which the notion rested.

Schrecker examined both the pre- and postwar views of science in physical education, and concluded that 'physical education as a whole can never conform in a great measure to a theory based mainly upon science',[78] since the knowledge generated by experimentation had, by virtue of its controlled, scientific nature, only limited application to the messy and uncertain realities of teaching. He stated frankly that 'physical educationists are making fools of themselves by advertising their work as something it cannot be', while scientists who 'deem it appropriate to disparage a thing because it cannot be fully verified and controlled with their own methods, are revealing that narrowness of thought which is the typical sign of an unphilosophic mind'. Schrecker argued that science had made a negligible impact on school physical education in the United States, which he regarded as the stronghold of scientific physical education, and asked whether this was:

> by any means astonishing, if one realizes the spirit which emanates not only from the 'Research Quarterly', but from the bulk of modern scientific literature on physical education? That spirit, staggering under the burden of statistically sifted evidence, is souless, chilling and barren, apt to stifle any enthusiasm for practical teaching in young physical educationists. The lesser evil of it is that many of those who succumb to it become prone to indulge in hair-splitting quibbling, thus detracting many a valuable thing. What is more serious is that a stickler for the chimera of a scientific physical education, when realizing its futility, as sooner or later he (sic) must, is inclined to lose confidence altogether, in himself and his work. This is, in fact, the tragedy of a great many physical education students today, and unduly prolonged study — not to speak of degree hunting — is for quite a number of them quite a convenient means of escape from the reality of teaching, for which they do not feel a match.[79]

This ferocious critique from Schrecker raised neither a murmur of disagreement nor concurrence in the literature, despite the fact that there was more than a grain of the truth in his accusations of status-seeking and hair-splitting quibbling.[80] At the same time, as we will see shortly, not all of the proponents and practitioners of scientific functionalism were entirely ignorant of the dangers and problems to which Schrecker alluded. But this lone dissenting voice was quite insubstantial compared with the overwhelming interest of male physical educators in the apparent benefits of scientific research to physical education, and it was in the context of this expanding field of interest and influence that the new view of physical fitness was located.

The Hard Core of Scientific Functionalism: Fitness, Strength, Endurance

Many of the proponents of scientific functionalism in physical education considered themselves to be swimming against a tide of popular prejudice and misconception regarding what they considered to be the proper function of physical education, and the actual effects of fitness training on the body. Mac-Queen argued in 1955 that 'prejudice dies hard, probably more so in Britain than elsewhere. The misconception that exercise with weights makes one slow, clumsy and 'muscle bound' is still held by many...yet there is not one scrap of scientific evidence to support this notion'.[81] They also situated themselves squarely in the camp of the progressivists to the extent that they supported wholeheartedly the individualization of physical education activities. The main reasons for individualization were not those proposed by the educational gymnasts, though, but were to do instead with the need for motivation which in turn required regular measurement, the maintenance of records and the production of norms and standards against which pupils could compare their own performances. One author suggested that 'measurement provides the fuel for the drives towards training; the aim of the method is self-improvement via increased demands'.[82] Another argued that the days of regimentation in the gym lesson had passed, but 'as long as we also claim that physical training and gymnastics should improve strength, physique and physical performance, these aspects are measureable and the sooner we assess our results the firmer will be the basis of physical education'.[83] The adoption of this rhetoric certainly presented the appearance of progressive values, though the final court of appeal, suggested in the latter statement, was expressed in the values of recording, measurement and achievement associated with the natural science paradigm. Moreover, as we will see with the development of circuit training, individual improvement was situated at the centre of a new form of pedagogy in which the teacher took a subsidiary role and the motivation to work harder involved a displacement of values from the externalized regulation of the group to the internalized drives of the individual.

The experimental methods and procedures of the natural science paradigm and the production of quantitative data derived from studies of strength, muscular endurance, cardio-respiratory endurance, and power formed the 'hard core'[84] of scientific functionalism. Within this core, the key assumption was that whatever else physical education may contain, the *basic* and *essential* element was functional physical activity. Implicit in the scientific functionalist's view of physical education was a hierarchy of aims and related types of activity, and the defining aim of any programme that deserved the label physical education was the improvement of the physical and physiological performance of an individual. This was the baseline, and after this aim had been met, other objectives were permissible, a point that was clearly articulated by McDonald, writing in 1957.

> During the past three decades or so, we have rapidly moved from a conception of Physical Training to one of Physical Education. Today the principle of 'education through the physical' is so well established that many feel the word 'physical' could well be discarded, the term Education alone being quite sufficient...It seems to me, however, that somewhere along this road of progress we have forgotten that our principle concern is with the physical...(and I) take strong issue with those in physical education who emphasize the social psychological objectives and neglect the development of muscle power and endurance ...The physical is basic and all students should be assured of a minimum amount of this basic quality.[85]

McDonald's insistence on physical activity as a basic requirement of physical education had the appearance of good common sense, but his request was not for physical activity of just any kind. If it had been, the educational gymnasts could easily have reassured him that things were not as desperate as they seemed. But what marked-off this statement as characteristic of scientific functionalism was the insistence by McDonald on a particular type of physical activity and a particular way of looking at physical education, in which the 'development of muscle power and endurance' were central.

The principle of progressive overload and its practical application through the idea of 'Progressive Resistance Exercises' developed by the American T L De Lorme in the field of exercise rehabilitation in the 1940s, was the key to developing both strength and endurance. De Lorme's studies[86] were widely cited by the British scientific functionalists and his ideas were applied particularly to the use of weights in strength training and in circuit training, and later to intermittent running. De Lorme himself was reportedly critical of physical educators and athletic coaches who neglected strength training, on the grounds that besides reducing the likelihood of injury, 'most activities will be performed more successfully and with less fatigue when greater strength and endurance are present'.[87] The British writers accepted this point uncritically. McDonald claimed that 'there is a realization of the fundamental fact that man (sic) needs strength and endurance. Whether it be the housewife, typist, labourer, factory worker or professional man, all need strength, enough at least to perform their daily tasks economically and without undue fatigue — and a little extra in reserve for the emergency that may overtake each or all of us at some time throughout life'.[88] MacQueen added to this the suggestion that Britain's failure to win a gold medal at the 1952 Olympic Games was due to the fact that 'the British athletes had not the sheer strength reserve of their foreign...rivals',[89] and echoed De Lorme's comment that there would be less injuries and a higher level of performance among performers of modest abilities if they undertook strength training. According to these accounts, strength was considered to be essential to all sections of the population, and the same methods centred on Progressive Resistence Exercises could be applied to each case to beneficial effect.

The publication of Morgan and Adamson's *Circuit Training*[90] in 1957 was arguably the single most important contribution of the decade to scientific discourse in physical education in terms of giving expression to some of the key ideas of the scientific functionalists, and in addition providing male physical educators with a set of practical principles and a technology for fitness development in schools. Morgan and Adamson developed circuit training on the basis of experimental work at Leeds University,[91] in their quest to discover a form of fitness training that held students' interest and improved their fitness at the same time. These experiments had been going on since the end of the second world war, and followed closely the procedures of natural science involving pre- and post-tests, experimental and control groups, a limited and carefully defined set of variables, quantitative measures and correlational analyses. Their claims for circuit training based on this work were that it:

> will meet a definite need in the physical education of boys and young men. It satisfies the modern demand that pupils shall be treated as individuals and not in the mass, and that they shall pursue their activity with the minimum of direction from the teacher. It calls for their intelligent co-operation at every stage. It is based on principles which are

biologically sound and its nature is such that performers are able to observe their own improvement. It has an undeniable recreative appeal. It is flexible enough to allow a bias towards one or another special aspect of fitness, while retaining the essential idea of all-round fitness for athletics and everyday life.[92]

Circuit training was, according to Morgan and Adamson, scientifically, technically and educationally progressive. In addition, they stressed the point that participants could see their improvement in measurable terms, and suggested that regular testing and the establishment of standards were a logical extension of the use of circuit training. They set these advantages in the context of school physical education programmes, arguing that while the educational, social and psychological dimensions of physical education had been justifiably emphasized through the 1940s and early 1950s, physical educators had neglected to develop 'the power of the human machine'. They saw circuit training as a means of redressing this imbalance that was, at the same time, consistent with progressive, child-centred principles. They also went to some lengths to stress that circuit training 'should not in any way supplant the training in skills which must be the supreme manifestation of physical education in schools'[93] and that it 'is not the whole of a boy's physical education, nor does it come early in his school career'.[94] They intended circuit training to be put to best use in schools with boys aged fourteen and over; 'it is at this age that boys become interested in their own development, physical as well as intellectual, and it is at this age...they begin to take part in pursuits which call for a high degree of strength and endurance'.[95] At this stage girls, unsurprisingly, did not figure in this scheme at all.

Morgan and Adamson's system achieved a high level of popularity among male physical educators in a relatively short period of time. In the June 1955 issue of *The Leaflet*,[96] two teachers reported an 'experiment' with circuit training in their schools. The following year, sixty-six men attended a conference on circuit training at Leeds University,[97] and in 1957 the theme of the PEA Christmas Conference was 'The Place of Strength and Stamina Training in PE'.[98] Morgan and Adamson had emphasized that circuit training was not designed primarily for sports performers, commenting that 'we are not all ambitious seekers after maximum physical fitness, willing to submit ourselves to the inexorable increase in the intensity of training',[99] and they strongly discouraged any attempts to make the circuit itself competitive. Nevertheless, they acknowledged that it was mainly sports performers who supported the circuits provided for students at Leeds University, and this use of circuit training as preparation for competitive sport became more frequent by the late 1950s. The Exeter based St. Lukes College rugby team reported on the beneficial effects of training and particularly circuit work on their performances,[100] and several conferences on 'Fitness for Sport' were organized during 1958 and 1959.[101] Female sports performers were also enthused by this new fitness work, with the CCPR organizing a conference on 'Fitness Training for Sportswomen' in 1958.[102] At the same time, interest in fitness was not confined to sports performers and by the end of the 1950s, the success of circuit training in highlighting the new view of physical fitness had also inspired a range of studies of the fitness of school pupils, which had the effect of introducing many of the scientific functionalists' notions about scientific research in physical education to teachers in schools.[103]

The significance of circuit training went far beyond its practical efficacy for developing physical fitness. It embodied the major tenets of scientific functionalism in physical education and signalled the power and potential of this way of thinking about physical activity to produce measurable results in relation to particular dimensions of sports performance and health. Not only did it mark a break with the old-fashioned pre-war view of the therapeutic purpose and effect of exercise on physical performance, but it satisfied, for its proponents at least, the main requirements of truly scientific work in physical education, and provided them with the legitimacy and status they so eagerly sought. Despite the fact that the hard core of fitness was defined by men for boys and men in masculine terms, the scientific functionalists absorbed some of the central notions of the child-centred gymnasts, projecting an image of circuit training and other forms of fitness training and their associated measurement tools as progressive, modern, individualized *and* scientific. Indeed, it was this absorption and appropriation of progressivist ideas like individualization that allowed the scientific functionalists to reconstruct the relationship between physical activity and health on the basis of their new view of fitness after the collapse of the medico-health framework. In the process, the male physical educators were one professional group among others responsible for stimulating social concern in the late 1950s over the less-than-wholesome spin-offs of affluence and technological innovation which were manifesting themselves in sedentariness and the resultant problems of obesity and coronary heart disease.

A New View of Fitness and Health

By the mid 1950s, the idea was becoming well established in British physical education discourse that people living in highly urbanized and industrialized areas were in greater need than their forebears of regular and self-consciously conducted exercise. Most often, this was seen to be part of an inevitable evolutionary process, in which increasing affluence and technological advancement contributed to physical deterioration. This perspective was clearly expressed in McDonald's 1957 comment that 'somewhere along the road of progress' in physical education:

> we have forgotten that our principal concern is with the physical. This is an omission, made all the more serious in this modern age of automation and sedentary living. Physically, man (sic) hasn't changed very much throughout the centuries — perhaps a little less surface hair, a narrowing of the jaws, not so much of the bent knee stance — but his way of life differs greatly from that of his more primitive ancestors. His muscles, for example, which thrive on movement, are today as a rule sadly neglected.[104]

Implicit in this critique of the physically degenerative effects of modern living was a view of the relationship between exercise and health that challenged the opinion of some sections of the medical profession. Schrecker related that 'according to Dr E. Jokl, it would seem that health and physical fitness have nothing to do with each other. Those physiological adaptations which are effected by physical training are supposed to be unimportant for our health because the structural and functional changes involved in them are apparently useless under pathological conditions'.[105] However, while the scientific functionalists conceded that fitness 'bore no relation to resistance to disease... physical education could stave off degenerative diseases and the products of the unnatural stresses of urban life'.[106] In the same vein, Peter McIntosh argued:

> surely the old idea that you could survive the winter without a 'cold' provided you did enough 'keep fit' exercises must be extinct by now. Health is a mental as well as a physical attribute. With more automation, urbanization and mechanical transport, the need to encourage pride in physical efficiency and to demonstrate the well-being and pleasure that come through the exercise of physical skill becomes increasingly important.[107]

Automation, mechanization, urbanization and sedentariness were the recurrent themes of this new view of the relationship between fitness and health, and the scientific functionalists considered that physical education in schools had a key role to play in combatting the evil side-effects of affluence. By the beginning of the 1960s news was beginning to reach the physical education profession that there was a relationship between obesity and coronary heart disease and between sedentariness and obesity.[108] Regular exercise, they were told, had a part to play in preventing the onset of the so-called risk factors associated with coronary heart disease, but this exercise had to be of a type that would inspire pupils to want to continue with it beyond their school years[109] and of sufficient intensity and duration to substantially affect the relevant physiological systems.[110]

However, the significance of this new relationship between exercise and health was more symbolic than practical during this time. Due to the way in which fitness had been reconstructed by the male scientific functionalists, with its hard core of strength and endurance training and concomitant tools of recording and measuring, the practical effect on school physical education of this news was, in the late 1950s and on into the 1960s, confined largely to male teachers and their pupils. And even among these teachers, competitive games and sports were, as we saw in Chapter 5, the major element of the physical education programme. Through the 1960s, circuit and weight training became established as indoor activities for older boys, taking up no more than twenty per cent of curriculum time of fifteen year old pupils allocated to what were regarded as minor indoor activities.[111] The application of the new scientific knowledge of the skill acquisition process, the mechanics of movement and the technology of fitness could be applied to improving the performance of games players, to be sure, and this became a major practical use of the new knowledge due to the overwhelming dominance of the 'traditional physical education' discourse, rather than its calculated use as a means of promoting the health of pupils.[112] Nevertheless, while the health connection played only a minor role in the physical educator's practice, the symbolism of the new connection between exercise and health served a vital function in the justificatory rhetoric for maintaining the physical educator's involvement in the health sphere, in a way that was seen to be contemporary and scientific.

The dominance of 'traditional physical education' in the form of competitive

team games among the male physical educators and the
progressivism of educational gymnastics among the fem⟨
during the 1960s to the influence of hard core scientific fⁱ
programmes.[113] There were also concerns from within ⁽
ranks of the scientific functionalists themselves over the eⁱ
work on pupils in the broader than merely physiological sense, -
the principles underpinning its practice. David Munrow, for instance, noteu ⟨
tendency to 'equate the taking of exercise with improved health' and cautioned
against this reduction of the meaning of health within physical education as
pertaining mainly to the physical.[114] He also expressed some concern, as early as
1956, over the kinds of attitudes boys may develop towards their individual
sexual identities given the heavily gendered character of so much of the work in
what he termed gymnastic programmes. While he supported the notion that a
fitness programme required physical challenges, testing and measurement to
work:

> such an approach, however, does carry with it potential dangers. Boys
> live in a general climate of opinion which tends to identify maleness and
> male characteristics with the mesomorphic physique. Some adolescent
> boys strive towards a physique which they cannot by any amount of
> exercise develop and they may acquire marked feelings of inferiority if
> this sort of gymnastic programme is badly presented.[115]

Girls, he felt, were likely to suffer problems of a different kind, although they
too were vulnerable to feelings of insecurity and disenchantment if their experience in physical education revealed that their own bodies could not match their
ideal of 'feminine beauty'.

> Feminine physical beauty is not allied markedly to any of Sheldon's
> somatotypes and there is thus no danger of whole hearted devotion to
> types of exercise which one can predict as highly unrewarding for
> certain individuals. On the contrary. Current standards of feminine
> beauty — purveyed to an enormous public through films and magazines
> are allied so often to standards of languid elegance — that women
> colleagues often find a considerable resistance in adolescent groups to
> any form of energetic movement at all.[116]

Although the actual effect on boys' and girls' participation in physical education activities may have been diametrically opposite in terms of results, Munrow
was suggesting that the concerns underlying their disparate behaviour were
motivated by a similar intensification of interest and anxiety invested in body
shape. Peter McIntosh provided an inkling of what these concerns might be
when he noted in 1963 that 'girls and, to a lesser extent, boys are more concerned
about the impression made by their shape than by the quality of their movements.[117] Certainly, for males the work of researchers like Sheldon had scientized
body shape by establishing his three categories of ideal types, endo, ecto, and
mesomorph, while for women, the movies and magazines had in parallel glamo-
rized body shape. In both cases, the body had become an object of desire, and

cular body shapes material manifestations of masculinity and femininity. The implications of these insights were not followed through at this time by physical educators although, as we saw in Chapter 4, the polarization of males and females through the ways in which the body and physical activity were conceptualized were well understood by many physical educators, and the educational gymnasts in particular. When critiques were mounted, their authors tended to adopt established attitudes on particular issues. For instance, one senior LEA Adviser for Physical Education attacked the work of N C Cooper on 'Fitness Testing of Junior School Children'[118] on the grounds that 'in recent years physical education has made a vital and distinguished contribution not only to the physical but to the mental, aesthetic and, indeed, even the moral development of children', and that the establishment of fitness standards was a 'reversion' to outmoded practices.[119] This continuing polarization of 'old' versus 'new' has indeed been a prominent characteristic of the struggles within physical education to define what are perceived to be the proper forms of practice appropriate to the subject, and so while these criticisms of Munrow and McIntosh were, to a certain extent from the inside, they were most likely to be enthusiastically endorsed by those who already understood these insights and studiously ignored by those in most need of them. This point could, indeed, be made with some conviction in relation to a particularly insightful comment made by Peter McIntosh to the 'Royal Society of Health' in the 1963 Chadwick Trust Lecture.

> My last word is one of warning. Fitness as a topic and as a personal requirement has in recent years been receiving more and more attention, especially in the USA. The more affluent the society, the more attention that is paid to fitness. This attention could become a preoccupation even an obsession. Fitness campaigns would then be a mark not of a virile and healthy society but of a decadent civilization.[120]

Notes

1 Thomson, I. (1984) 'Almond of Loretto: Origins and development of his system of health education', *Scottish Journal of Physical Education*, **12**(1), 32–36.
2 For example, between 1850 and 1900, the percentage of the world's population living in cities of 20,000 people or more increased from 4.3 per cent to 9.2 per cent, and 100,000 or more from 2.3 per cent to 5.5 per cent; in Giddens, A. (1982) *Sociology: A Brief but Critical Introduction*, San Diego: Harcourt Brace Jovanovich, p. 7.
3 Thomson, I. (1978) 'The origins of physical education in state schools, *Scottish Educational Review*, **10**(2), 15–24.
4 Jolly, W. (1876) *Physical Education and Hygiene in Schools*, London: John Kempster and Co. Ltd, p. 19.
5 Jolly, note 4, p. 21.
6 Thomson, I. (1979) 'Over-pressure and physical deterioration factors leading to the acceptance of physical education 1880–1895', *Physical Education Review*, **2**(2), 115–122.
7 Thomson, note 6.
8 Under the payment-by-results scheme.
9 McIntosh, P.C. (1968) *PE in England Since 1800*, London: Bell (Second Edition); Thomson, note 3.

10 Williams, A. (1988) 'The historiography of health and fitness in physical education', *PEA Research Supplement*, **3**, p. 1.
11 This is confirmed by Thomson, note 6.
12 Thomson, I. (1986) 'Militarism and Scottish schools in the Boer war era', *Physical Education Review*, **8**(2), 110–119.
13 While the agitation for drill came to a head in Scotland, the Royal Commission generated an Interdepartmental Commitee which produced the first Syllabuses for Physical Training in 1905 for both England and Scotland.
14 Board of Education/Scotch Education Department (1903) *The Royal Commission on Physical Training (Scotland)* London: HMSO.
15 Thomson, note 3, p. 21.
16 Thomson, note 12, p. 117.
17 Michel Foucault's investigations of professional knowledges, which give particular prominence to the rise of medical science in the nineteenth century, illustrate the ways in which it was possible to exercise power over the materiality of the body through a range of institutions such as schools, hospitals, asylums and factories. See especially the chapter entitled 'Body/Power' in Gordon, C. (1979 Ed.) *Michel Foucault: Power/Knowledge*, The Harvester Press, and Turner, B. (1984) *The Body and Society*, Oxford: Blackwell.
18 Graves, J. (1942) *Policy and Progress in Secondary Education*, London: Thomas Nelson, p. 85.
19 Board of Education (1933) *Syllabus of Physical Training for Schools*, London: HMSO, p. 12 emphasis in original.
20 Newman, note 19, p. 6.
21 Newman, note 19, p. 8.
22 Newman, note 19, pp. 6 and 9.
23 Williams, note 10, p. 1.
24 McIntosh, P.C. (1963) *Sport in Society*, London: Bell, p. 108.
25 *The Leaflet*, **45**(6), 1946, pp. 123–4.
26 Relating mainly to age, types of medical treatment, social class and associations with the working classes.
27 Sutherland, R. (1946) 'Public health — Modern methods of fighting disease', *Journal of Physical Education*, **38**, 124–133.
28 This point of view is confirmed in this comment from Dalzell-Ward, A.J. (1960) 'Trends in health education', *Physical Education*, **52**, 76–79. 'It was...understandable that the medical interest was mainly pathological in character and that the educationist's interest was either what was the effect of pathology in education or how could pathological conditions be avoided. The promotion of health by physical education obviously depended first upon the eradication of pathological conditions since underweight, anaemia, discharging ears, tuberculosis or rheumatism relegated activity and movement to a secondary position', p. 78.
29 Dunlop, J.L. (1949) 'The educational gymnast and the school health service', *Journal of Physical Education*, **41**, 129–134.
30 Dunlop, note 29, p. 130.
31 Dunlop, note 29, p. 131.
32 Dunlop, note 29, p. 134.
33 Dunlop, note 29, p. 132.
34 Spafford, P. (1947) 'Gymnastics, modern teaching methods in Great Britain', *Journal of Physical Education*, **39**, p. 103.
35 *The Leaflet*, **45**(6), 1946, p. 121, report on a lecture by David Hardman MP, Parlimentary Secretary to the Minister of Education; 'Physical fitness was of increasing importance as a factor in good health and improved industrial production.' Mr Ellis Smith, Labour MP, *TES* 6 August 1954, p. 760.

36   Report of a comment made by a Dr Balme at the Ling Association's New Year Conference in 1947, in *The Leaflet*, **49**(2), 32–34, 1948.

37   Report on the National Panel Meetings held in November 1948 in *The Leaflet*, **50**(1), 1949.

38   Report on the Ling Association's New Year Conference in the *TES* 1 January 1949, p. 1.

39   *TES* 30 April 1949.

40   *The Leaflet*, **53**(6), 1952.

41   Miss N Chatterton, Remedial Organizer for Hertfordshire; Chatterton N (1954) 'The problem of foot health in schools', *Journal of Physical Education*, **46**, p. 39.

42   Letter from 'Gymnast of the old school' in *The Leaflet*, **58**(9), 1957.

43   Letter in *The Leaflet*, **58**(10), 1957.

44   Sutherland, R. (1949) 'Some aspects of health education', *Journal of Physical Education*, **41**, 24–30.

45   Brown, D. (1949) 'Health education in the grammar school', *Journal of Physical Education*, **41**, 71–81.

46   Commenting on the Plowden Report, published in 1967, Peter McIntosh cited the evidence of surveys showing 30 per cent of population had foot defects originating in childhood, and noted that the task of prevention proposed by the Committee was awarded to chiropody and remedial exercise, but no mention was made of a possible contribution by the physical education profession. McIntosh maintains this shows the extent of change in primary physical education between 1900 and 1968; McIntosh, note 9, p. 279.

47   Brown, H.C. (1958) 'The training of the man teacher of physical education', *Physical Education*, **50**, p. 93.

48   Sutherland, note 44, p. 27.

49   *The Leaflet*, **61**(1), 1960.

50   *The Leaflet*, 1952, p. 68.

51   *The Leaflet*, **66**(1), 1965, p. 3.

52   McIntosh, note 9, p. 250; and as Brigadier Wand-Tetley commented 'fighting fit and fit to fight', Wand-Tetley, H.T. (1946) 'Purposeful physical training in the army', *Journal of Physical Education*, **38**, 140–143.

53   See Schecker, K.A. (1954) 'Physical fitness', *Journal of Physical Education*, **46**, 45–52/55, for a contemporary analysis.

54   For example, according to Sutherland, note 44, p. 27, 'So far as men are concerned, it is important that physical activity should have a purpose; and I believe men enjoy physical activity which has an element of aggression in it. It allows them to rid themselves in the easiest way of the impulses towards aggression which otherwise might display themselves in more unpleasent directions'. For David Munrow 'Systems of exercises, with their implied promise of poise and graceful carriage, will persists in their appeal for many women and girls. Again, just as the sthenic (sic) emotions are stronger in the male, so are the activities more numerous with which he can satisfy those emotions; some of them, as for instance, boxing, are particularly masculine and, correspondingly, we may expect to find some peculiarly feminine activities'. Munrow, A.D. (1942) Physical Education in the Universities. Paper presented at the Conference on Physical Education in Post-War Reconstruction, London, February, p. 5.

55   McLaren, A. (1895) *A System of Physical Education: Theoretical and Practical*, Oxford, (Revised Edition).

56   See Moyse, Y. (1949) 'A brief outline of some of the activities of the Ling Physical Education Association', *Journal of Physical Educaton*, **41**, 31–53 and 77–89.

57   Munrow, note 54, p. 6.

58 See Munrow, A.D. (1963) *Pure and Aplied Gymnastics*, London: Arnold. When the degree course at Birmingham eventually arrived in 1948, it was an elective subject within the Bachelor of Arts degree.

59 Wand-Tetley, note 52, p. 141.

60 Wand-Tetley, note 52, p. 143.

61 For instance, *The Leaflet* ran a series of three articles by the Navy (July 1955), the Army (October 1955) and the RAF (March 1956).

62 McIntosh, P.C. (1948) 'Skill and Physical Education', *Journal of Physical Education*, **40**, 130–137.

63 Munrow, A.D. (1952) 'Transference of Training', *Journal of Physical Education* 44, 49–54.

64 McLurg, Anderson, T. (1952) *Human Kinetics and Analysing Body Movements* London: Heinemann.

65 McLurg, Anderson, T. (1955) *The Leaflet*, **56**(3), p. 6.

66 This is not to say that Anderson himself saw the development of human kinetics as solely or even mainly for this purpose. Interestingly, he straddles the older therapeutic view of exercise and the more recent natural science view of knowledge production — see McLurg, Anderson, T. (1952) 'Problems in physical education', *Journal of Physical Education*, **44**, 55–60.

67 For example, Cyriax, V. (1949) 'The physiological effect of physical exercise', *Journal of Physical Education*, **41**, 145–151; and some of the papers read at the European Congress on Physical Education, Lisbon, 1947, listed in *The Leaflet*, **48**(6), 135–138, 1947.

68 See, for example, Asmussen, E. and Boje, O. (1950) 'Body temperature and capacity for work', *Journal of Physical Education*, **42**, 48–66; De Lorme, T.L. and Watkins, A.L. (1951) *Progressive Resistence Exercise: Technics and Medical Applications*, New York: Appleton-Century-Crofts; Adamson, G.T. (1952) 'Effect of systematic overload on the strength, physical fitness and physical efficiency of schoolboys', *Journal of Physical Education*, **44**, 109–112; Adamson, G.T. (1953) 'Effect of developmental training on physical fitness', *Journal of Physical Education*, **45**, 22–25.

69 *The Leaflet*, **50**(1), 1949; some in attendance at the meeting expressed the fear that science training may overwhelm the arts work.

70 *The Leaflet*, **51**(10), 1950, p. 210.

71 *The Leaflet*, **53**(10), 1952, p. 159.

72 *The Leaflet*, **54**(8), 1953.

73 Munrow, A.D. (1955) *The Leaflet*, **56**(1), p. 6.

74 Henry, F.M. (1965) 'Physical education as an academic discipline', *The Leaflet*, **66**(1), 6–7.

75 Henry, note 74, p. 6.

76 Henry, note 74, p. 7.

77 For some writers like James Oliver, 'research' and experimental methods *were* synonymous. 'It will be sufficient here to say that...research can be described as the scientific method of finding answers to questions and that research in physical education is the scientific method of finding answers to questions pertaining to physical education. It is by means of quantitative research that truth is uncovered and from the results of small samples generalizations are made for larger populations'. This is 'what research means'. Oliver, J. (1961) 'Research in physical education', *Physical Education*, **53**, 67–80.

78 Schrecker, K.A. (1952) 'Scientific physical education?' *Journal of Physical Education*, **44**, 113–121.

79 Schrecker, note 78, p. 119.

80 See, for example, the interchange between Woods and Segwick over strength training in *The Leaflet*, **62**(5) & (9), 1961.

81 MacQueen, I.J. (1955) 'Progressive resistance exercise in basic training for sport and athletics', *Physical Education*, **48**, p. 50.
82 Duthie, J.H. (1955) 'The measurement of strength in schools', *Physical Education*, **48**, 61–63.
83 Bull, K.R. (1955) 'Physical tests in the secondary school', *Physical Education*, **48**, 83–87.
84 Morgan, R.E. and Adamson, G.T. (1957) *Circuit Training*, London: Bell, p. 14; 'The contention here put forward is that the hard core of fitness is the efficiency of the muscular and circulo-respiratory systems. These may be regarded as the engine which determines the work output of the body and their efficiency may be expressed in terms of strength, muscular endurance, circulo-respiratory endurance and power'.
85 McDonald, A. (1957) 'Some reflections upon the "physical" in physical education', *Physical Education*, **50**, p. 33.
86 DeLorme and Watkins, note 68.
87 MacQueen, note 81, p. 50.
88 McDonald, note 85, p. 33.
89 MacQueen, note 81.
90 Morgan and Adamson, note 84.
91 Adamson, note 68.
92 Morgan and Adamson, note 84, pp. 5–6.
93 Morgan and Adamson, note 84, pp. 67–68.
94 Morgan and Adamson, note 84, p. 71.
95 Morgan and Adamson, note 84, p. 69.
96 *The Leaflet*, **56**(5), 1955.
97 *The Leaflet*, **57**(3), 1956.
98 *The Leaflet*, **58**(8), 1957.
99 Morgan and Adamson, note 84, p. 74.
100 *The Leaflet*, **58**(6), 1957.
101 *The Leaflet*, **59**(7), 1958.
102 *The Leaflet*, **59**(4), 1958.
103 Campbell (1958) 'Youth fitness project', *Physical Education*, and Campbell and Pohndorf (1961) *Physical Education*, pp. 48–56; Bull, note 83; Duthie, note 82; Cooper (1962) 'Fitness testing of junior school children', *The Leaflet*, **63**(7).
104 McDonald, note 85, p. 33.
105 Schrecker, note 53, p. 51.
106 Cove-Smith in the *TES* 25 July 1952, p. 636.
107 McIntosh, P.C. (1957) 'From treadmill to spring board', *The Leaflet*, **58**(5).
108 For example, McIntosh, note 24.
109 Dr Barlow (c.1960), cited in Swain, M.O.B. (1988) *Physical Education in England, America, and NSW and Allied Subjects*, NSW: ACHPER.
110 McIntosh, note 24, particularly Chapter 3.
111 According to Whitehead, p. 28 in Whitehead, N. and Hendry, L. (1976) *Teaching Physical Education in England*, London: Lepus. This was also the case at Birminham University, see Munrow, A.D. (1958) Physical Education in the Universities. Proceedings of the Second British Empire and Commonwealth Games Conference, Barry, Glamorgan, p. 3.
112 For example, *The Leaflet*, **64**(7), 1963 'A circuit for rugby players'; *The Leaflet*, **65**(1), 1964 'Modified interval running as training for contact sports'; *The Leaflet*, **65**(9), 1964 'An objective test of baseball ability'.
113 It quickly gained ascendancy in tertiary programmes though, through the introduction of the BEd degree.
114 Munrow, note 111, p. 3
115 Munrow, A.D. (1956) *Physical Education*, 18–24.

116 Munrow, note 115, p. 23.
117 McIntosh, P.C. (1963) 'Practical aspects of physical education'. The 1963 Chadwick Trust Lecture, reprinted in *The Leaflet*, **64**(8), 62–64.
118 Cooper, note 103.
119 Letter in *The Leaflet*, **63**(9), 1962, p. 67.
120 McIntosh, note 117, p. 64.

Chapter 7

The Social Construction of Physical Education: Connecting Past, Present and Future

> There was a long-drawn-out battle over terminology. Physical training (PT), which had grown out of 'drill', became physical education (PE). Even PE was sacrificed by the fanatical 'movementiers' as they sailed through the art of movement, basic movement training and human movement studies. For the sake of peace, and to enable the PE people, the dance people and the sports studies people to work happily, the term 'movement studies' is now generally accepted.[1]

Anthony was, of course, correct in his observation that there has been a 'long-drawn-out battle over terminology' in physical education. But the participants in the battle did not have to be 'fanatical' to favour one term over another, and the battle is far from over.[2] This is because the act of naming is not a simple, straightforward nor obvious matter. On the contrary, it is a profoundly political act which projects a definition of the subject and its aims, content and pedagogy, and it is for this reason that the battles Anthony refers to have been so hard and acrimoniously fought. Some physical educators, to be sure, have had a difficult time accepting this point, that such battles are not episodes of abnormal chaos punctuating a normal state of calm tranquility and consensus, but are instead a common and entirely healthy feature of social life. Of course, there is always the danger that conflict can become unhealthy and destructive, but with questions of degree we might as usefully ask 'how long is a piece of string?' Moreover, the issue of unhealthy conflict does very much depend on which side you happen to be on.

In this chapter, I want to bring together the various threads of the position taken in this book by first of all reviewing and summarizing briefly the analysis presented in Chapters 4 to 6, and highlighting some of the key issues in this struggle as I see them. I then want to swing the analysis back around full circle to pick up some of the themes presented in Chapter 1 in relation to the recent public debate over physical education and school sport, and to argue that the 1970s and early 1980s witnessed an elaboration of the structuring discourses in physical education laid down in the postwar period in such a manner that allowed physical education to be used as part of the Thatcherite strategy to win consent for the Conservative's educational reforms, which in themselves formed a central plank in the Tories' plans for re-election at the 1987 General Election. Finally, in the last section, I will draw out what I consider to be the possible repercussions of these recent events for the future, and to suggest in particular that the public debate of the late 1980s has merely been the beginning of a new phase in the struggle to define physical education.

Contestation and Power: Reconstructing the Past

The reconstruction in Chapter 4 of the debate over gymnastics, a debate which polarized female and male physical educators and their respective definitions of physical education, revealed questions of aims, content and pedagogy to be inescapably linked to the broader question of power. In this context and in its relational sense, power refers to the capabilities of vying parties to access particular resources that allow one to bring about changes which advantage it over others, or in Giddens' terms to the 'transformative capacity...to get others to comply with their wants'.[3] In the case of physical education and as the debate unfolded, the male physical educators' ability to discredit the underlying principles of educational gymnastics and very quickly to restrict the females' influence to primary schools and the indoor programme in girls' secondary school classes was not a simple matter of the males *having* power and the females being power-*less*. Rather, the ascendency of the male discourse of scientific functionalism reflected the strategic positioning of males and females in society and their access to the resources required to bring about change. The fact that women dominated the physical education profession until after the war and the introduction of mass secondary schooling had much to do with the fact that few men considered physical education teaching to be a worthwhile career. Their entry to the profession was bound to represent a challenge to the female gymnasts. But with all of the cards apparently stacked in their favour, including control of their professional association, journals, the Inspectorate and Advisory Service, and fifty years of tradition and a close-knit sisterhood, the gymnasts were immediately caught on the back-foot after the war. From the outset of the debate, the male physical educators held the strategic high ground by virtue of the fact that they were males in a patriarchal society. This point is more than self-evidently and trivially axiomatic. What this meant was that male physical educators had more ready access to allegedly high status activities such as higher degree study and experimental science research, their careers were not susceptible to disruption by parenthood, which in turn made them more acceptable than women as leaders, and their rapid appropriation of competitive team games was built on existing patriarchal domination in sport more broadly. When changes to the structure of the college system were mooted, the males did not have what quickly became for the females the *dis*advantage of tradition to impede their responses. Indeed, since the positions of power and influence in society were almost entirely occupied by males, with most of these being protestant, white, and Anglo-Saxon, it is unremarkable that the values of similarly privileged male physical educators should just happen to be consistent with the broader definitions of worthwhile activity in society. It was precisely this group which had a major role in defining what was to count as high status in the first place.

In other words, the dice were loaded in the debate over gymnastics, and every time they were rolled they favoured the male physical educators. But this was not a straightforward matter of inevitable and absolute victory for the males; if it had been, there would have been very little debate at all. The female physical educators were not powerless, and the ascendency of the male definition of physical education was only achieved over a long and protracted period of struggle, during which the females' distinctive progressivist discourse gradually lost ground and was finally fenced-in to the category of girls' dance and gymnastics. Moreover, the prominence of the male version of physical education was maintained only through constant vigilance and contestation. Each significant new change in political, cultural and educational spheres presented new threats, and their arguments had to be reconstructed in new forms to meet the exigencies of the new situations. In some cases, the female physical educators' discourse was appropriated and absorbed into an apparently oppositional discourse, such as the positioning of the liberal humanistic sentiment of treating pupils as individuals and tailoring programmes to their needs, at the heart of circuit training. While the actual practices in educational gymnastics and circuit training which were motivated by this sentiment could not have been further apart, in terms of the effects and outcomes teachers might have hoped would derive from them, we cannot claim that this appropriation represented a straightforward example of male victory or female defeat. The example suggests, instead, that there is always potential for challenge and transformation of the dominant discourse, and this dominance is merely contingent and must be constantly renewed.

At the same time, the fact that domination is not a static or absolute state, but a process and a matter of contingency and circumstance, does not deny that in the case of physical education, the scientific functionalism which privileges males gradually eroded the progressive discourse of the educational gymnasts over time. By the end of the 1960s, it was clear that competitive team games were almost as prominent a part of girls' secondary school programmes as they were of boys', and the new BEd degrees for both males and females were being structured around the core of the new scientific knowledge. For the most part, the female physical educators were not dragged, kicking and screaming, to adopt team games over gymnastics. Instead, they were won over to the male version of physical education on the basis of the 'rationality' of the male arguments and the 'naturalness' of the values these arguments projected. Not only was the male definition of physical education perceived to be clear and obvious, but the proponents of oppositional discourses were, as Anthony reminded us in his statement quoted at the beginning of this chapter, 'fanatical'. Since the meaning of physical education was clear, opposition to the consensus was irrational and destructive. The discourse of scientific functionalism in particular promoted the idea of the destructiveness of conflict, and in this it was very much in keeping with one of the dominant cultural themes of the postwar period outlined in Chapter 3, the view that Britain had matured into a conflict-free society. Indeed, contemporary physical educators' difficulties with the notion of contestation over the meaning of physical education are in large part an outcome of the major cultural themes of egalitarianism, consensus and nationalism which emerged during the period under study.

These themes were most prominently in evidence in Chapter 5, and were projected through competitive team games which formed the core of physical education in the mass secondary schools. The appropriation and reconstruction by the male physical educators of the educational ideology surrounding the public school tradition of team games, and the invention of 'traditional physical education', was in itself a constituent part of the wave of cultural renewal that followed the war. In keeping with this spirit of social reconstruction, the elitism and separatism of the public schools' use of team games was turned on its head, so that team games became the natural inheritance of all, and the common denominator that proved British society was 'equal'. The association of school sports teams with the fate of elite international teams provided a mechanism for the widespread fostering of national identity through the mass secondary schools, and promoted the idea that success or failure in international sport was somehow indicative of Britain's current standing as a world power. The fact that Britain continually fared badly in both arenas during the 1950s gave added impetus to the sports lobbiests to argue for higher levels of government involvement in the running of British sport, which in turn led to the ruling class investing more and more importance in 'traditional physical education' as a predictor of Britain's future performance in elite sport and the international market-place.

The process of reconstructing the public schools' games ethic for use in the mass secondary schools may have wrought radical changes to the upper class ideology of team games, but it did not eradicate the preoccupations and interests of its creators. The values that were built into the rules, conduct and the very structure of team games projected these interests in barely modified form, legitimating as 'natural' competitiveness and aggression, the need to identify with the team against a common foe and in so doing sublimate 'I' for the abstracted 'We', and to accept the verdict of the neutral umpire or referee. Applied to the masses, as a cluster of interconnecting groups rather than as a collection of discrete individuals, these values clearly favoured the interests of the already privileged minority, since they promoted national over sectional interests, consensus over conflict, conformity over difference, and at the same time demonstrated that all members of a controlled, stable society have an equal opportunity to rise above their current situations.

As the discussion in Chapter 5 revealed, this structure of values and associations was already in place by the end of the second world war, a factor that accounts for the speed with which the newly arrived male physical educators found acceptance of their role as champions of team games in the mass secondary schools. The emerging discourse of scientific functionalism greatly assisted this acceptance, since the new knowledge of fitness training, skill acquisition and biomechanics had an apparently clear and direct contribution to make to enhancing elite sports performance. The use of experimental methods and concomitant quantitative measures was entirely consistent with the postwar view of society as conflict-free, since science promoted similar notions of objectivity, political neutrality, and consensus. The positioning of experimental, empiricist science, as the foundation of the male physical educators' professional knowledge and at the heart of his professional identity, thus served to embed these values within male discourse.

The discussion of the new view of fitness and health in Chapter 6 illustrates the empirical literalness that ran through the male discourse in physical education. In conceptualizing the relationship between physical education and health, the scientific functionalists 'naturally' stressed the primacy of exercise and the physiological transformations that take place in the body as a result of exercise.

While the Swedish gymnasts had also held a functional view of the physical education/health relationship, their location in girls' private schools forced them to extend the scope of their teaching to incorporate emotional and social factors. Even the protagonists for physical education in the state elementary schools considered exercise to be only one component in four in promoting health. While the male scientific functionalists no doubt were also aware of the range of forces that impact on health, their increasing concerns with the microscopic physiological changes that were taking place in the body during exercise made it difficult for them to draw wider emotional or social considerations into their frame of analysis. The outcome was a reductionist conception of physical education's relationship to health which was overwhelmingly preoccupied with the development of strength and endurance and their measurability. The concern for measurement and the ability to quantify in 'precise' terms the physical capacities of the body illustrates the crude empiricism at the root of their view, and the assumption that physical endurance and strength are metaphors for, and the literal embodiment of, health.

Consolidation and Incubation: Merging Past and Present

While there were many developments both in physical education and in the wider political, cultural and educational spheres during the 1970s and early 1980s, I suggest that up until the mid 1980s there were no radical discontinuities within, or additions to, physical education discourse. Instead, this period witnessed the further elaboration of the themes I have just summarized and their consolidation in institutionalized practice at primary, secondary and tertiary education levels. The debate in the second half of the 1980s represented a peak in the development and consolidation of the postwar discourses. 'Traditional physical education' continued to grow in prominence in tandem with a concern for elite sport and scientific functionalism, while the progressive concerns of the educational gymnasts were pushed further to the margins of physical education discourse, surviving mainly in girls' gymnastics and dance. With the emergence of the health-based physical education movement in the early 1980s, progressivism began to lose its pre-eminence in primary schools also. At the same time, as we have seen in Chapter 1, the humanist concern within progressivism for the individual child spilled over from educational gymnastics and dance to form a counter-rhythm to elitism and functionalism in games teaching and some forms of health related fitness, and also informed developments in leisure based programmes in the upper secondary years and some outdoor/adventure programmes. Despite this diffusion of progressivism and its infiltration of other areas of subject matter within physical education programmes beyond gymnastics and dance, the dominant discourse has been that of 'traditional physical education', and its key concern (and justification) the enhancement of sports performance, through teaching and coaching programmes, by the application of principles derived from scientific studies of human movement. In the forty year period between 1945 and 1985, it is this structuring discourse that has underwritten the practice of most physical educators, first mainly males and increasingly, females also.

   While the analysis presented in Chapters 4 to 6 showed that the female progressivist discourse was already in the process of being marginalized from the 1950s on, it was still able to co-exist, albeit uneasily, with 'traditional physical education' and scientific functionalism, protected within girls' physical education. During the 1970s, the female and male physical educators effectively adopted stand-off tactics. But by the end of the decade, the female discourse was significantly weakened by the influx of new women teachers to the profession who had little experience of the socializing effects of what Sheila Fletcher called the 'female tradition', and had instead been inducted into physical education discourse through the academically-orientated degree courses that began to proliferate from the mid 1970s on.[4] It was also weakened by the introduction in some places of co-educational physical education classes, which no longer provided the protection for the progressivist discourse that the single-sex arrangement had done. By the end of the 1970s, this uneasy co-existence of diametrically opposed discourses was about to end, and the progressivist influences caricatured as ideologically motivated, trendy, and in some cases, actually dangerously subversive.

Events in the wider spheres of politics and educational policy hastened this process of marginalization along. The so-called Great Debate initiated by the Labour Prime Minister James Callaghan's speech at Ruskin College in 1976:

> signalled a fundamental shift in the debate about educational means and ends. It marked, at the highest political level, the formal end of the long postwar phase of educational expansion which had been largely promoted by the party of which he (Callaghan) was leader. The speech was therefore a declaration — a public redefinition of educational objectives — as well as a response to the more immediate events of economic crisis, cuts in public expenditure and the polemical weight of the Tory critique of Labour's educational past.[5]

According to the CCCS writers, Callaghan's speech embodied concerns for the cost-effectiveness of the government's involvement in public education, including the close supervision of teachers, the monitoring of teachers' and pupils' performances and the installation of a 'core curriculum of basic knowledge' to ensure the maintenance of national standards, and the more explicit use of schools and tertiary institutions to service the needs of industry.[6] By casting the Great Debate in these terms, Callaghan's speech framed the boundaries of policy initiatives in the years that followed in a way that was scarcely distinguishable from the position of the Labour Party's Tory critics.[7] And even though the Great Debate hardly registered in physical education literature,[8] it nevertheless had important implications for physical education discourse.

In the short term, the logic of recession and economism that saturated Callaghan's speech led to physical education being overlooked by both the DES and HMI in England in a number of key curriculum policy documents that appeared towards the end of the 1970s and beginning of the 1980s,[9] while in Scotland the Munn Report of 1977 on the curriculum in years three and four of the secondary school adopted the logic of 'traditional physical education' in suggesting that 'physical education, with its heavy emphasis on non-cognitive aspects, should within two weekly periods, be able to establish a basis for continuing development through the informal curriculum and other school activities'.[10] As the educational agenda of the late 1970s was focused on the issue of drawing schooling and industry closer together through the promotion of science, technology and commercial subjects, and initiatives such as work experience, industrial training and vocational education, the progressivist discourse in physical education could only be marginalized further since it had little to contribute to the debate in the terms it had been framed. With concerns for survival of physical education in schools rarely far from the surface of professional debate in physical education,[11] the discourse of 'traditional physical education' seemed to offer the most readily acceptable public category for the subject.[12]

The terms of the Great Debate set by Callaghan fitted the purposes of the Conservative opposition of the late 1970s well. Indeed, educational issues were a key component of the Conservative's platform leading up to the General Election victory in May 1979, in particular the matters of parental (consumer) choice in schooling and a resolve to halt the alleged decline in educational standards by resurrecting a selective system over the corpse of the comprehensive school. Richard Johnson[13] has argued that in what he calls the first phase of Thatcherism with respect to educational policy, between May 1979 and mid 1981, there was only limited achievement of the government's policy aims. The effect of pursuing these aims during this period produced the negative outcomes of cost-cutting and strategic underfunding, but did not result in their translation into actual restructuring. In the next phase, Johnson claims the Thatcher government met the head-on resistance of the educational professionals between 1981 and 1983, resulting in a series of crises within the government itself and the replacement of Mark Carlisle with Keith Joseph as Secretary of State for Education. In phase three, in the months before and after the 1983 General Election, a number of solutions to these crises were proposed through Joseph's office in terms of vouchers and loans, but Johnson claims these plans merely served to deepen the crisis within the Conservative party. It was during the next phase, steered in its latter stages by Kenneth Baker, leading up to the 1987 General Election and in the face of unprecedented industrial action by teachers and other educational professions, that the school sport and physical education debate was brought into the play.

The CCCS writers had argued in 1980 in *Unpopular Education* that the future prospects for the Thatcher government's educational policy aims depended considerably on securing economic success, but also, significantly, on winning popular consent for its plans to restructure what had been, since at least 1945, a deeply and broadly *un*popular system of state schooling.[14] However, despite this unpopularity with the general public, the radical and controversial nature of Conservative plans had provoked a great deal of public anxiety by the mid 1980s. Thatcherite education policy squarely challenged the teaching profession across a range of concerns such as working conditions, salaries and career structures, and the administration and control of the curriculum itself, and the resulting prolonged industrial action did nothing to foster the consent the Tory policy aims required for their successful implementation. Opposition from the general public and the educational professionals was bad enough, but the real danger to Thatcherite educational reform came from the deepening divisions that were appearing within the Conservative Party itself. In the fourth phase of Thatcherism in education, in the year to eighteen months leading up to the 1987 General Election, Johnson argues that the solutions proposed by Keith Joseph, in terms of vouchers and loans, had to be rejected in order to clear the way for the search for new policy initiatives. It was at this point that the debate over school sport and physical education becomes a significant part of this process, towards the end of 1985 and at a time when the Conservatives were most vulnerable to disintegration through internal divisions. The major function the physical education debate served was not primarily to win consent from the general public nor from teachers for the Thatcher reforms, but to marshall the Conservative forces both outside and inside the Party, and to provide a focus for Conservative critique to sharpen and re-kindle resolve and conviction. It was through the example of school physical education that internal differences among the New Right could be overcome and a renewed moral outrage against the (alleged) excesses of left wing subversion directed. The public debate over school sport and physical education was, in other words, a call to Conservative forces to rally around the flag for the sacred triad of Queen, Country and the Economy.

Physical education was an appropriate candidate to serve this function for Thatcherism due to the dominance of the 'traditional physical education' discourse as a professional ideology and, more importantly and relatedly, as a definition of physical education instantly recognizable and acceptable to the general public. The ambiguities and complexities of physical education discourse, with its oppositional and alternative elements, while recognizable and important to most physical educators, were irrelevant to this public portrayal of school physical education. Critics were able to appeal to (what was for most physical educators) a simplistic notion of the relationship between school sport and physical education precisely because of the success of the 'traditional physical education' discourse within physical education itself. As we saw in Chapter 1, there had been no actual demise in school sport, nor had there been an effective left wing, progressivist subversion of physical education. But such was the educational climate in 1985, thoroughly saturated as it was with nationalism and economism, that the presence of *any* seemingly counter-hegemonic elements to the discourse of 'traditional physical education' could be eagerly drafted in to the cause of the New Right, as a symbol of the continuing threat to traditional moral standards and ways of life, the ongoing deterioration of quality in the teaching force and the consequent need for government intervention, and the ever-present dangers of subversion of the sacred values of economic prosperity, national pride and chauvinistic patriotism.

A Yet to be Concluded Story: Prospects for the Future

The General Election victory of 1987 and its immediate aftermath in terms of the 'Baker Bill' (Johnson's fifth phase of Thatcherism in education), marks not the end-point in this study of the postwar social construction of physical education, but the beginning of a new moment, and so merely an episode in a yet to be concluded story.[15] As such, it is not possible to predict the likely repercussions of recent events for the future of school physical education beyond sketching briefly, in the light of the historical evidence this study has marshalled, some of the broader forces that may exert a prominent influence. I suggest that there are a number of issues that might be considered important at this stage.

The first of these is the inclusion of physical education in the national curriculum in England and Wales and in the new examination structure in Scotland (which predated the English/Welsh developments by several years), an event which may shift the concerns of professional physical educators away from practical physical activity (including sport), towards the construction of an academic subject. One of the off-shoots of scientific functionalism in physical education in the late 1960s and through the 1970s was the academicization of physical education as a degree level subject in tertiary institutions. The arrival of the predominately school-based Certificate of Secondary Education (CSE) in England and Wales in the mid 1970s presented the opportunity for the application of the new knowledge of human movement in schools, and this trend has continued with growing pressure from some sections of the physical education profession for A Level studies (in England) in physical education or a related topic such as Sports Studies.[16] Comparative evidence from other countries such as Australia, where this process of academicization began to exert a major influence on school physical education in some states as early as the mid 1970s, suggests that there is the danger of a trend over time to first of all gradually reduce the amount of time spent within programmes on practical physical activity, and then to continue to increase the scientific, bio-physical aspects of the subject at the expense of socio-cultural knowledge. In the case of some states in Australia, this process has been fuelled by an ongoing struggle for academic status in tertiary institutions, resulting in a redefinition of studies in physical education as scientifically-based, and a gradual distancing of high status university programmes from school physical education.[17]

In light of the dominance of scientific functionalism in British physical education since the second world war, I suggest similar potential dangers exist in Britain. One particular danger is that high status courses in British tertiary institutions may gradually abandon their concerns for the training of teachers for the more currently prestigious professionals fields of sports coaching, recreation management, sports journalism, and exercise therapy. The outcome for physical education teacher training may be a second class status alongside these other courses. On the other hand, there is little danger of the discourse of 'traditional physical education' disappearing from schools. The power of this discourse and its popular appeal as a definition of physical education is, I suggest, clearly evident from the arguments presented in this study. But this popularity and dominance does not guarantee that the three or four year trained physical education teacher will necessarily have a prominent role in teaching competitive games and sport in schools. One possible future scenario is that this responsibility will be taken on, more and more, either by other teachers (some of whom *may* have trained as physical educators) who have specialist coaching qualifications, or by professional coaches employed specifically to coach games and sports and organize school teams. Meanwhile, the physical education teacher may be permitted a minor role in teaching games and sports, but will find his or her time consumed by teaching and assessing the new academicized physical education subject. Perhaps the 'low-achiever' or the sixth form recreation programmes will also be entrusted to the degree-qualified physical educator, but these will be seen as low-status and infinitely less important than the competitive games and sport programme. Indeed, a model for this system has long been in place in a not dissimilar form in the private schools, and could with little difficulty be instituted, especially in the former state schools that decide to 'opt out'.

I suggest, then, that the discourses of 'traditional physical education' and scientific functionalism will continue to exert a potent influence on ways of thinking about and practising physical education in schools into the next century. However, in the fall-out created by the Baker reforms of state schooling, it is clear that the physical education profession is undergoing a series of transformations which may render it unrecognizable, in relation to its current form, by the year 2000. These transformations have much to do with the tensions that exist between these two dominant discourses, since the academization of physical education in schools, fed by the growth of scientific functionalism since the end of the second world war, is in some important respects incompatible with 'traditional physical education'. Not the least of these incompatibilities is the perceived practical (that is, overtly 'physical') nature of 'traditional physical education', in contrast to the academic (that is, 'intellectual') nature of courses underwritten by scientific functionalism, and its popularly accepted symbolic qualities, which is the much more powerful discourse of the two in the public sphere. At the same time, scientific functionalism as a professional ideology has been viewed by physical educators as complementary to competitive sport, promoting the idea that sports science can make a significant contribution to improving elite performance, a notion that has recently begun to gain some credibility with the general public as well. Nevertheless, the legitimacy of physical education as an academic school subject based in scientific functionalism is weak compared with the public acceptability of 'traditional physical education', since it is the 'practical' nature of sports performance that makes it such a powerful medium for projecting the various representative qualities attributed to physical education during the debate leading up to the 1987 General Election. This tension may present something of a dilemma for the future of physical education, since a case will need to be made for 'scientific physical education' as a school subject appropriate for school pupils irrespective of their sporting abilities, on the basis of what has essentially, since the 1950s, been an elitist discourse.[18]

At the same time, the currently dominant 'traditional physical education' discourse cannot be guaranteed a smooth passage into the next century either. It seems clear that the relationship between school sport and elite sport, particularly at international level, can only become more problematic. Given the increasing commercialization and commodification of sport and the massive growth of media sport,[19] pressure on school sport to emulate media sport will continue. School sport may have to become better organised, employ professional coaches, and perhaps accept corporate sponsorship all the way down to individual school level, if it is to be a genuine and effective 'nursery for elite talent'. The development of special sports schools for talented elite sports performers may present another strategy to satisfy this requirement. In addition, the ethno-centerism of 'traditional physical education' itself may be a source of major tensions. Part of the popular acceptability of this discourse in the public sphere, as we have seen in Chapters 1 and 5, has been the potent nationalistic sentiments it projects. As the analysis in Chapter 5 makes clear, this nationalism is explicitly racist, celebrating the superiority of 'the British' over other nationalities; this has been the key to its potency and popularity. But the problematic nature of nationalism within the 'traditional physical education' discourse is clearly evidenced in sporting confrontations between Irish, English, Scots and Welsh, when these 'other nationalisms' break through. And since the end of the war, the tensions surrounding nationalism have been exacerbated by the failure of this discourse to accommodate the rapid rise to prominence of black athletes in British sport. The extent to which 'traditional physical education' can continue to celebrate the racial superiority of 'the British' is clearly rendered problematic with the continuing success of black athletes, particularly when the numbers of elite black sports performers becomes too large to be simply or easily overlooked as exceptions and become instead the rule.

Within this matrix of possibilities, the future prospects for health related fitness and other health based physical education programmes appear uncertain. As we saw in Chapter 6, the male physical educators' interests in fitness were at the leading edge of the rise of scientific functionalism in the postwar period. The new view of fitness developed during this period marked a distinctive break with previous conceptualizations of the relationship between exercise and health, inscribing the notion of fitness with functionality and purposiveness. Much effort and ingenuity was devoted by scientific functionalists to the development of ways of improving sports performance and to the creation of degree courses during the 1960s and 1970s. The more recent emergence of health based physical education programmes in schools during the 1980s witnessed a fusion of the scientific functionalists' concerns for physical fitness and the educational gymnasts' concerns for the individual learner. This was an important development since it provides substance to Foucault's claim that the 1950s marked the beginning of a broader cultural shift from public to individual and external to internal forces of social control, in this case manifest in an individuation and internalization within individuals of a moral responsibility to keep fit, which by implication meant keeping healthy.[20] Indeed, the desire to individualize fitness programmes was a key issue for Morgan and Adamson in the 1950s when they were developing circuit training, and so the recent emergence of this fusion in the form of health related fitness is not at all new, and could rather be viewed as the latest development in an ongoing process that had its genesis in the 1950s.

What is new, however, at least in some of the health based physical education initiatives,[21] is an attempt to locate exercise and health within the context of the pupil's total lifestyle. In this version of health based physical education, the danger of reducing physical education programmes to those activities that are functionally related to the development of physical fitness is less likely to occur, since the maintenance of health over a prolonged period of time must account for factors beyond the merely physical and physiological, such as work, recreation, emotional condition, diet, and so on. The importance of such a holistic approach to health based physical education has been demonstrated recently by studies which have suggested that programmes focusing solely on functional concerns risked leaving unchallenged, or in some instances tactily endorsing, behaviour and attitudes characteristic of such conditions as anorexia, bulimia and excessive exercising.[22] The problem for the survival of health based physical education programmes that are sensitive to such issues and are able to incorporate sociocultural modes of analysis alongside functional, bio-physical knowledge, is that they may be less likely to find support in schools since they do not offer the seductive promise of the quick-fix, of solving society's spiralling health care costs by quickly and efficiently producing fit children. Where health based physical education programmes are able to find spaces in the school system, in primary schools or as alternatives to sports or academic programmes for so-called low-achievers in secondary schools, they may suffer from the ills that beset low-status activities such as poor resourcing, under-funding and so on. Or they may, in some cases, be drafted in to the service of some higher good, such as providing fit players for school sports teams.

Postscript

Crystal-ball gazing is a notoriously hazardous occupation, the chances of success slim indeed in the face of an infinite number of possible futures. Acknowledging this, the purpose of the previous section was not to predict in specific terms what will happen to physical education in the future, but more modestly to sketch the outlies of the broad issues, as I perceive them, which may be important in shaping physical education discourse in the aftermath of the recent public debate. However the future unfolds, the prospects for a version of school physical education that has the potential to release people from some of the neuroses of modern living such as the tyrannical cult of slenderness,[23] to provide a means of overcoming self-alienation and physical inhibition, or to address problems of structured and institutionalized gender, racial and class oppressions, seems to me to be limited. There are few signs in the recent turns which physical education has taken to suggest that the field of practical knowledge the subject embraces can promote social democratic principles at a time when it has been used, effectively and successfully, as a symbol of traditional Conservative values, as a bench mark for a way of life that celebrates economism, possessive individualism and chauvinistic, racist patriotism.

And yet, some of the teachers who appeared in the 1987 *Panorama* programme, the successes of the health based physical education movement (in its holistic forms), and some of the other alternative and oppositional forms of physical education such as outdoor activities and socio-culturally based programmes,[24] offer some hope for a more humanistic, socially and politically aware profession in the future. All educational professionals, including teachers, administrators, policy makers and researchers, share a culture in Thatcherite Britain where socialist and humanistic values are not encouraged, and certainly not rewarded. To speak up as Richard Swinnerton (see Chapter 1) did in the *Panorama* programme requires a certain degree of conviction, and courage. However, as Connell[25] has recently argued, people who attempt by themselves to critique the dominant discourses in their professions and in society more broadly stand little chance of being successful, and more than a very good chance of being shouted down and, perhaps, too demoralized to go on. Physical educators who are uncomfortable with the prospect of a subject that promotes so-called traditional values as they were framed by the New Right in the public debate need, instead, to begin to form alliances with other oppositional groups, not only with the political left but with what Richard Johnson[26] has called the New Politics, a third political force consisting of a cluster of oppositional groups such as feminists, Greens, and anti-racists. Connell's analysis of oppositional trends in education and politics in the 1970s and 1980s suggests that they will also need to abandon alternative forms of physical education that merely co-exist with more dominant versions of the subject, where, as in the case of educational gymnastics, they were liable, at the very least, to be easily marginalized. Connell argues that democracy is mainstream not marginal, and it is only by contesting mainstream definitions and practices that there is any chance of effective transformation or restructuring. In order to mount such challenges, socialist, democratic and feminist physical educators need to furnish themselves with informed arguments that raise questions about the vested interests which lie at the heart of particular definitions of worthwhile knowledge, and which privilege some groups while oppressing others. It is here that this study is intended to make a contribution.

In this book I have presented one view of the social construction of physical education in postwar Britain. It is an interpretation that is as much open to contestation and dispute as the various versions of physical education that it has outlined. It is, however, an account which I hope at the very least illustrates a number of key issues. The first of these is that the form which physical education takes in schools, its aims, content and pedagogy, is crucially bound up with the interests of particular groups in society. This point, I suggest, must surely by now be beyond dispute, given the whole weight of material that has appeared recently in the sociology of school knowledge field, the physical education studies cited, and the evidence presented, in this book. Change, struggle, and conflict are the normal state of affairs in social life, and all educational action is also a form of political action.[27] It seems to me that these are inescapable conclusions that this study supports.

At the same time, while sectional interests are sometimes actively and consciously pursued by clearly identifiable parties, more often knowledge is structured by forces which advantage some groups over others in ways that are taken for granted, as natural, obvious and immutable, a process that goes on outwith the consciousness of many of those who are advantaged and is sometimes willingly supported by some of those who are disadvantaged. This is a key feature of hegemony. Who gains and who loses is a far from straightforward matter and, as I have argued already in this chapter and elsewhere in this book, hegemony needs constantly to be maintained through struggle and contestation. This factor in itself should be enough to dissuade us from too simplistic formulations of who the dominant and subordinate groups are in society, and what the outcome of struggles will be. More than this though, that school knowledge is structured in ways which benefit unfairly some parties over others needs to be treated as problematic. It needs to become the starting point for research and professional practice in education, the subject of investigation and reflection rather than of willing or grudging acceptance. Accepting this conclusion, that the form and content of school knowledge and its pedagogy and evaluation are inextricably bound up with the exercise of power and the political process, in relation to how the goods produced by society are distributed, to whom and on what basis, requires us to move beyond stock images of the political left and right. The fact that educational action is political and intimately related to the circulation and exercise of power now needs to be problematized and investigated, not disputed.

Where does this analysis leave us in terms of the recent public debate over school physical education; what messages are there from this study for contemporary struggles over the meaning of school knowledge? I argued in the first chapter that the immediate postwar period represented something of a watershed for physical education in Britain. The introduction of mass secondary schooling was probably the single-most significant event in stimulating the developments that followed since, as a secondary school subject requiring specialist teachers, physical education quite suddenly appeared as a much more attractive career prospect to males than it had ever done before. Given the state of play in physical education up until 1945, with the existence of three recognizably dissimilar versions of physical education, each created to meet the specific classed and gendered needs of its clients, a clash of ideologies of dramatic proportions was inevitable. In connecting up the events of the postwar period with the contemporary situation, I suggest that the contentious issues may be many years older, but they are still, recognizably, the same issues. Political, cultural and educational conditions have certainly altered in the intervening period, and so have the various alleged crises to which physical educators are required to respond. But the old tensions and conflicts which surrounded the opposing definitions of physical education have not come out in the wash of the last forty-five years. On the contrary, they form the undercurrents to the contemporary debates; they are the structuring discourses in physical education today, embodying the basic assumptions and expectations of the profession.

In the process of professional socialization, physical educators are brought into contact with these structuring discourses, just as professionals in other fields are initiated into preferred discourses about themselves. Much of this sedimented knowledge is transmitted and absorbed unconsciously by the field's initiates, since the profession's own story about itself, encapsulated in these structuring discourses, tends to be told reflexively, through its actions, its attitudes and tones of voice. Less often are these fundamental beliefs consciously and explicitly articulated. One of the key ways in which this study might connect with contemporary situations in physical education is to articulate, to put in to words, some of these unspoken tales. This doesn't mean to say, though, that by simply raising people's awareness of these structuring discourses that all will suddenly be well. On the contrary, it is to be hoped that this awareness will problematize the ways in which physical educators understand themselves, their subject and their profession.

One of the first victims of the process of problematizing these structuring discourses must be the abstracted 'We'. Who are the 'physical education profession'? Is it possible for physical educators to speak with one voice about themselves and to agree what the term physical education means? The account presented here would suggest not, since the structuring discourses of contemporary physical education were created out of division and conflict, particularly between males and females. The next question which follows from this is the matter of who claims to speak for the profession (the Physical Education Association?), and what definition of physical education do they project? Does this definition reflect interests that unjustly advantage some groups over others? If so, which students are most likely to succeed in these physical education programmes, and which are most likely to fail? Is it possible to cater for all interested parties in the construction of a school subject, or must some inevitably be disadvantaged? If so, who has the right to make these decisions: individual teachers; school departments; academics; the PEA; the government; the CCPR; the commercial sponsors of elite sport? Is a consensus between these factions possible or desirable? These questions embrace just some of the ways in which this account of the social construction of physical education can impact on contemporary actions. By problematizing the discourses that saturate contemporary practice, and by stepping outside what Phillip Adams referred to as the 'lurid NOW', a range of issues are exposed that might otherwise remain part of the sedimented and received wisdom of the field.

The recent debate over physical education was unprecedented in so far as it aired issues in a much more public way than had ever happened before. But I suggest that it was not a one-off event, and that matters which previously have been debated in the relative privacy of professional and learned journals and the educational press, and at conferences and inservice seminars will be, more and more often, the subject of wider exposure. This is in part due to the insidious role mass media play in our daily lives, and the way in which the electronic media has encroached increasingly on our private lives in its relentless search for news. In addition, as this and other discussions have shown, organized physical activity is crucial, functionally and symbolically, to the maintenance of the social order and to supporting and legitimating the hegemony. As such, it seems to me that school physical education will continue to be positioned as a key site of struggle within debates about egalitarianism, not just in terms of social class but increasingly in relation to gender and race, nationalism and social control. Unfortunately, there are no formulae or recipes for engaging in struggles over the definition of physical education, or for that matter, over the definition of a just society. To be sure, there will be an increasingly urgent need for educational practitioners of all kinds to develop strategies for their engagement in these struggles, but such strategies will only emerge from the development of an informed, coherent and committed pedagogical and political position. This book is a contribution to the development of such a position.

Notes

1 Anthony, D. (1980) *A Strategy for British Sport*, London: Hurst, p. 47.
2 See for example McKay, J., Gore, J. and Kirk, D. (1990) 'Beyond the limits of technocratic physical education', *Quest*, **42**(1), 52–76; Kirk, D. (1990) 'Knowledge, science and the rise and rise of human movement studies', *ACHPER National Journal*, **127**(Autumn), 8–11.
3 See Giddens, A. (1979) *Central Problems in Social Theory*, London: MacMillan, p. 93, and Giddens, A. (1976) *New Rules of Sociological Method*, London: Hutchinson, pp. 110–113.
4 Fletcher, S. (1984) *Women First* London: Althone; Dewar, A. (1987) 'The social construction of gender in physical education', *Women's Studies International Forum*, **19**(2), 453–465.
5 Centre for Contemporary Cultural Studies (1981) *Unpopular Education*, London: Hutchinson, p. 218.
6 Callaghan, J. (1976) 'Towards a national debate', *Education*, **148**, 17.
7 The so-called 'Black Papers' are probably the best statements of the right wing view; see Cox, C.B. and Dyson, A.E. (1969, Eds) *Fight For Education: A Black Paper*, London: Critical Quarterly Society; Cox, C.B. and Dyson, A.E. (1970, Eds) *Black Paper 2: The Crisis in Education*, London: Critical Quarterly Society; Cox, C.B. and Boyson, R. (1975, Eds) *Black Paper 5: The Fight for Education*, London: Dent.
8 Proctor's papers in the *Physical Education Review* are probably the best attempt to

work through the implications of the 'Great Debate' for physical education; see particularly Proctor, N. (1984) 'Problems facing physical education after the great debate', *Physical Education Review*, **7**(1), 4–11.

9   See, for example, Her Majesty's Inspectorate (1977) *Curriculum 11–16*, London: HMSO; Her Majesty's Inspectorate (1979) *Curriculum 11–16, Supplementary Working Papers, Physical Education*, London: Department of Education and Science; Department of Education and Science (1980) *A Framework for the School Curriculum*, London: HMSO; Department of Education and Science (1981) *The School Curriculum*, London: HMSO.

10 Scottish Education Department (1977) *The Structure of the Curriculum in the Third and Fourth Years of the Scottish Secondary School*, Edinburgh: HMSO, p. 47.

11 For example, Hargreaves, D. (1982) 'Ten proposals for the future of physical education', *Bulletin of Physical Education*, **18**(3), 5–10; and Proctor, note 8.

12 Williams, E.A. (1985) 'Understanding constraints on innovation in physical education', *Journal of Curriculum Studies*, **17**(4), 407–413; Kirk, D. (1986) 'Health related fitness as an innovation in the physical education curriculum', in Evans, J. (Ed.) *Physical Education, Sport and Schooling: Studies in the Sociology of Physical Education*, Lewes: Falmer Press, pp. 167–181.

13 Johnson, R. (1989) 'Thatcherism and English education: Breaking the mould, or confirming the pattern?' *History of Education*, **18**(2), 91–121.

14 See CCCS, note 5, and Johnson, note 13, pp. 95–101.

15 This heading is borrowed from *Unpopular Education*, p. 241, (see note 5).

16 For example, Carroll, R. (1986) 'Examinations in physical education: An analysis of trends and developments, in *Trends and Developments in Physical Education*, London: E and FN Spon, pp. 233–239.

17 Kirk, note 2; Fitclarence, L. and Tinning, R. (1990) 'Challenging hegemonic physical education: Contextualizing physical education as an examinable subject, in Kirk, D. and Tinning, R. (Eds) *Physical Education, Curriculum and Culture: Critical Issues in the Contemporary Crisis*, Lewes: Falmer Press, pp. 169–192; McKay, Gore and Kirk, note 2; Kirk, D., McKay, J. and George, L. (1986) 'All work and no play? Hegemony in physical education', in *Trends and Developments in Physical Education*, London: E and FN Spon, pp. 170–177.

18 McKay, J. (1986) Sport Science: The Study of Elites by Elites for Elites? Paper presented to the XXIII FIMS World Congress of Sports Medicine, Brisbane.

19 Hargreaves, J. (1986) *Sport, Power and Culture*, Cambridge: Polity Press.

20 See the chapter entitled 'Body/Power' in Gordon, C. (1979 Ed.) *Michel Foucault: Power/Knowledge*, The Harvester Press, and Kirk, D. and Colquhoun, D. (1989) 'Healthism and physical education', *British Journal of Sociology of Education*, **10**(4), 417–434.

21 A good example of an early holistic programme is Whitehead, J. and Fox, K. (1982) 'Student centred physical education', *Bulletin of Physical Education*, **19**(2), 21–30.

22 Kirk, D. and Colquhoun, D. (1989) 'Healthism and physical education', *British Journal of Sociology of Education*, **10**(4), 417–434; Tinning, R. (1985) 'Physical education and the cult of slenderness', *ACHPER National Journal*, **107**, 10–13.

23 Tinning, note 21.

24 For an example of the latter, see Fitzclarence and Tinning, note 17. See also Hellison's recent overview of alternative views of physical education pedagogy that may be capable of challenging current orthodoxies, in Hellison, D. (1988) 'Our constructed reality: Some contributions of an alternative perspective to physical education pedagogy', *Quest*, **40**(1), 84–90.

25 Connell, R.W. (1988) 'Curriculum politics, hegemony and strategies of social change', *Curriculum and Teaching*, **3**(1&2), 63–71.

26 Johnson, note 13.
27 'Making the pedagogical political and the political pedagogical'; Aronowitz, S. and Giroux, H. (1985) *Education Under Siege*, London: RKP; see also Connell, R.W., Ashenden, D., Kessler, S. and Dowsett, G. (1982) *Making the Difference* Sydney: Allen and Unwin, p. 208; Kirk, D. (1988) *Physical Education and Curriculum Study: A Critical Introduction*, London: Croom Helm, pp. 24–42.

Index